To my favorite chef...
Michael!
Dad
Christmas 1987

SOUTHWEST TASTES

SOUTHWEST TASTES

FROM THE PBS TELEVISION SERIES
GREAT CHEFS® OF THE WEST

BY ELLEN BROWN

HPBooks

Cover: *Shrimp San Pedro, The White Dove,*
Tucson, Arizona, page 114

Published by HPBooks
A division of HPBooks, Inc.
© 1987 Tele-Record Productions, LTD.
Printed in the U.S.A.
1st Printing

Library of Congress Cataloging in
Publication Data

Brown, Ellen.
   Southwest tastes.

   Includes index.
   1. Cookery, American—Southwestern
style.   I. Great chefs of the West.   II. Title.
TX715.B8491455   1987   641.5979
87-14865
ISBN 0-89586-578-5

Notice: The information contained in this book
is true and complete to the best of our
knowledge. All recommendations are made
without any guarantees on the part of the
author or HPBooks. The author and publisher
disclaim all liability in connection with the use
of this information.

TABLE OF CONTENTS

When work on "Great Chefs of the West" began, we planned to produce a thirteen-part series featuring well-known chefs from the West and Southwest. The format was similar to the "Great Chefs of New Orleans" I and II, "Great Chefs of San Francisco" and "Great Chefs of Chicago." As was done for these series, we intended to offer a small paperback companion cookbook.

Eighteen months later, the series had turned into twenty-six programs featuring sixty chefs from sixteen cities. Instead of featuring one chef per program, "Great Chefs of the West" offers a different chef for each dish. The book grew from a 112-page paperback to what you are holding now.

Ellen Brown had written the *Great Chefs of Chicago* cookbook, and when we approached her to write *Southwest Tastes*, we suggested that she expand its scope. Consequently, in addition to the recipes, she has given us history, techniques, menus for entertaining, and wine selections.

Direct translation of a restaurant recipe to the home kitchen is not always practical or possible. These recipes represent some editorial adjustment, but they are for the most part accurate versions of the chefs' dishes.

You can cook confidently from *Southwest Tastes*, but to fully avail yourself of the chefs' expertise, watch the "Great Chefs of the West" on public television. This video cooking class will bring the recipes to life.

Without the financial assistance of our underwriters, Procter & Gamble's Crisco, True Value, and Weber, who believe not only in public television but in the new Southwest cuisine, we would never have been able to complete this ambitious and expensive project.

Credit should also go to our official hotel, Sheraton, who left the selection of the chefs entirely up to us, and to our official airline, Frank Lorenzo's Continental, whose main concern was, and still is, whether their passengers are going to expect Southwest cuisine on all their flights.

Last, but not least, credit should go to you, our viewer and reader. A portion of the proceeds from every copy of *Southwest Tastes* goes toward purchasing additional programming on public television as well as helping to pay for future "Great Chefs" television productions. We thank you for the support.

JOHN SHOUP
Executive Producer
GREAT CHEFS TELEVISION PRODUCTIONS

Writing a book such as this is not a solitary effort, but one made easier with the support and help of others. I would like to express my thanks:

To the chefs, who shared of themselves and their creativity, and who are preserving our culinary traditions as they are developing new ones.

To Terri Landry, that able television producer of "Great Chefs of the West," whose attention to detail, meticulous observations in the kitchens, and help while writing this book were invaluable.

To John Shoup, executive producer of "Great Chefs of the West," for having enough faith in the project to explore this exciting culinary region so fully in the video and in this book.

To John Mariani and David Vaughan for sharing their insights and knowledge.

To Eric Futran, whose glorious photographs enliven these pages.

To Mimi Luebbermann, for her editorial assistance.

To those many people who have aided in the testing of the recipes; and to my friends, whose support, as always, was deeply felt and appreciated.

To Sam Cat the Magnificent and George Washington Park Cat, who kept me company for many long nights at the computer and in the kitchen, and ate all the mistakes.

ELLEN BROWN
Washington, D.C.

FOREWORD

BY JOHN F. MARIANI

Had anyone asked me a decade ago to assess the dining-out scene in the west, I would have been tempted to quote Horace Greeley—no, not his famous exhortation to "Go West, young man!" but instead his speech at the Houston Fair Grounds in 1871, in which he said that Texas was "in urgent need of . . . fifty thousand cooks." And that didn't begin to consider the needs of California, Arizona, New Mexico, and other states.

Ten years ago I might have reeled off the well-known names of deluxe dining rooms in the west serving Continental or French cuisine of a high order: Ma Maison and Chasen's in Los Angeles, Ernie's and Jack's in San Francisco, Tony's in Houston, Dudley's in Denver, the Orangerie in Scottsdale, and many other fine establishments. I might also have listed some of my favorite barbecue, Mexican, and hamburger stands that are part of a long, honorable tradition of western prole food. But I would have been hard pressed back then to prophesy the kinds of changes and directions western cooking would take or even to suggest that there would be any legitimacy to the idea of a "new California cuisine" or a "new Texas cookery," much less mark the revolutionary character of restaurants like Denver's Rattlesnake Club or Dallas' Routh Street Cafe. These, and many of the other restaurants and cooks featured in *Southwest Tastes* from "Great Chefs of the West" show the manifest destiny of American cuisine for the future. From the simple beauty of *enchiladas verdes* at Houston's Ninfa's to the elegant refinement of a wild-mushroom gratin at San Francisco's Campton Place, we are now seeing a cuisine that displays a remarkable diversity of flavors, techniques, and traditions, both for those who grew up chewing on *jalapeño* peppers for breakfast and those who wouldn't know a *burrito* from a *chimichanga* (something that still eludes me whenever I order the combination platter).

This is exciting food, and exciting men and women cook it. This is luscious food, often spicy, sometimes seasoned with bravado, and always enticing. These dishes demonstrate the superiority of American chefs in the techniques of grilling and smoking over hardwoods and of marrying hot flavors with sweet and sour ones. And, perhaps most important, the young chefs in this book have maintained their respect for their older colleagues and for the revered, delectable traditions that have brought western cookery to this extraordinary plateau.

The producers of the television series have done a wonderful job of evoking not just the flavor of the food but of the people and regions that the food springs from. And Ellen Brown, who must by now have enough Frequent Flyer mileage to take her to Mars and back, has performed a backbreaking labor of true oral history by interviewing these chefs and in making domesticated sense of the most disparate methods and ingredients so that any cook from Sheboygan to Shreveport can master even the most unfamiliar dish.

Southwest Tastes from "Great Chefs of the West" is a milestone in American cookery, and, like those signposts out in the middle of the desert in all the Western movies, it points the way in which American cooks inexorably are headed.

The History of Southwest Tastes

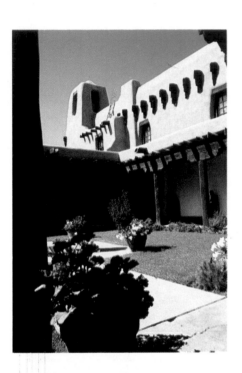

Traditional Southwest cuisine, with its assertive clear flavors and bright colors, evolved more by circumstance than design. It is the result of the serendipity that led Spanish, Mexican, and Anglo settlers to a region of what is now the United States where a native American civilization was already flourishing.

While each of the new ethnic groups brought with them specific dishes to be integrated into the region's cookery, the disparate elements were related by the crops the Indians grew in that area. Dishes had to be adopted to the ingredients that were available, and the dishes that resulted from this process are the nucleus of Southwest tastes.

Crops unknown to the Spanish—corn, squash, and beans— became the basis for the region's larder. The Spanish brought the seedlings for previously unknown fruit trees, and received the chili pepper in return.

While the new settlers may not have found the orchards of fruit trees they left behind in Segovia and Savannah, there was no shortage of food. Capt. James H. Cook, a direct descendant of the famous British navigator, wrote of hunting wild turkey during his early days as a cowboy in Texas: "Great flocks of this king of all game fowl roamed about ... quail were abundant and never having been hunted, they were not so wild as they are today." He also talked about the wild hogs and, of course, the buffalo. During the 1700s, it is estimated that more than 60 million buffalo roamed freely on the prairie and served as the basis of the diet for those building the railroads across the Great Plains. Their number was less than a thousand by the time the government began protecting the bison in 1889.

Different ethnic settlers exerted their culinary influence in different areas of the Southwest. The Acadians were an important force in the East Texas area around Beaumont, so gumbos are still prevalent in the region. And it is not uncommon even today to find tacos served with shredded cabbage instead of lettuce in the area around San Antonio, where a contingent of German immigrants followed the Spanish.

The geographic isolation of Southwestern settlements allowed such pockets of ethnicity to flourish. Arturo Jaramillo, the owner of Rancho de Chimayó in Chimayó, New Mexico, was raised in that town, now merely a 30-minute drive from Santa Fe. He recalls, however, that prior to World War II, cars were virtually unknown there, and a trip to the state capital was made only a few times a year, since it was a day's trip over arduous mountain roads.

Today, distinctions between the cuisines of the Southwest have blurred. One is likely to find Arizona-bred *chimichangas* in Dallas or Texas-born *nachos* in San Diego. What differentiates the once region-tied specialties is how they are presented. In California one is likely to find citrus slices garnishing a plate, and it's likely that the *salsas* served in Texas will be based on cooked rather than raw tomatoes.

Within the array of Southwest tastes, there are subcultures that transcend regional variations. The chuck wagon cookery that nourished the cowboys, those modern nomads so romanticized in folklore, developed wherever they were herding cattle to market.

Another constant, regardless of the meats or seasonings used, was the barbecue. The word *barbecue* is derived from the Spanish word *barbacoa*, which, in turn, came from the Indian word for a framework of green wood used to support meat or fish over the coals. While grilling, the oldest form of cooking, has come of age in sophisticated restaurant kitchens and forms an

Goat Cheese Rellenos, Gordon's, Aspen, Colorado

important part of new Southwest cooking, it originated in this method of long cooking over low heat, which was used by Indian tribes from Canada to the Patagonian pampas.

The most important Indian presence in the development of Southwest cooking was that of the Pueblo tribes. The Pueblo Indians, living in about thirty towns in New Mexico and Arizona, number about ten thousand today. They achieved a way of life that many anthropologists believe was the highest level of civilization among the Indians in what are now the boundaries of the United States. The Southwest is scattered with the remains of their sturdy communal dwellings, their elaborate irrigation projects, and their dynamic linear artistic style.

The backbone of their cuisine was corn, supplemented by beans for protein and by chilies, squash, and tomatoes for taste and vitamins. The gathering of corn is still celebrated by the Hopi, the Pueblo tribe of Arizona, at Niman, the most important *kachina* ceremony of the season. It forms the basis for *piki*, the brittle Indian bread that is the predecessor of the tortilla.

And the all-important tortilla, which we now know as the bread for Southwest and Mexican cookery, was an Indian invention. The Indians heated whole corn grains in water containing a little dissolved lime to make the skins come off. Then they ground the softened kernels into a smooth dough called *masa*, which the women tossed and patted into thin cakes.

We have few extant cookbooks on Indian cooking, since recipes were passed down as part of the tribes' oral history. One of the best is by Juanita Tiger Kavena, an Oklahoma-born Creek Indian who was adopted by the Hopi tribe after her marriage to a Hopi in 1948. She spent more than twenty-five years chronicling that tribe's culinary culture. She writes in *Hopi Cooking* that the Hopis added chamiza shrub ashes to dishes made with blue corn to enhance its blue color. The ashes have a very high mineral content, which augmented the Indian diet, usually devoid of all dairy products and low in animal proteins.

Indeed, the Indians' use of meat could be viewed by some as rather quirky. Before their habits were changed by European influence, the Indians only ate the organs of the animals they hunted for food, and left the muscles for predatory animals.

The Pueblo tribes used blue corn more often than any other of the brightly colored species they raised, and had a fascination with the color blue in general. Anthropologists credit this to a parallel made with the benevolence of the blue sky.

The Indian heritage is part of the matrix of Southwest taste, but in Texas it is secondary to other influences.

The food in the expansive state is as varied as the topography—from arid desert to lush seaside beaches. Even within the state, dishes vary according to the local proportion of Spanish and Mexican settlers. While the Mexicans used native chilies and flavorings such as *epazote*, spices such as cumin were a prize hoarded by the Spaniards for themselves. In San Antonio, spices were locked in the governor's palace to remain the possession of the powerful.

Some of the best Southern-style cooking in the country comes from east Texas, where ranchers who had migrated from the South both before and after the Civil War lived largely on the mottled kidney beans called pinto beans, hot breads, and "chicken-fried" steak. The cooking on these ranches was characterized by a lavish use of fresh, rich ingredients. And as the decades progressed, the cultures began to blend. The use of chilies has worked its way into typically Anglo dishes such as corn bread and even potato salad.

Nuances of Texas food abound, but nationally we associate the state with chili con carne. In San Antonio, where the dish most likely originated, "chili queens" and their pots used to appear daily in the Military Plaza after the produce merchants vacated the spaces for the day. They found a national spotlight when a coterie visited the Columbian Exposition of 1893 in Chicago with the San Antonio Chili Stand.

The state health department made the chili queens and the tamale vendors history following World War II, but national societies to preserve and protect what Frank X. Tolbert glorified as "a bowl of red" have materialized. The Chili Appreciation Society International, founded in 1951 and based in Dallas, now has chapters internationally, as does the International Chili Society based in Newport Beach, California.

The first chili cook-off was staged in 1967 by Tolbert, and now, between the two rival chili societies, it's estimated that thousands stir cauldrons annually.

"Real" Texas chili con carne is made with small cubes of meat, which, along with the use of *ancho* chilies, distinguishes it from other Southwestern versions, which use shredded beef. All chili con carnes are an amalgam of Mexican spices the European tradition of long simmered stews.

Along with chili con carne, another Texan specialty now gaining popularity nationally is the *fajita*, traditionally made with skirt steak that is marinated and then grilled with onions and chilies.

While *fajitas* might be considered merely a variation on the Mexican *tacos al carbon*, grilled steak wrapped in tortillas, another Texas dish, *nachos*, is a U.S. version of the myriad Mexican tortilla specialties.

A cafe owner in El Paso is credited with their invention, and while the embellishments can be almost anything, the basic snack of crispy tortilla chips topped with refried beans, cheese, and slices of *jalapeño* has become so common that it is sold at convenience stores and in airports throughout the country.

Texas is also the home of the mesquite tree. Hot-burning mesquite wood, usually plucked from the ground young since the trees rob the arid soil of moisture, has become synonymous with grilling in the region.

It's important to recall that unlike New Mexico and Arizona, Texas has a 375-mile stretch of coastline on the Gulf of Mexico, and the most important commodity gleaned from the waters is shrimp. In fact, shrimping has given rise to a subculture akin to that of the cowboys. Texans have not embraced the fish preparations of the Yucatán peninsula as have Californians, but they have invented many preparations for this prized catch using chilies and Mexican sauces.

Equally distinctive as Texas cookery are the dishes native to New Mexico. Long the domain of the Pueblo Indians, New Mexico was settled by Spaniards moving north from Mexico, who began to establish outposts after the first forays by Spanish explorer Francisco de Coronado in 1540. They had moved along the Rio Grande by 1598, only to find they were virtually isolated from the rest of the world by the desert and frequently hostile Indian tribes.

It was nearly a century later that fifteen hundred colonists emigrated to Santa Fe, and El Camino Real secured contact between the capital of New Mexico and Mexico City. The *ranchos* they built showed the mark of European parentage: orchards of apple, apricot, and peach trees as well as vineyards.

While the dishes from these New Mexican kitchens are basically Spanish, they are more closely aligned with Mexican and Indian foods than those of either Texas or Arizona.

New Mexicans have adopted the Indians' buttery piñon nuts, using them in pastries, just as they burn the aromatic wood, whose piney smoke fills the thin air around Santa Fe. The New Mexican settlers also developed *sopaipillas*, puffy pillows of fried flour dough based on the Indian fry breads common to the Pueblo and Navajo.

Another specialty of New Mexico, *posole*, a hominy and pork stew enlivened with chilies, was a substantial meal for the cold nights of the mountains. Along with tamales, *posole* is a traditional Christmas dish, and it is believed to bring good luck for the new year.

The local variation on Texas chili con carne is *carne adovada*, in which meat is simmered in a sauce made from the same dried chilies that form the decorative *ristras* seen in kitchens and outside the front doors of adobe houses.

They are kept in a dark place until the peppers show spots of orange, then they are tied into strings and placed in the brilliant sun. After three weeks they are dry and crimson red.

In addition to adding color to houses, the chilies are used in almost all chili sauces in New Mexico. They can either be steamed or soaked until pliable, at which time the pulp is scraped away from the skin, or the dried pods are simply ground to a powder.

The state has also added desserts to the Southwestern repertoire. *Natilla,* an egg custard topped with beaten meringue, is their version of floating island; and the traditional Christmas sweets of *biscochitos,* crispy anise-flavored cookies, and *empanaditas,* small turnovers filled with a mixture of dried fruits, pork, and frequently piñon nuts, have become traditional across the region.

One cannot discuss the food of New Mexico, however, without mentioning the use of slate-blue cornmeal in the region around Santa Fe, a culinary practice derived from the Indians. It forms a background for vivid red chili sauces, and connoisseurs say blue corn tortillas are more delicate than their yellow counterparts.

While settling New Mexico was a goal of the Spanish, they virtually ignored the adjoining land of Arizona for a century longer, until the advent of large-scale copper mining and cattle raising made settlement of the territory advantageous.

Part of what we now know as the cooking of Arizona is that staple of the diet, tortillas made from wheat, a grain introduced by the Spaniards. The flour tortilla forms the basis for many of the specialties we associate with Arizona: *chimichangas, burros,* and burritos.

In general, Arizona food is based on the cooking of Sonora, the desert section of Mexico right across the border. It is milder than the cuisine of most Mexican provinces, with many dishes calling for no chilies at all, but it also lacks the elegance of cooking from more prosperous regions. Along with the cooking of the nearby provinces of Chihuahua and Nuevo Leon, the style is called *"nortena"* in Mexico, and includes beans stewed with cumin and cilantro, and *menudo,* a tripe stew flavored with *poblano* or *ancho* chilies. *Menudo* is credited with curing hangovers and is therefore served as breakfast on Sunday mornings.

To anyone who has seen the desert around Tucson, with giant cacti rising like pillars from the mesas, it is not surprising that Arizona cooks use cactus pads both in salads and as garnishes for their food.

These three states are the major sources of Southwest traditional cooking. States such as Colorado, which was settled centuries later, and California, which was settled by the Spanish but lacked the synergistic blending of cultures, made few contributions to Southwest tastes. These states' variations on the classic dishes of Texas, New Mexico, and Arizona are due more to ingredient variations than cultural influences.

Colorado's first settlers were not *caballeros,* but frontiersmen of French or Anglo origin who came westward across the plains early in the nineteenth century to trap beavers. By the 1830s, miners had replaced trappers, but the population remained sparse. Denver, founded in 1858, a year before the "Pike's Peak or Bust" rush to Colorado's goldfields, is a city of rambling Victorian mansions rather than haciendas.

And while the history of California goes back to the Spanish missions, the Mexicans in the southern part of the state have been the dominant influence on the cuisine. When translated to California, Southwest cuisine becomes lighter, more like the seafood-based cookery of the Yucatán and Veracruz provinces than the desert specialties of Sonora.

Monterey jack, native to California and used nationally as a substitute for Mexican *asadero* cheese, is one of the state's contributions to Southwestern cooking. From farther south in the state, Anaheim chilies have become as common for *chiles rellenos* as the traditional *poblano.*

The plains of the Southwest gave rise to a new category of nomadic people once the Indians were settled on their reservations. The famed cowboys of the nineteenth century, such as Kit Carson and Doc Holliday, had in common with their less celebrated compatriots the school of chuck wagon cookery.

The first chuck wagons, dating to right after the Civil War, were two- and four-wheeled vehicles drawn by oxen, mules, or horses with the contents stowed and covered with hides or tarpaulins. *Chuck* was slang for food, or "grub," and the wagon served as a kitchen on the move.

The key to its design was a large device called the chuck box set at the wagon's rear, with a back that swung down like the tailgate of a station wagon to become a work surface where the "cookie," or "coosie" (from the Spanish word *cocinero,* for cook), would work.

Most of the chuck wagon cooks were older cowboys who still possessed the stamina to rise long before dawn to start the fire for breakfast. Lore has it that these cooks ruled their constantly moving camps with a hand as hard as their cast-iron skillets. An old proverb in the Southwest says: "Only a damned fool would argue with a skunk, a woman, or a roundup cook."

The cooking itself was done on open fires, usually in a pit to allow the coals to retain their heat, and the basic utensil was the Dutch oven, which could be converted to an oven in which to bake pies or the biscuits that formed the basis of the cowboys' breakfast; used as a braising pot for roasts, stews, and the pinto beans that were a staple on the trail; or serve as a deep-fryer for chicken-fried steaks.

In *Out Where the West Begins,* Arthur Chapman eulogized the chuck wagon and its rudimentary accouterments: "The old Dutch oven never failed to cook the things just right./T'was covered o'er with red-hot coals, and when we fetched her out,/the biscuits there were of the sort no epicure would flout."

The larder of most chuck wagons contained some canned goods, mainly tomatoes, but most traveling pantries were kept to the basics: flour, coffee, sugar, and dried fruits. Onions and potatoes were about the only perishables included among the provisions, and foods such as eggs or fresh vegetables were rare.

Regardless of where they roamed, the food of the chuck wagons retained its own integrity. Even today, when helicopters have replaced riding the range, the same cobblers and platters of chicken-fried steak are on ranch tables.

Techniques

Not long ago I gave a recipe for *guacamole* to a friend who looked in horror at the *serrano* chilies listed as an ingredient. Although a most accomplished cook, she had never delved into Southwestern cookery, since she abjectly refuses to deal with a recipe in which a line of the instructions reads "put on rubber gloves."

The warnings regarding the potent oils from hot chilies, along with the roasting of chilies and various ways of handling tortillas, are integral parts of the traditional cooking of the Southwest as well as the lighter versions of Southwestern food developed by innovative chefs.

Cooks trained in the European tradition don't think twice about slowly cooking flour and butter to form a roux, or melding egg yolks and cream to a thickened custard, since these procedures are essential steps in many dishes. In the same way, once you have roasted and peeled chilies a few times, that operation, too, will become second nature.

What I have done is to take a few of the techniques used most frequently in Southwestern cooking and explore them step by step. You will see in many recipes a notation to consult this chapter rather than delineating the process each time. However, take heart. After a few times there will be no need to refer back; you will have mastered the techniques.

In addition, there are some pieces of equipment used by the devoted Southwestern cook—such as special wire baskets with which to create crispy bowls from flour tortillas, or tortilla presses—that would be frivolous investments for those cooking the cuisine infrequently. Part of this chapter details substitutions for these specialized gadgets.

The step-by-step photos were taken in the Dallas kitchen of Anne Lindsay Greer, the noted Southwestern food writer who has pioneered so many aspects of the new style of Southwestern cooking. My thanks to her for her time and attractive hands.

At the end of this chapter are basic recipes for stocks, which I consider essential to every kitchen. When people say that restaurant food tastes better than home-cooked food, what they are frequently noticing is the depth of flavor given to soups and sauces by long-simmered stocks. It is no more difficult to make stocks than it is to boil water, and keeping the freezer "stocked" should become part of every cook's routine.

Making stocks can also be economical. I keep four bags in my freezer: one each for poultry, meat, and fish scraps, and the last for those slightly "tired" vegetables such as a limp sprig of parsley. When one of the protein bags is full, it's time to make the stock, so a few quarts cost virtually nothing. ∎

HANDLING FRESH CHILIES

Many recipes using fresh hot chilies such as *serranos* or *jalapeños* call for either seeding, or seeding and deribbing them. The variation occurs because some chefs like the added hotness imparted by leaving the ribs attached to the flesh, while others do not. The ribs and seeds are the hottest part of all chilies, and the individual chili is hotter at the stem end than the tip end.

When handling hot chilies, the main thing to keep in mind is to avoid contact with the oils. The easiest way to do this is to wear rubber gloves; however, I find them cumbersome when using sharp knives. The second method is to coat your hands with oil and wash your hands immediately after handling the chilies, remembering not to touch your skin with your hands until you have washed them well.

Do not handle chilies under running water, since the vapors can carry the oil to your face, and use a plate rather than a cutting board since the oils can lodge in wood fibers or in the cut surface of plastic.

For larger chilies, such as *poblanos* or bell peppers, an easy way to remove the seeds and ribs is to cut away the flesh. Cut a slice from the bottom so the chili will stand flat, then slice down from the stem end with a sharp paring knife, using the indentations of the ribs as a guide. You will be left with the stem attached to the cage of ribs and seeds, with the flesh freed.

For smaller chilies, slice off the stem end and cut the chili in half. Use a sharp paring knife to cut around the core, removing the ribs. The seeds will come out with the ribs.

ROASTING, PEELING, AND SEEDING CHILIES

You will notice that some recipes call for chilies (or bell peppers) to be roasted, peeled, and seeded while at other times the seeds are left in. The basic procedure for roasting and peeling is easy to master.

I find it convenient to do a batch of chilies at one time. It takes virtually no more time to roast a dozen chilies than it does one, and this means that you have a cache for a few days. (The same is true for such tasks as chopping onions, peeling and seeding tomatoes, or mincing cloves of garlic. It makes sense to do a large quantity ahead, so that at the actual time of cooking the process goes both more smoothly and more quickly.)

How you will roast the chilies depends on the cooking methods at your disposal. Make a small slit with a paring knife near the stem of each chili to allow steam to escape while the chili is roasting, as it may explode when roasted otherwise. (This is not necessary with bell peppers.) It is important that all parts of the chili are evenly charred; this might entail holding it with tongs and turning it so the flame can reach the bottom and top of the chili.

The purpose of the roasting process is to blister and char the skin of the chilies, which will cause a separation between the skin and the flesh. While you want the skin to blister and char, chilies should be turned frequently with tongs so that the flesh underneath the skin does not burn.

This blistering allows the steam from the partially cooked flesh to further disengage the skin, so that it can easily be peeled off. Here are the ways chilies can be roasted:

1   2   3

1. In these illustrations, the chilies are being roasted on a gas stove, although there are many options, as detailed. They are turned with tongs as the skin chars, until the entire surface is blackened.

2. As they are done, place the chilies in a plastic bag so that the steam will complete the process of separating the skin from the flesh.

3. Place the chilies in a bowl of ice water and, when cool enough to handle, peel the skin away with your fingers and discard.

On a Gas Stove

Place the chilies on a metal grid such as a cake rack or a very open broiler grid and turn the flame on high. Turn the chilies frequently with tongs.

On an Electric Stove

Use the same sort of metal grid and set the burner to medium-high. You may have to adjust the heat frequently to maintain that delicate balance of charring without burning.

In an Oven Broiler

This is perhaps the easiest method of roasting, especially if you are doing a large quantity; however, the chilies have a tendency to overcook. Preheat the broiler for at least 10 minutes with the door ajar; the purpose is to heat the element but not the oven. Place the chilies on the grid of a broiler pan about 4 inches from the flame or gas broiler. Turn frequently with tongs.

With large bell peppers, you may have to move the pan down when charring the bottoms, since they may be taller than 4 inches.

In a Dry Skillet

While this method works well with small chilies such as *serranos*, I don't recommend it for big bell peppers that give off a large quantity of liquid. If there is moisture in the pan, the peppers will stew rather than blister.

Heat a heavy skillet or griddle over medium-high heat. When the pan is hot, place the chilies in it, turning them frequently.

On a Charcoal or Gas Grill

This is my favorite way to roast chilies, since the charcoal or wood taste adds depth to the finished dish they are part of. For a large batch of chilies, it's worth it to light the grill just for them, or to grill some chilies around the periphery of the grill as meat is grilling over the hotter part of the fire.

Let the fire burn down to medium, about 10 minutes after you would have placed a steak on it. Turn the chilies frequently, and do not allow the flesh to burn. The amount of time depends on the temperature of the coals. For a gas grill, it will take the same amount of time.

In Hot Oil

This is an easy way to achieve a blistered skin, and it also retains the color of bright chilies such as red bell peppers or *poblanos*. It's also a good choice if the chili is not evenly shaped, since the oil will penetrate into all crevices.

Heat oil in a Dutch oven or deep-fryer halfway up the sides to a temperature of 375°; make sure the oil is hot enough or the chilies will not blister but will cook and become greasy. Make sure the chilies are dry or they will sputter in the hot oil. Add the chilies, not crowding the pan or they will lower the oil temperature. Remove them with a slotted spoon when the skin is blistered (this will only take a minute or two), or turn them if they have not been completely submerged, then remove. The skins will be blistered but not charred. Drain on paper towels.

Peeling

Regardless of the method used for roasting, all chilies can be peeled in one of two ways. Either place the charred chilies in a heavy plastic bag, seal the top with a twist tie, and allow the chilies to steam for at least 20 minutes, or until cool enough to handle. Alternately, you can plunge them into a bowl of ice water to cause the skins to dislodge and stop the cooking action. Using either method, once the chilies are cool enough to handle, peel the skin away gently with your fingers.

For chilies such as *poblanos* to be used for *chiles rellenos*, the second method is recommended since the flesh will not continue to cook, but if the chilies are going to be pureed, then the first and more traditional method will work fine.

Seeding

If the chilies are going to be chopped or pureed, seeding is a snap; break off the stem, then remove the seeds and ribs with your fingers, rinsing the chili under running water. Then proceed with the cooking.

If, however, you want to keep the chili whole, start by making a slit down one side, starting and ending ½ inch from the ends. Carefully remove the seeds with the tip of a knife or a demitasse spoon, and cut the ribs out, if desired, with a pair of nail scissors.

MAKING CORN TORTILLAS

With the convenience of tortillas—both corn and flour—in the refrigerator case of the supermarket, few of us take the time and effort to make our own. However, as with making puff pastry or pasta, also readily available now, it's good to have the skill to make them should the need arise.

For 16 tortillas

1½ cups *masa harina*
½ cup cornmeal
1½ tablespoons oil
1⅓ cups warm water

Mix all the ingredients together in a large bowl and beat with a wooden spoon until thick and smooth. Scrape the sides of the bowl, and cover the surface of the dough with plastic wrap while pressing and frying individual tortillas so the dough will not dry out.

To form the tortillas, wet your hands and pull off a lump of dough about the size of a golfball. Roll it into a ball. Tear off 2 pieces of plastic wrap about a foot long. Either in a tortilla press, or between 2 dinner plates, place the ball between the 2 sheets of plastic wrap. Press down with the palm of your hand to flatten slightly, then press firmly to form a thin circle.

Use the first tortilla to test the consistency of the dough. If the edges of the tortilla are uneven and crumbly, the dough needs a little more water. If the sheet of plastic sticks to the dough and it is very soft, add a few tablespoons of *masa harina*.

Repeat with the remaining dough, leaving individual tortillas between the sheets of plastic wrap.

Heat a heavy skillet over medium-high heat until hot. Peel off the top sheet of plastic and invert the tortilla into the hot pan. Grill until stiffened, about 30 seconds; turn for 1 minute or less, until the side is slightly browned, then turn to the first side for 30 seconds. The time for grilling each tortilla is less than 2 minutes.

Repeat with the remaining tortillas.

1

2

3

1. Beat the ingredients together with a wooden spoon until the dough is thick and well blended.
2. Using a tortilla press, place a scoop of dough (formed with an ice cream scooper) between two sheets of plastic wrap and pat gently by hand before pushing the press down.
3. Tortillas can also be pressed between two dinner plates, if you don't own a press. Use the same method and place the dough between two sheets of plastic wrap. Use even pressure when pressing down on the top plate to form a round tortilla.

ROLLING ENCHILADAS

Once corn tortillas have cooled, they become stiff and will break if you try to roll them into cylinders around an enchilada filling. They will need to be softened in order to become pliable.

Heat ½ cup of oil in a skillet or sauté pan over medium heat to a temperature of 275°. Using tongs, place a tortilla in the oil and fry for about 15 seconds on a side, or until they are lightly colored but still soft.

Remove and drain on paper toweling.

You can do up to 6 tortillas at a time and then complete filling and rolling them; however, don't do more than that or they may stiffen again.

To complete the enchiladas, dip the softened tortillas into the enchilada sauce, fill with whatever filling you have prepared, and then roll. Place them closely together in a baking dish, spoon more sauce over the top, and sprinkle with cheese.

1   2   3

1. Soften corn tortillas briefly in warm oil so they can be rolled without breaking.
2. After softening, dip the tortillas in the sauce that will also top the enchiladas.
3. Roll the filling inside the softened and sauced tortillas, then spoon additional sauce and some grated cheese on top before heating them in the oven.

FRYING CORN TORTILLAS

There's nothing as addictive as a bowl of spicy *salsa* and a basket of freshly fried tortilla chips. The difference between just-fried tortilla chips and packaged corn chips is like the difference between a fresh crisp Oriental stir-fry and canned chow mein.

It's easy to make your own chips, and also to fry tortillas into curved shapes for tacos shells or decorative baskets for salads or various fillings.

It's best to use either stale tortillas, or let the tortillas dry at room temperature for a few hours, since the moisture from fresh tortillas will cause splattering in the hot grease.

1

2

3

4

5

1. Cut corn tortillas into shapes depending on their intended use. Strips are fried to garnish soup, small chips accompany *salsa*, and the larger triangles become *nachos*.

2. When the oil has reached the proper temperature, a test chip will cause a ring of white bubbles and will float on the surface and reach a nutty brown color within a few seconds.

3. To make a taco shell, fold the tortilla in half using tongs, and hold it in place while it stiffens and crisps.

4. To form a tortilla basket, push the center of the tortilla down into the hot oil with tongs. The sides will naturally curl upward.

5. Drain fried corn tortilla shapes well on paper towels.

For *nachos:* Cut each tortilla into sixths; for chips, cut them into eighths. As a garnish for soups such as Sopa Azteca, page 26, cut them into strips.

Heat oil slowly over medium heat in a Dutch oven or deep-fryer to a temperature of 375°. Have a slotted spoon and paper towels ready.

For chips or strips: Add a handful at a time, being careful not to crowd the pan or the oil temperature will be lowered and the chips will become greasy without becoming crisp. Fry completely submerged in oil for 20 to 30 seconds, or until lightly browned and crisp. Remove with a slotted spoon and drain on paper towels. Repeat with remaining chips or strips.

For a taco shell: Place a tortilla into the hot oil and carefully fold it in half with tongs. Keep the folded-over tortilla submerged in the oil until brown and crisp. Shake over the pan to remove oil from the center, then drain upside down on paper towels, patting the outside to remove excess oil.

For a basket: You can buy an appliance to make a perfectly round basket (see Mail Order Sources), or you can make a triangular basket with a meat pounder or tongs. Place a tortilla in the hot oil, then immediately push the center down into the oil, holding it in place until the sides have curled up around the cooking implement and are stiff and brown. Remove with tongs, drain off the excess oil, and drain upside down on paper towels, patting the outside to remove excess oil.

MAKING FLOUR TORTILLAS

While only the true connoisseur can tell a homemade pressed corn tortilla from a good machine-made one, the difference in fresh flour tortillas is more pronounced. These feathery light breads are well worth the minimal effort needed to create them.

Another advantage to making your own flour tortillas is that you can easily make them in miniature sizes for hors d'oeuvres.

Since tortillas freeze well, you can make a batch on a leisurely day and have a supply on hand.

To make 12 tortillas

2 cups unbleached all-purpose flour
1 teaspoon salt
¾ teaspoon baking powder
⅓ cup vegetable shortening
⅔ to ¾ cup very hot water

Mix the flour with the salt and baking powder. Using your hands, mix in the shortening until the mixture becomes a coarse, even meal. Mix in ⅔ cup of the water, adding it all at once, and knead for 2 minutes, or until the dough has the consistency of a stiff bread dough. If dry and crumbly, add extra water; if too moist, add a few tablespoons of additional flour.

Cover the dough and allow it to rest for 20 minutes. Heat a skillet, sauté pan, or griddle over medium-high heat until hot enough that a drop of water immediately sizzles and evaporates. You will be rolling and then cooking each tortilla, rather than rolling them all and then cooking them.

Pinch off a piece of dough the size of a golfball, and dust your hands and the dough ball with flour. Place the ball on a lightly floured surface and flatten the ball with your hands into a circle ½ inch thick. Then, using a rolling pin, roll it twice in the same direction. Keep rolling, turning the dough 90° each time, until you have formed a circle ⅛ inch thick and about 8 to 9 inches in diameter.

Immediately place it in the hot skillet and cook it for 30 to 45 seconds, or until bubbles begin to form on the top. If the tortilla puffs up into a pillow, push it down with a spatula. Turn and cook 20 seconds, remove with a spatula, and keep warm by placing it in a tea towel and covering it with the towel.

Roll and cook remaining tortilla dough in the same way.

1 2 3

4 5

1. The consistency of the dough for flour tortillas should be like a stiff bread dough.
2. Break off pieces of the dough and roll in well-floured hands into balls.
3. Pat them into a circle between the palms of your hands, and roll them first into an oval and then into a circle.
4. Cook the tortillas on a hot dry griddle or in a skillet until bubbles start to form on the top. Then turn them over so the second side is cooked.
5. Flour tortillas can be kept warm in a decorative pottery bowl while others are fried.

To Soften Flour Tortillas

Flour tortillas, like corn tortillas, become brittle when cold, and must be softened to become pliable for bending into *quesadillas* or rolling for *chimichangas*.

To soften, heat a dry skillet, sauté pan, or griddle over medium heat. Heat a tortilla for about 30 seconds, or until bubbles start to appear on top. Turn and heat the second side for about 15 seconds. Fold or roll immediately.

STOCKS AND STOCK-REDUCTION SAUCES

Long-simmered stocks are hardly a chef's secret; they are well within the culinary skills of anyone who has ever boiled water. Stocks provide, however, the depth of flavor you find in soups and sauces made in restaurants.

I cannot stress enough the importance of "stocking" your freezer with a larder consisting of poultry, meat, and seafood stock. The main ingredient in making stocks easily and economically is forethought.

Keep self-closing bags in your freezer to serve as the repository for scraps, so that every time you bone a chicken breast or take the neck and giblets out of a fresh chicken, every time you trim the bones and fat from a cut of veal or beef, and every time you peel a shrimp or fillet a fish the stock-making materials get added to the appropriate bag. When the bag is full and you're home for the day, it's time to make stocks.

Some of the stock should be frozen in ice cube trays; you can learn the capacity of your trays by melting a cube and measuring. Once frozen, transfer the cubes to a plastic bag, so you don't have to chip away at a glacier for 2 tablespoons. For saving space, however, I usually freeze most stock in 2-cup containers, since soups call for a minimum of that amount.

The general rules of stock making are to bring the liquid to a boil over medium heat and to skim the surface of scum as it rises during the first hour. Stock should simmer rather than boil briskly, so the fat in the pot does not become incorporated into the stock. Stock should be at room temperature before it is covered so it does not sour.

Strain the stock and allow it to reach room temperature. Then chill it so the fat that has risen to the surface will harden and can be removed. This hardened fat is pure cholesterol. I usually save chicken fat in a separate container for making *confit* of duck. I know people who save beef or veal fat and consider it the ultimate for cooking French fries.

Please note that there is no salt in the following stock recipes. Since stocks may either be used at simmered strength for soups, or may be greatly reduced for sauces, it's better to salt the finished product than to risk having too much salt in a reduction.

Chicken or Meat Stock

(Makes 3 quarts)

6 quarts water
4 pounds chicken bones and skin (you can fill in with inexpensive chicken backs sold in packages in the supermarket if you don't have enough) *or* 6 pounds of a combination of primarily veal bones and scraps with some beef bones and scraps (fill in breast of veal, cut into chunks, and some beef shank)

2 carrots, scrubbed and halved
2 medium onions, peeled and halved
3 celery stalks, with leaves
3 thyme sprigs, or 1 teaspoon dried thyme
6 parsley sprigs
2 bay leaves
3 garlic cloves, halved
12 black peppercorns

Bring the water to a boil over high heat (this will make the stock come to a boil faster).

For meat stock, preheat the oven to 450°. Roast the bones and meat for 30 minutes, or until brown, in a shallow roasting pan. For brown chicken stock, follow the same procedure. For regular chicken stock, do not.

Add the meat to the water and turn the heat down to medium. When it comes to a boil, skim frequently until the scum stops rising, then add the remaining ingredients and simmer, uncovered. Add additional water if the stock level falls below the level of the ingredients.

Chicken stock develops a good flavor after 3 hours, while meat stock should simmer for a minimum of 6 hours.

Strain and discard the solids. Let the stock reach room temperature, then refrigerate. Remove the fat layer from the top and freeze the stock.

Demi-glace and Glace de Viande

There's no magic about it. *Demi-glace* and *glace de viande* are nothing more than unsalted meat stocks that have been degreased and then reduced over medium-low heat until they become rich and syrupy. The concentrated flavor adds richness and depth to sauces and stews.

Bring 2 quarts of veal or beef stock to a boil and simmer uncovered over medium-low heat until it has reduced to 1 cup. Strain and freeze in ice cube trays.

Both *demi-glace* and *glace de viande* will keep frozen almost indefinitely.

Fish Stock

(Makes 3 quarts)

4 quarts water
1 cup dry white wine
4 pounds fish trimmings (including shellfish shells and lobster bodies, broken apart)
2 onions, peeled and halved
2 tablespoons fresh lemon juice
3 thyme sprigs, or 1 teaspoon dried thyme
6 parsley sprigs
2 celery stalks, including leaves, cut into sections
6 black peppercorns

Bring all the ingredients to a boil and simmer, uncovered, for 3 hours. Proceed as above, except that chilling to remove fat is not necessary since the fat content is so small.

Specialty Stocks

A few of the recipes in this book call for special stocks made from the primary ingredient of the dish, ranging from smoked rabbit to venison. Some recipes in the book contain specific stock recipes; if not, follow this general recipe.

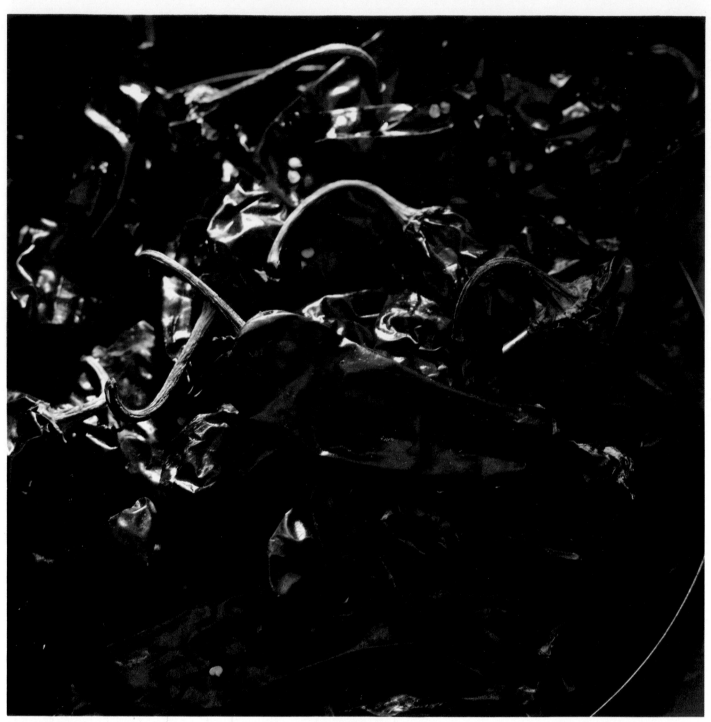

Dried Chilies

To make 2 quarts Specialty Stock:

4 quarts water
3 pounds meat trimmings (bones, skin, fat, gristle, and anything else you can
   trim away), or as much trimmings as yielded plus extra meat
1 medium onion, halved
1 carrot, scrubbed and halved
2 celery stalks, including leaves, cut into sections
3 thyme sprigs, or 1 teaspoon dried thyme
3 parsley sprigs
6 black peppercorns

Follow directions for meat stock, either roasting or not roasting the bones as the
main recipe calls for.

ODDS AND ENDS

Removing Silver Skin

Many recipes call for removing the silver skin, an almost iridescent membrane
covering a tenderloin or saddle of meat. The silver skin is different from the fell
covering a leg of lamb. That is a solid layer of fat, while the silver skin is a thin,
tough membrane. If it is not trimmed away, the meat will curl as it cooks rather
than lying flat in the roasting pan. Some butchers and supermarkets remove the
silver skin for you, while others sell meat that still requires this final trimming.

To remove the silver skin, first trim the meat of fat and trim away any
irregular edges to form an even piece. With the blade of a sharp paring knife,
scrape away at the end of the silver skin while pulling with your fingers down
the length of the meat. Repeat this process, turning the meat as necessary, until
all the silver skin has been scraped and pulled away.

Toasting Nuts

Toasting not only brings out the flavor in nuts, since it slightly cooks the nut
oils, it also makes removing their skins much easier, if that is called for in
a recipe.

To toast nuts, preheat the oven to 350°. Spread the nuts out in a single layer
on an ungreased cookie sheet and bake in the center of the oven for 5 to 7
minutes. Remove from the oven.

If you want to remove the skins from nuts such as hazelnuts or almonds,
wrap the nuts in a cloth tea towel and allow them to steam for 5 minutes. Then
roll the nuts around inside the towel to rub off the skins.

Peeling and Seeding Tomatoes

Many recipes call for pulp from tomatoes that have been peeled, seeded, and
diced. This is an extremely easy technique, and it's easier to do a batch of
tomatoes than one or two at a time.

Bring water to a boil in a Dutch oven or stockpot and add a few tomatoes at
a time with a slotted spoon. Allow them to poach for 30 to 40 seconds, then
remove them with the slotted spoon to a bowl of ice water.

Once blanched, the skins should slip easily off the tomatoes.

With your paring knife, cut the core out of the tomato. Holding the tomato
in the palm of your hand over the sink or a garbage can, with the core end
down, squeeze the tomato and the seeds will emerge. Then dice or slice the pulp
as called for in the recipe.

Once the tomatoes are peeled and seeded, they can be stored in the
refrigerator, covered with plastic wrap, for up to 3 days.

Regional Favorites

The centuries-old traditional dishes of the Southwest have been preserved primarily by the teaching of one generation to the next. Within the comfort of the home kitchen, mothers taught their daughters how to press tortilla dough and how to achieve puffy *sopaipillas*. This oral instruction maintained both regional and familial variations in even the simplest dishes.

Restaurants have broadened the exposure of these foods during this century. Usually the people working in the kitchens are not trained chefs, but home cooks sharing their dishes with the public and adapting their ancestors' recipes to be served on a larger scale. While some restaurants in the Southwest feature the dishes of several states and regions, the dishes in this chapter are primarily drawn from those restaurants specializing in dishes native to the region and cooked by people who learned them in childhood.

Included among the *enchiladas verdes* and *biscochitos* are dishes drawn from the Southern Anglo heritage of foods brought by settlers pushing west and served both in their homes and from chuck wagons on the prairie. For some specialties in the genre, we present prize-winning recipes from the cooking contests of the State Fair of Texas.

This chapter represents the classical base from which the new Southwest cooking chefs are improvising. ■

Chile con Queso, La Louisiane, San Antonio, Texas

This is a classic Southwestern appetizer that can be served as a cocktail party hors d'oeuvre by placing the cheese mixture in a chafing dish or fondue pot and letting guests dip chips.

Chile con Queso

La Louisiane, San Antonio, Texas

(Serves 8)

2 cups oil
8 large corn tortillas, cut into quarters
1 large tomato, cored and chopped
1 small onion, peeled and chopped
6 to 8 *serrano* or *jalapeño* chilies, seeded and chopped finely
2 garlic cloves, peeled and minced
Salt and pepper to taste
½ cup dry white wine
4 cups grated American or Cheddar cheese

Pour the oil into a large heavy skillet and heat to 375°. Fry the tortilla sections until crisp and lightly brown, about 2 minutes. Remove with a slotted spatula and drain on paper towels. Keep warm until ready to use.

Pour all but 2 tablespoons of the oil out of the skillet and add the tomato, onion, chilies and garlic. Sprinkle with salt and pepper and sauté over medium heat until the onions are soft and translucent, about 5 to 7 minutes. Add the wine to the pan and reduce slightly. Reduce the flame to low, add the cheese, and stir until melted.

Spoon over the tortilla wedges and serve immediately.

Note: You can prepare the cheese mixture up to 2 days in advance and reheat it slowly in the top of a double boiler. The tortillas should be fried the day they are used; however, they can be done in advance and reheated in a 300° oven. ■

This spicy mixture of seafood and beef is served in Arizona in a paviada, a terra-cotta pedestal heated with charcoal. Most of us do not have one in the pantry, but fear not. Any heated serving platter will do just as well.

Parilla

La Paloma/Atlas, San Diego, California

(Serves 6 as an appetizer, 3 as an entree)

10 ounces beef fillet, cut into strips
6 large shrimp, peeled and deveined
Two 7-ounce shelled lobster tails, sliced into medallions

Marinade

Juice of 2 grapefruit (about 1½ cups)
Juice of 1 orange (about ½ cup)
2 tablespoons olive oil
2 bay leaves
¼ red bell pepper, seeded, deribbed, and cut into fine julienne
1 small *jalapeño* chili, seeded and chopped
2 small *poblano* chilies, seeded and cut into thin strips
1 garlic clove, peeled and minced
1 Tabasco chili, seeded and chopped (or a *serrano* can be substituted)
¼ cup roughly chopped cilantro leaves
1 medium onion, peeled and sliced
1 teaspoon Tabasco sauce

To finish the dish

4 tablespoons olive oil
2 *jalapeño* chilies, seeded and sliced into strips
½ onion, peeled and sliced
3 ounces tequila

Garnish

Guacamole, page 138, in lettuce cups
Refried beans, page 38, in corn tortillas

Prepare the meat and seafood and mix the marinade ingredients together. Marinate for 2 to 3 hours.

Remove the meat and keep it separate from the seafood. Heat 2 tablespoons of the olive oil in a sauté pan or skillet over high heat and, when hot, sear the beef on all sides. Add the *jalapeños* and onion and sauté briefly, then deglaze the pan with half the tequila. Reserve the mixture and keep it warm.

In a second sauté pan or skillet, heat the remaining olive oil until hot and sauté the lobster and shrimp with some of the vegetables in the marinade. Flame with the remaining tequila and remove from the heat.

Fill a *paviada* with hot coals, or heat a serving platter. Place the beef mixture and seafood mixture in the center, and flank with lettuce cups of *guacamole* and refried beans wrapped in tortillas.

Note: Do not marinate the food for more than the time allotted, since the acid in the fruit juice will break down the fibers. ∎

JOAQUIN GONZALEZ
shown with owner George Dareos
La Louisiane, San Antonio, Texas

The Acadians, who helped to develop Creole cuisine, settled in Texas as well as Louisiana, and La Louisiane in San Antonio, where Joaquin Gonzalez has been chef for the past thirty-two years, plays on Creole flavors, with the chef adding Southwestern accents on occasion.

The restaurant, founded in 1935 by Turkish-born Max Manus and now owned by his brother-in-law George Dareos, is one of the oldest restaurants in San Antonio. When it first began, Manus' wife would do the shopping and deliver groceries to the kitchen door.

Chef Gonzalez was born in Mission, Texas; however, his family moved back to Mexico during the Depression. When he arrived in Houston in 1947, he knew no English, and his first job, after determining that he did not like the construction business, was as a dishwasher in a restaurant.

"I've had no formal schooling in cooking, but learned from the chefs along the way," he says.

He is fond of using artichoke hearts and mushrooms with quickly sautéed dishes, such as Chicken Gonzalez and Red Snapper George, named for the restaurant's owner. Both are variations on Creole dishes, although the chef adds more spices.

"People in this part of the country, no matter what they are eating, like a little bit of spice," he says.

Mary Trevino is known for the soups she makes on weekends; they could easily be whole suppers or lunches. The broth is flavorful, and the ingredients combine many textures and flavors, from creamy avocado to crisp-fried tortilla strips.

Sopa Azteca

El Mirador, San Antonio, Texas

(Serves 12)

1½ tablespoons olive oil
2 medium onions, peeled and sliced
6 garlic cloves, peeled
2 pounds ripe tomatoes, cored and cut into chunks
1½ tablespoons dried oregano
1½ tablespoons dried basil
1 tablespoon ground cumin
1 teaspoon ground black pepper
10 cups water
2 pounds meaty chicken pieces
3 bay leaves
1 *epazote* sprig (optional)
One 6-ounce can tomato paste
1 red bell pepper, seeded, deribbed, and cut into thin slices
1 cup sliced celery
1½ cups diced zucchini
1 large carrot, peeled and thinly sliced
Salt to taste
1 medium potato, peeled and diced
1 cup vegetable oil
15 corn tortillas, cut into ¼-inch strips
½ pound fresh spinach, washed, stemmed, and cut into strips
1 avocado, peeled, cubed, and sprinkled with lemon juice to prevent discoloration
1 pound mozzarella or Monterey jack cheese, shredded

Place the oil in a large sauté pan or skillet over medium heat. Add the onions and garlic and sauté until the onions are translucent and soft, about 10 minutes, stirring frequently. Add the tomatoes, oregano, basil, cumin, and pepper. Continue to cook until the tomatoes are soft, about 10 minutes, then puree the mixture in a blender or a food processor fitted with a steel blade. Set aside.

Bring the water to a boil in a large soup pot and add the chicken pieces, bay leaves, and *epazote*, if used. When the water returns to a boil,

skim off the foam that rises to the surface, then add the pureed vegetable mixture and tomato paste. Simmer over low heat, uncovered, for 20 minutes, or until the chicken is cooked and tender. Remove the chicken pieces with a slotted spoon and, when cool enough to handle, discard the skin and bones and shred the meat. Set the meat aside.

Add the bell pepper, celery, zucchini, and carrot to the broth and cook about 10 minutes, or until tender. Remove the vegetables, set aside, and salt broth to taste.

While the soup is cooking, parboil the diced potato in salted water until tender. Drain, and pat the cubes dry on paper towels. Heat the oil in a sauté pan or skillet, and fry the potato cubes until brown. Remove,

drain on paper towels, and set aside.

In the same oil, fry the tortilla strips in small batches until crispy, removing them from the hot oil with a slotted spoon to drain on paper towels; repeat the process until all the strips are fried. Set aside.

To serve, divide the vegetables and potato cubes among the soup bowls. Add to each, in order, the tortilla strips, spinach, shredded chicken, cubed avocado, and cheese. Pour the boiling broth into soup bowls and serve immediately.

Note: Everything except the cubing of the avocado can be done in advance. Reheat the vegetables in the soup; the other ingredients will be reheated sufficiently by the boiling stock. ■

Caldo Xochitl, El Mirador, San Antonio, Texas

The problem with most chicken broth soups is the flavorless broth itself—regardless of what else it contains. In this case, the broth is spicy and delicious, and the fresh salsa added at the end gives it freshness.

Caldo Xochitl

El Mirador, San Antonio, Texas

(Serves 12)

1 frying chicken, cut into pieces
10 cups water
Salt to taste (about 2 teaspoons)
1 teaspoon ground black pepper
1 tablespoon ground cumin
1 *epazote* sprig (if available)
1 basil sprig, or ½ teaspoon dried basil
3 bay leaves
4 whole cloves
1 tablespoon dried oregano
5 garlic cloves
2 cups sliced zucchini
1½ cups diced carrots
1½ cups diced celery
1½ cups diced green bell peppers
1 medium onion, peeled and chopped
One 17-ounce can garbanzo beans, drained and rinsed
½ cup cilantro leaves, tightly packed
½ cup chopped green onion, white part only
1 to 2 *jalapeño* chilies, seeded, deribbed, and finely chopped
3 cups hot cooked rice
2 ripe tomatoes, seeded and diced
1 ripe avocado, finely cubed and sprinkled with lemon juice to prevent discoloration

Place the chicken, water, salt, pepper, cumin, *epazote*, basil, and bay leaves in a large soup pot. Bring to a boil over high heat, skimming off the foam that rises to the surface. In a blender, puree the cloves, oregano, and garlic with a little water and add to the soup. When the soup comes to a boil, lower the heat to a simmer and cook the soup until the chicken pieces are very tender, about 40 minutes.

MARY TREVINO

*shown with husband Julian
El Mirador, San Antonio, Texas*

San Antonians know that if it's the weekend, Mary Trevino is making Sopa Azteca at El Mirador. The restaurant has become a local favorite and has received national press in the *New York Times* and *Bon Appetit*, especially for its soups, rich spiced chicken stocks with chicken and vegetables that are really a meal in themselves.

Mrs. Trevino, now seventy, whose husband Julian makes all of the meat dishes in the restaurant, is a native of Guanaquato in central Mexico and was raised in San Antonio. When they bought the restaurant in 1968, she had no intention of cooking, but began "doing things the way I remember my mother cooking it."

Her food is a mix of Mexican and Tex-Mex. The enchiladas, for example, are done with chile con carne, as is common in Texas, except on Fridays when they are made in the Mexican fashion with no onion and a red chili sauce. Her chile con carne is Texan, also, since she uses cumin, not found in authentic Mexican chili.

El Mirador is only open for breakfast and lunch, and features many Southwestern breakfast specialties, including *huevos rancheros* and eggs cooked with spicy chorizo sausage.

garbanzo beans to the soup and simmer until the vegetables are tender but still slightly crisp, about 15 minutes. Return the chicken to the soup.

In a small bowl, mix the cilantro, green onion, and chopped chilies.

To serve, place ¼ cup of rice in the bottom of each soup bowl and ladle the soup over it. Garnish with the cilantro mixture and cubes of tomato and avocado.

Note: Everything except the vegetable garnishes can be made up to 2 days in advance. Bring the soup to a boil over medium heat and it will be sufficient to reheat the rice. ■

This is the classic dish on which so many chefs are now improvising, with fillings ranging from goat cheese to lobster mousse. While it is usually served as a light meal, I prefer it as a side dish to accompany grilled foods.

Chiles Rellenos

La Tertulia, Santa Fe, New Mexico

(Serves 6)

12 fresh chilies such as *poblano,*
    Hatch, or Anaheim
6 American cheese slices
4 eggs, separated
Pinch of salt
Oil to grease pan
Flour for dipping

Roast, peel, and stem the chilies (see page 28), leaving the seeds in. Don't worry if you have small tears in the flesh, since the flour and batter will cover them. Cut each slice of cheese into 4 strips and insert 2 strips into the top of each chili. Set aside.

Beat the whites with a pinch of salt to form a stiff meringue. In a separate bowl, beat the egg yolks until thick and lemon colored, about 15 minutes. Add the yolks to the whites, beating on low speed briefly to incorporate, then proceed immediately since the batter deflates quickly.

Heat a skillet over high heat and grease it with a little oil. Dip the chilies in flour, shaking off any excess, then dip into the egg batter. Fry in the hot skillet until brown on one side, about 2 minutes, then turn and brown the other side. Add oil to the skillet if the chilies start to stick. Repeat until all the chilies are fried. Layer the chilies in a baking dish or on an ovenproof platter with a piece of aluminum foil between each layer, and keep them warm in a 150° oven while frying the remaining chilies.

Note: For the best flavor, the chilies should be fried at the last minute; however, the time-consuming roasting can be done up to 2 days in advance. Keep them covered with plastic wrap in the refrigerator. ∎

JUNE AND WILLIE ORTIZ
La Tertulia, Santa Fe, New Mexico

In Michener's *Iberia,* a *tertulia* was a gathering place for good food and good conversation. June and Willie Ortiz named their restaurant in Santa Fe after that concept. La Tertulia is housed in a century-old adobe building that was part of the Guadalupe Mission Church on the Camino Real, the road that led to Mexico City.

The dining rooms were formerly the convent's dining room and chapel, and the Ortizes' collection of religious art dating back to the 1700s is housed in an alcove in the two-story waiting area.

Willie Ortiz had retired after a long career in military intelligence when he and his Tennessee-born wife decided to go into the restaurant business. "I felt it was really a shame that there wasn't a restaurant serving native specialties in the city, and people were beginning to visit the city and they couldn't taste what we were eating at home," he says.

The food served at La Tertulia is all based on dishes recalled from his childhood in Chimayó, New Mexico, where his father was an Indian trader. They feature such staples as *posole,* a pork and hominy stew, *carne adovada,* the New Mexican version of chile con carne in which pork is simmered in a red chili sauce, and *chiles rellenos* stuffed with cheese and fried in a light egg batter.

For the past eleven years of the fourteen-year history of the restaurant, the dishes have been prepared by Isadora Martinez, a native of Pecos, New Mexico, about twenty-five miles from Santa Fe.

Huevos rancheros *are the traditional Southwestern breakfast, with a moderately hot chili sauce adding spice even to that hour of the day. They make a wonderful brunch dish, or a casual supper entree if a few more dishes are added.*

Huevos Rancheros with Green Chili Sauce

Rancho de Chimayó, Chimayó, New Mexico

(Serves 6)

Sauce

½ pound lean beef, coarsely ground or finely chopped
1 pound Anaheim or *poblano* chilies, seeded and chopped
1 quart water
2 teaspoons finely chopped onion
1 garlic clove, peeled and crushed
½ teaspoon Worcestershire sauce
1 tomato, cored and finely chopped
2 tablespoons cornstarch, mixed with ¼ cup cold water
Salt and freshly ground black pepper to taste

Eggs

½ cup (1 stick) butter
6 corn tortillas
12 eggs

Garnish

Refried beans, page 38
Spanish rice
Shredded lettuce
Tomato wedges
Tortilla chips

In a sauté pan or 12-inch skillet, brown the beef over medium-high heat, stirring frequently, until the beef is well browned. Pour off the grease and set aside.

In a saucepan, combine the browned beef with the chopped chilies, water, onion, garlic, Worcestershire sauce, and tomato. Bring the mixture to a boil over medium heat and simmer for 20 minutes, stirring occasionally. Add the cornstarch mixture and stir until it returns to a boil and thickens. Simmer over low heat for 5 minutes, add salt and pepper to taste, and set aside.

SHARON MOONEY
State Fair of Texas Winner
Arlington, Texas

Fried chicken with cream gravy and a basket of biscuits are as at home in Texas as they are in Tennessee. All through the Southwest certain Southern classics are part of the heritage, and the variations on cooking them were passed down through the generations.

Sharon Mooney is a Louisiana native who moved to Ft. Worth at age twelve. "I thought I had gone to heaven; I'd never seen so much green grass or anything as clean," she says. Mrs. Mooney learned her method of cooking prize-winning chicken from her mother-in-law.

"The secret, so that you taste the chicken, is to not add many spices or a heavy batter. You soak the chicken first with baking soda and salt to give the chicken flavor, and then you fry it covered for most of the time," she says.

Mrs. Mooney, who became a Girl Scout at the age of seven, says, "I could cook anything over a campfire before my mother would ever let me cook in the kitchen." She entered her first cooking contest seventeen years ago, when a neighbor suggested it. In 1985, she won the Best in Show at the State Fair of Texas for a cobbler. She especially enjoys the ethnic food contests.

"I am married to an American Indian, and I have done a lot of research into their cooking. The Indian dishes I make for contests are all authentic, but I make them modern. I'll use green beans in stews instead of *nopales*," she says.

Preheat the oven to 200°. Cut the butter into 1-tablespoon sections, and heat one section in a skillet. When hot, soften a tortilla by frying it over medium heat for 20 seconds on a side, turning with tongs. Remove from the pan, reserve in the preheated oven, and repeat with the remaining tortillas.

Heat a tablespoon of butter in the pan and add 2 eggs. Sprinkle with salt and pepper and fry them over easy. Remove with a spatula and place on a heated tortilla. Place the plate in the oven to keep warm and repeat with the remaining 5 servings.

Assemble each serving by ladling sauce over the eggs. Add the refried beans and Spanish rice, arrange the shredded lettuce around the eggs, and garnish with the tomato wedges and tortilla chips.

Note: The sauce and garnishes can be prepared a day in advance and kept refrigerated. Reheat the sauce over low heat, stirring occasionally. ∎

Covering the pan while the chicken fries creates moist and tender chicken with a crispy brown crust. For a real Southern meal, serve biscuits, page 41, with the gravy.

Southern Fried Chicken with Cream Gravy

Sharon Mooney, Arlington, Texas

(Serves 4)

One 3-pound fryer, cut into serving pieces
1 teaspoon salt
1 teaspoon baking soda
2 pounds shortening
1½ cups unbleached all-purpose flour
1 teaspoon poultry seasoning
1 teaspoon paprika
Dash of cayenne

Cream gravy

2 tablespoons reserved chicken grease
2 tablespoons reserved seasoned flour
1 cup evaporated milk
1 cup water

Place the chicken in a mixing bowl and cover with cold water. Add the salt and baking soda to the water and allow to sit for 1 hour.

Melt the shortening in a heavy deep-sided skillet over medium-high heat, and heat until it reaches a temperature of 350°. Mix the flour with the poultry seasoning, paprika, and cayenne. Drain the chicken pieces well and roll or shake them in the seasoned flour. Allow to sit for 5 minutes, then roll again in the flour and carefully place the chicken in the hot fat.

Cover the pan and cook until browned, about 12 to 15 minutes.

BERTIE VARNER

shown with ranch hands
Y.O. Ranch, Mountain Home, Texas

While Bertie Varner does not have to operate out of a chuck wagon and cook over an open fire, as the cook for the historic Y.O. Ranch she is upholding the tradition of chuck wagon cookery.

Breakfast is mounds of homemade biscuits, bacon, and eggs. Lunch and dinner is a rotation that always includes, in the course of a week, fried chicken, chicken-fried steak with cream gravy, and peach cobbler, and each day there is a bowl of ranch beans on the table.

"This is not only what the people like, but I have to fix what's easiest since I've got a lot of people to feed and no help," says Mrs. Varner, who was born in Arkansas fifty-eight years ago but considers herself "more a Texan than the people who were born and raised here."

Her chuck wagon is a one-story cottage, with long banquet tables covered with red-checked plastic cloths and an open kitchen from which she serves huge pots of food cafeteria style.

Mrs. Varner was working in a local restaurant when she joined the Y.O. Ranch staff in 1976. Since then, she has been feeding thirty-five to 120 people a day, cooking everything from scratch.

And she runs the kitchen with an iron hand. "Nobody ever tells me what they want to eat. I decide, and a lot depends on how many people we're feeding that day. I may look at cookbooks to get ideas, but then I do my own thing. I know what my people like to eat," she says.

Turn when brown, then re-cover and cook an additional 12 to 15 minutes. When tender, remove the cover to crisp the chicken.

Drain well on paper towels and cover lightly with aluminum foil to keep warm; do not cover tightly or the chicken will lose its crispiness.

To make the cream gravy, pour all but 2 tablespoons of grease from the skillet and add the flour. Reduce the heat to low and stir constantly for 2 minutes to cook the flour, scraping up any brown bits on the bottom of the pan. Slowly add the evaporated milk and then the water, whisking constantly to keep the gravy smooth. Season with salt and pepper.

Note: There's no getting around it. The best fried chicken is made right before serving. However, the chicken can be recrisped in hot fat. ∎

Fried chicken holds a dear place in the heart of all Texans. This version creates chicken that is incredibly crisp, with moist and juicy meat.

Fried Chicken

Y.O. Ranch, Mountain Home, Texas

(Serves 8)

2 frying chickens (2½ pounds each), cut into serving pieces (save the backs and necks for making stock)
Salt and ground black pepper to taste
7 eggs
¾ cup evaporated milk
3 cups unbleached all-purpose flour
Shortening for deep-frying (about 2 pounds)

Season the chicken pieces with salt and pepper and place them in a colander over a bowl.

Break the eggs into a mixing bowl and whisk in the evaporated milk. Place the flour in another mixing bowl. Melt the shortening to a depth of not more than half the pan in a deep heavy skillet or Dutch oven and heat to a temperature of 350°.

Dredge the chicken pieces heavily with flour, then dip in the egg batter and once again in the flour. Place a few pieces in the hot fat, not crowding them in the pan, and fry until golden brown, about 15 minutes total time, turning with tongs when needed. The chicken is done when it floats in the hot fat rather than sinking to the bottom of the pan.

Remove the chicken with tongs, drain on paper towels, and keep it warm in a 150° oven while frying the remaining pieces. ∎

The nature of these enchiladas changes greatly depending on which filling is served. With pork they are quite hearty, and much more delicate with chicken, a filling called pollo guisando. Either way they are a great hit, and a good dish for a casual supper.

Enchiladas Verdes

Ninfa's, Houston, Texas

(Serves 4)

Pork filling

1 chunk Carnitas, diced, page 38
3 ounces cream cheese, optional

Chicken filling

One 2½-pound chicken, baked or poached
½ cup (1 stick) butter
1 *jalapeño* chili, chopped (with seeds)
½ cup chopped onion
2 large tomatoes, peeled, seeded, and diced
1 cup tomato sauce
Salt and pepper to taste

Enchiladas

12 corn tortillas
½ cup vegetable oil
2 cups grated Monterey jack cheese
Salsa Verde, page 13
Sour cream
Paprika

If using the pork filling, dice the *carnitas* and mix with the cream cheese, if desired. If the pork is cold, reheat it before filling the enchiladas.

If using the chicken filling, remove the meat from the chicken, either discarding the bones and skin or saving them to use later for stock. Shred the meat and set aside.

Heat the butter in a sauté pan or skillet and, when hot, sauté the *jalapeño* and onion over medium heat until the onion is translucent. Add the tomatoes and sauté an additional minute. Add the tomato sauce and cooked chicken, season with salt and pepper, and allow to simmer for 2 minutes to blend the flavors. Set aside.

Preheat the oven to 400°. To make the enchiladas, heat the oil in a heavy skillet over medium heat. Using tongs, hold a tortilla in the hot oil just long enough to make it pliable, about 10 seconds. Drain on paper towels and place some of the filling in the center of the tortilla. Roll it and place it in an ovenproof baking dish, seam side down. Repeat with the remaining tortillas, either filling a large baking dish or 4 individual ones.

Sprinkle the cheese over the enchiladas and place in the oven until

Enchiladas Verdes, Ninfa's, Houston, Texas

NINFA LAURENZO
Ninfa's, Houston, Texas

It's a story in the Horatio Alger tradition. From a taco stand in the barrio of Houston, Ninfa Laurenzo, a widow with five children, has created a chain of eleven of the most respected restaurants in the country.

The strength of Ninfa's is twofold: a menu made up of the foods of her childhood, such as *fajitas* and green chili enchiladas, made with high-quality ingredients and artfully presented.

All of the Ninfa's are decorated in a colorful manner, with *serapes* covering the banquettes, flowers stenciled on the walls, and a woman making flour tortillas in view of the diners.

Mrs. Laurenzo was born in Harlingen, Texas, and moved to Houston with her husband, Dominick, when they married in 1948. When he died, her five children ranged in age from six to twenty-one, and she realized the tortilla business that supported them was not sufficient.

"The Mexican food in the city was strictly Tex-Mex, and I started doing the dishes my Mexican grandmother had done at home," she says. *Carnitas,* slowly simmered pork, and flan, the traditional caramel custard, are done to her family's recipes.

All of her five children are now involved in the business founded to support them. It is reflective of Ninfa's that the symbol for the chain is a colorful parrot.

"In Mexico, the parrot is the symbol of love," Mrs. Laurenzo says. "And this whole operation started because of my love for my children."

the cheese melts. Place some *salsa verde* and sour cream on the tortillas, and sprinkle with paprika for color.

Note: The tortillas can be filled a day in advance and kept, covered with plastic wrap, in the refrigerator. Reheat them in a 250° oven until hot, then top with cheese and raise the oven heat. ∎

Legend has it that Kit Carson's dying words were "If there were only time for one more bowl of chili." This recipe was probably what he envisioned. With all the controversies over the definitive chili, the judges at the State Fair of Texas voted for this one.

Grand-Prize Chili

Ray Calhoun, Dallas, Texas

(Serves 8 to 10)

¼ cup vegetable oil
3 pounds beef chuck or round, cut into ¼-inch cubes or "chili ground" (very coarsely ground, available in some markets)
1 onion, peeled and finely chopped
4 garlic cloves, peeled and finely chopped
1 tablespoon paprika
5 to 6 tablespoons chili powder
1 tablespoon ground cumin
1 teaspoon dried oregano
One 8-ounce can tomato sauce
1 teaspoon salt
1 cup water or more
1 *jalapeño* chili, seeded and halved, or 1 teaspoon cayenne (optional)
3 cups cooked pinto beans (see Ranch Beans, page 38)
Finely minced onion
1 cup grated Cheddar cheese

In a covered saucepan or Dutch oven, heat the oil over medium-high heat and cook the beef until it is evenly browned and no pink shows. Add the onion and garlic and sauté until the onion is translucent, about 5 minutes.

Add the paprika, chili powder, cumin, and oregano and stir for 3 minutes to cook the spices. Add the tomato sauce, salt, and water and stir to combine. Add the extra chili or cayenne if you want a hotter chili.

Bring to a boil and simmer, covered, over low heat for 2 hours, stirring occasionally and adding more water as needed, up to 1 cup depending on the rate of simmer. To serve, place some pinto beans in the bottom of bowls and ladle in the chili. Sprinkle with chopped onion and cheese.

Note: The chili can be made up to 3 days in advance, and it freezes extremely well. ∎

The jalapeños *in this beanless chili are sure to clear your sinuses. This recipe will totally delight true "chili heads."*

Sweat-Hot Chili

Aunt Chilada's, Phoenix, Arizona

(Serves 4)

3 tablespoons lard
10 ounces beef sirloin or tenderloin, trimmed and cut into ¾-inch cubes
1¾ cups Green Chili Sauce, page 42
4 *jalapeño* chilies, seeded and cut into thin rings

Garnish

¼ cup grated Monterey jack cheese
¼ cup grated Cheddar cheese
4 tablespoons chopped green onions, white part only
4 cilantro sprigs

In a heavy saucepan or Dutch oven, heat the lard over medium-high heat. When hot, add the cubed beef and brown on all sides. Add the green chili sauce and *jalapeño* rings to the pot and simmer, uncovered, for 30 minutes.

To serve, ladle into bowls and top with a sprinkling of the two cheeses, green onions, and a sprig of cilantro.

Note: The sauce can be prepared up to 3 days in advance, or it can be made in advance and frozen. The dish itself can be prepared in advance and reheated, but the chilies will lose pungency. ∎

RAY CALHOUN

State Fair of Texas Winner
Richardson, Texas

Nearly every inch of fabric on Ray Calhoun's red vest is covered with embroidered emblems and chili pepper–shaped pins. They are his souvenirs and medals from the chili cookoffs he enters each year, more than forty in 1986. In addition to competitions sponsored by the Chili Appreciation Society International, the organization of avid "chili heads" that sponsors the contests, he has won both the Texas and Oklahoma state fair events.

Calhoun, who has worked as a data manager for Texas Instruments since 1963, started entering chili contests in 1978, although his interest in cooking led to classes in food service years before. The fifty-four-year-old Arkansas native says, "You can't duplicate a pot of chili, and no two pots cook the same way. The secret to good chili is to keep it simple. You improve your chili by removing ingredients from the recipe."

Through competition, Calhoun has learned the variations of cooks in other states. "You see more tomatoes away from Texas, and we kid California people about bell peppers, celery, and other strange stuff they put in their chili," he says.

While he eats chili at home, the pots prepared for judges differ. "I use coarsely ground chili-grind meat at home because I think it makes a better tasting bowl of chili, but it doesn't look as pretty so I do the little cubes for contests," he says.

While the version and method used by Josephine Castillo is traditionally Texan, tamales can be filled with everything from picadillo *to barbecued shrimp.*

Tamales

Josephine Castillo, Houston, Texas

(Serves 10 to 12)

5 to 6 dried *ancho* chilies

Dough

1½ pounds fresh *masa* dough, or
   3 cups *masa harina* mixed with
   1½ to 2 cups lukewarm water
   and ½ teaspoon salt
1 cup lard
2 to 3 tablespoons reserved *ancho*
   chili pulp
½ cup reserved chili juice

Filling

¾ pound chuck roast, completely
   cooked
1½ pounds pork roast, completely
   cooked

¼ teaspoon ground cumin
3 garlic cloves, peeled
1 teaspoon salt
¼ teaspoon whole peppercorns
1½ teaspoons water
1 tablespoon lard
¼ cup reserved chili juice
Reserved *ancho* chili pulp

To complete the dish

1 package dried corn husks, soaked
   in water overnight
2 cups water

It's best to start this recipe by treating the *ancho* chilies used for both the dough and filling. Wash the dried *anchos* and place in a pot with water to cover. Bring to a boil and simmer until the chilies are soft and bright red. Drain, reserving the liquid, and discard the seeds and caps from the chilies. Using a teaspoon, scrape the pulp from the skins, then discard the skins.

To make the dough, mix all the ingredients together with your hands, adding more chili juice if the dough does not start to hold together. Allow the dough to sit for at least 15 minutes, while making the filling.

To make the filling, cut the beef and pork into chunks and chop finely in a food processor fitted with a steel blade (or grind in a meat grinder). Do this in batches as necessary. Crush the cumin, garlic, salt, peppercorns, and water to a paste in a mortar. Melt the lard in a skillet over medium heat and, when hot, add the meat, seasoning paste, and chili juice. Process 1 cup of the meat with the remaining *ancho* chili pulp. Add to the meat in the pan and simmer for 5 minutes to blend the flavors.

To make the tamales, place 1 tablespoon of the dough on the smooth side of a corn husk, covering the entire width of the husk and three-fourths of the length. Place 1 tablespoon of the meat filling down the center lengthwise and roll tightly, folding the excess husk under. Tie with a strip of corn husk. Repeat until all the filling is used.

Line a steamer or the bottom of a deep pot with excess corn husks and place the tamales in the steamer fold side down, so the tamales are standing upright. Cover with a layer of corn husks and a damp towel.

Pour water around the sides of the pan and cover tightly. Steam over medium heat for 40 to 50 minutes, and serve immediately.

Note: Both the filling and dough can be prepared a day in advance, and the tamales can be rolled up to 6 hours in advance. Bring the dough to room temperature and heat the filling before rolling. ∎

Tamales, Josephine Castillo, Houston, Texas

The name of this staple of the South and the Southwest says it all—beef fried in the same batter cooks use for chicken. The cream gravy is part of the dish, and it's usually served with a pile of mashed potatoes and a basket of hot biscuits (see page 41).

Chicken-fried Steak with Cream Gravy

Y.O. Ranch, Mountain Home, Texas

(Serves 6)

Six 7-ounce portions of tenderized
    beef (either cube steaks or
    tenderized round steak)
Salt and pepper to taste
5 eggs
One 12-ounce can evaporated milk
2 to 3 cups shortening or oil
Flour for dredging plus 3 tablespoons
    all-purpose flour
About 2 cups water

Sprinkle the meat with salt and pepper and set aside. Beat the eggs and ½ cup of the evaporated milk together in a bowl. Heat the shortening or oil in a heavy deep-sided skillet to a temperature of 350°.

Dredge the steaks with flour and dip them in the batter, then in flour again, lightly shaking off the excess. When the oil is hot, add the steaks a few at a time, being careful not to add too many or they will lower the temperature of the oil. Fry for 4 minutes on one side, or until golden brown, then turn with tongs or a slotted spatula and fry the other side. Drain on paper towels and keep warm in a 150° oven.

To make the gravy, pour all but 4 tablespoons of the fat from the skillet and turn the heat to low. Add the 3 tablespoons of flour and cook over low heat, stirring constantly, for 3 minutes; do not let it burn. Add the remaining evaporated milk, whisking until smooth and scraping the bottom of the pan to get up the small bits clinging to it, then add the water gradually, stirring constantly, until the gravy is smooth and of desired thickness. Add salt and pepper to taste and pour the gravy into a bowl to pass along with the chicken-fried steaks. ■

JOSEPHINE CASTILLO
Houston, Texas

When Josephine Castillo, a thirty-six-year-old home economist and food consultant, makes tamales, she is reliving a culinary memory of Christmas each year in her Brownsville, Texas, home.

"My grandmother was from Monterrey, Mexico, and tamale making was to her what baking cookies is to Scandinavians. Every Christmas she would make a minimum of fifty dozen, so she would have her friends and her sisters come over and they would set up an assembly line," she recalls.

While the tamales she now makes call for a spiced meat filling, Castillo said that the fillings can vary from poultry to all pork, all beef, or a sweet and spicy filling such as *picadillo,* beef with raisins and spices. Tamales are frequently also sweet, and can be filled with coconut and pineapple, at which time the *ancho* chili is omitted from the *masa* dough.

At the same time that Castillo carries tamale making to the next generation, she also experiments with her own recipes based on traditional foods. "While *fajitas* are now all the rage in restaurants, they are nothing new to my family. Everyone in my part of Texas ate them at home," she says.

But what they were eating was beef *fajitas* made from inexpensive skirt steaks. Castillo uses the same process of marinating and grilling pork tenderloin for a subtle and delicious result.

This is perhaps the most famous dish originating in Arizona: the Southwestern equivalent of the eggroll. It is filled with a spicy beef filling, deep-fried so the flour tortilla becomes a crisp pastry, and topped with a chili sauce and garnishes for extra texture and flavor.

Chimichangas

Aunt Chilada's, Phoenix, Arizona

(Serves 6)

Boiled beef

4 pounds beef tenderloin or eye of
    round
1 large onion, roughly chopped
2 celery stalks, roughly chopped
1 carrot, roughly chopped
1 gallon water

Beef filling

5 tablespoons lard
Reserved boiled beef
1¼ cups reserved beef stock
2 garlic cloves, peeled and minced
½ teaspoon ground black pepper
¼ teaspoon dried basil
¼ teaspoon dried oregano
½ teaspoon ground cumin
Salt to taste
1 green bell pepper, seeded, deribbed,
    and diced
1 medium onion, peeled and diced
6 green onions, trimmed and sliced
2 mild green chilies (*poblano* or
    Anaheim), seeded and diced
5 tomatoes, seeded and diced

To finish the dish

Six 14-inch flour tortillas
6 cups vegetable oil for deep-frying

Garnish

Green Chili Sauce, page 42
Guacamole, page 138
1 tomato, seeded and diced
3 tablespoons green onions, white
    part only, chopped
½ cup grated Monterey jack cheese
½ cup grated Cheddar cheese

Place the boiled beef ingredients in a stockpot and bring to a boil, skimming any scum that rises to the surface. Lower the heat and simmer, uncovered, for 3 hours. Remove the beef and allow to sit until cool enough to handle. Reserve 1¼ cup of

the stock for use later in this recipe, and freeze the rest for future use. Shred the beef loin.

To make the filling, melt 3 tablespoons of the lard in a large sauté pan or skillet and add the meat, beef stock, and spices. Simmer for 15 minutes to reduce.

While the meat is simmering, heat the remaining lard in another sauté pan or skillet and sauté the vegetables for 5 minutes; they should remain firm.

Add the vegetables to the meat and simmer an additional 5 minutes.

To make the *chimichangas*, place a scoop of the meat mixture in the center of a tortilla and roll it like an eggroll, tucking in the ends. Secure with toothpicks and repeat with the remaining tortillas.

Heat the oil to 375° in a deep, heavy pan and add the rolls, not crowding them in the pan. Holding them submerged in the oil with tongs, fry until golden brown, and drain on paper towels.

To serve, place on plates with dollops of the sauces and a sprinkling of the other garnishes.

Note: The filling can be prepared up to 3 days in advance and kept refrigerated; however, the rolls should be made and fried just before serving. ∎

While the traditional carne adovada was meat actually cured in a red chili paste, this version served at La Tertulia tenderizes the cubes of pork through a long cooking process before adding the sauce. The restaurant uses a brand of commercial sauce, Bueno Red Chile Pork Sauce, and after many experiments, the recipe below replicates the taste.

Carne Adovada

La Tertulia, Santa Fe, New Mexico

(Serves 8 to 10)

10 pounds pork shoulder meat, cut
    into 1-inch cubes
½ cup water

Chimichangas, Aunt Chilada's, Phoenix, Arizona

Red chili sauce

12 to 14 large dried New Mexico
   chilies
2 teaspoons garlic powder
1½ teaspoons dried oregano
2 teaspoons dried cumin
2 teaspoons salt

½ cup flour
2 tablespoons oregano
2 tablespoons garlic powder
1½ tablespoons salt
1½ cups water

Place the meat in a large pot with the water and fry, uncovered, for 2 hours over low heat, stirring occasionally and adding a little more water if the meat appears to be sticking.

While the meat is frying, make the red chili sauce. Stem, seed, and rinse the chilies, then place them in a pan with water to cover. Bring to a boil. Simmer for 15 minutes until tender, covered, then remove from heat. Drain, reserving the chili juice. Puree the chilies in a blender or food processor with 2 cups of the reserved chili juice and the seasonings. Strain and set aside.

Drain any excess water from the pan in which you have cooked the meat, then sprinkle the flour over the meat, tossing to coat evenly. Cook about 10 minutes over medium heat, stirring occasionally, then add the seasonings and the chili sauce. Add the 1½ cups water and simmer 30 minutes.

Note: The recipe can be prepared up to 3 days before serving, and it also freezes well. ∎

Carne Adovada, La Tertulia, Santa Fe, New Mexico

Fajitas *made from succulent pork tenderloin are a delightful variation on* tacos al carbon *(a grilled meat and tortilla sandwich). They are also more unusual than traditional* fajitas, *which are made from skirt steak.*

Pork Fajitas

Josephine Castillo, Houston, Texas

(Serves 8)

2½ pounds pork tenderloin
¼ cup *mole* paste (available in Latino
   groceries or by mail order, page
   196)
½ cup fresh lemon juice
4 garlic cloves, peeled and crushed
¼ teaspoon crushed black
   peppercorns
1 tablespoon water
1½ teaspoons salt, or to taste

To serve

16 corn tortillas
1 lemon, cut into wedges
1 cup shredded iceberg lettuce
1 tomato, seeded and diced

½ cup chopped onion
Guacamole, page 138 (optional)
Sour cream (optional)

Trim the tenderloins of excess fat and silver skin. Mix the remaining ingredients and marinate the tenderloins, covered with plastic wrap, in the refrigerator overnight.

Light a charcoal or gas grill, and grill the tenderloins until done, about 15 minutes, turning them once or twice during the grilling period. Allow them to rest for 10 minutes before slicing.

To serve, heat the tortillas, wrapped in aluminum foil, in a 300° oven. Place sliced pork down the center of each tortilla, and add the remaining garnishes to suit personal taste.

Note: The pork can also be cooked in a 450° oven for 15 to 30 minutes, depending on the size. Two or 3 tenderloins will take only 15 minutes. ∎

Like a confit of duck, these chunks of pork are braised in fat and are so tender they fall apart. They form the basis for Enchiladas Verdes, page 31.

Carnitas

Ninfa's, Houston, Texas

(Serves 6)

5 pounds pork shoulder, cut into six
    12-ounce chunks
1¾ pounds lard
1 tablespoon salt
¾ teaspoon black pepper
1 teaspoon garlic powder
¼ cup milk

Garnish

2 avocadoes, peeled, cored, and sliced
    into wedges
½ onion, peeled and sliced into rings
2 limes, quartered
1 cup sour cream
Salsa Verde, page 43
12 to 18 flour tortillas, wrapped in
    aluminum foil and heated in a 300°
    oven for 15 minutes

Cut the pork into 12- to 16-ounce chunks, cutting away as much fat and gristle as possible. Heat the lard in a deep, covered skillet to a temperature of 200°.

Mix the salt, pepper, and garlic powder and rub the mixture on all sides of the pork chunks, shaking them to remove any excess.

Add the pork to the heated lard and sear to brown on all sides. Reduce the heat to the barest possible simmer, and cook the pork for 1½ hours, turning it every 20 minutes. After 1 hour of cooking time, add the milk to the skillet.

Drain the pork on paper towels, then place on a platter and garnish with wedges of avocado, rings of onion, lime, sour cream, and Salsa Verde. Serve with flour tortillas.

Note: The pork can be cooked up to 6 hours in advance and kept at room temperature. If not being served immediately, drop it into hot fat to crisp, then drain. ∎

This recipe is as traditional to the Texas prairie as tumbleweed; it is served as a side dish and is the basis for refried beans (see page 38). Pinto beans, one of the many gifts to Southwestern cookery from Mexico, are a staple of the Southwestern diet.

Ranch Beans

Y.O. Ranch, Mountain Home, Texas

(Serves 8 to 10)

2 cups dried pinto beans
4 bacon slices, diced
Salt and pepper to taste

Place the beans in a colander and wash them in cold running water for 3 minutes, picking over them well to discard any pebbles, broken beans, or beans that are shriveled or discolored.

Place the beans in a large pot and fill it with hot water 4 inches above the level of the beans. Add the bacon, bring to a boil, and simmer covered for 3 to 3½ hours. Add water as necessary, 1 cup at a time, during the cooking process to keep the beans covered. For the last hour of cooking, uncover the pot to allow the juices to thicken, and add salt and pepper at that time. ∎

Refried beans, like guacamole, *is one of the most versatile staples of the traditional Southwestern repertoire. It is served as a side dish with almost all meals, and can be used as a topping with grated cheese on crispy* nacho *chips as an hors d'oeuvre.*

Refried Beans

El Mirador, San Antonio, Texas

(Serves 8 to 10)

1½ cups lard or bacon fat
2 cups chopped onions
4 garlic cloves, peeled and minced
¼ cup flour
8 cups cooked Ranch Beans, page 38
Salt and pepper to taste
1 cup grated Monterey jack cheese
    (optional)

Heat the lard or bacon fat in a heavy deep-sided skillet over medium-high heat. Add the onions and garlic and sauté, stirring frequently, for 5 minutes. Lower the heat, add the flour, and stir for 3 minutes to cook the flour and form a roux.

Raise the heat to medium-high and add the beans. Using the back of a large wooden spoon or a potato masher, mash the beans into the

Ranch Beans, Y.O. Ranch, Mountain Home, Texas

bottom of the pan, stirring frequently so they do not stick. When the beans are broken up, but still have visible pieces, simmer for a few minutes, season with salt and pepper, and serve, sprinkled with grated cheese, if desired.

Note: If making a large quantity of beans for a party, mash some as noted above, and chop the remainder in a blender or food processor fitted with a steel blade, using a pulsing action so they are chopped but not pureed. The beans can be made in advance and reheated, covered, in a 250° oven. ∎

Potato salad is one of the side dishes most often served with ribs and barbecue in Texas. This one, made by marinating the potatoes, is particularly delicious. The barbecue sauce at The Salt Lick is a secret, but this recipe is similar to it.

Potato Salad

The Salt Lick, Driftwood, Texas

(Serves 4 to 6)

5 large Idaho baking potatoes
Salt and pepper to taste
1 teaspoon celery seed
1 large onion, peeled and diced
½ cup juice drained from dill pickles
⅓ cup barbecue sauce
⅓ cup vinaigrette salad dressing
½ to 1 cup mayonnaise, or to taste

The day before serving, scrub the potatoes and boil them in salted water until tender but still slightly firm when pierced with a knife point; they should not be mushy. Plunge them into ice water, and when cool enough to handle, peel them and cut them into ¾-inch dice.

Season the potatoes with salt, pepper, and celery seed. Marinate the onion in the pickle juice for a few hours, or overnight in the refrigerator. To serve, drain the juice and add the onions to the potatoes. Add the barbecue sauce and salad dressing, tossing to coat evenly. Place back in the refrigerator at least 1 hour before serving, and just before serving, add the mayonnaise. Adjust the seasoning and serve. ∎

HISAKO ROBERTS AND TIM ADER

The Salt Lick, Driftwood, Texas

When Hisako and Thurman Roberts' children became of school age, the Texas native and his Hawaiian-born wife decided to change their nomadic life of traveling around the state while he built bridges.

They drew up a list of what they could do support the family from the resources of their 750-acre farm in Driftwood, a town of two hundred about thirty miles from Austin. At the top of the list of more than fifty options was starting a barbecue restaurant, and for more than twenty-five years, The Salt Lick has been serving up beef barbecue and potato salad.

The barbecue sauce, a secret recipe that flavors the potato salad and is mopped on the briskets and ribs as they grill, is a sweet and sour salad dressing with more than fifteen spices and Worcestershire sauce.

The Salt Lick takes two days to barbecue brisket. Each morning, Tim Ader, who has been using Roberts' method since he started cooking at the restaurant four years ago, starts by placing cardboard boxes under the grills and creating a huge fire to burn off the barbecue sauce. He then creates a fire with mesquite wood, and rubs the whole briskets with a mixture of salt, black pepper, and cayenne.

On the first day, they are cooked for twelve hours. After an initial searing of thirty minutes to seal the meat, they are turned over a 200° fire every forty-five minutes, and are basted almost constantly with barbecue sauce.

That night, the briskets are chilled, and the next day they are placed over an even lower part of the fire, at the back of the grill, and are cooked for four to five hours.

Hot chilies and cheese are what separates this Southwestern corn bread from its Southern cousins. It's the perfect accompaniment to roasted or grilled foods.

Jalapeño Corn Bread

Y.O. Ranch, Mountain Home, Texas

(Makes 24 servings, and can be frozen)

2 *jalapeño* chilies, finely chopped (seeds and ribs left in)
One 17-ounce can creamed corn
½ teaspoon baking soda
½ teaspoon salt
1 tablespoon sugar
2 eggs
¾ cup buttermilk
⅓ cup oil
1 cup grated Longhorn cheese
2 cups yellow cornmeal

Preheat the oven to 350°. Heavily grease a 17½-by-12-inch baking pan.

In a large bowl, mix the finely chopped *jalapeños* with the corn. Beat in the baking soda, salt, and sugar, then add the eggs one at a time, beating well. Add the buttermilk and oil, then whisk in the cheese and cornmeal.

Pour the batter into the prepared pan, distributing it evenly, and bake in the center of the preheated oven for 30 to 40 minutes, or until the top is brown and a toothpick inserted in the center comes out clean. Cool in the pan and serve in squares. ■

Sopaipillas, Rancho de Chimayó, Chimayó, New Mexico

I think these feathery-light pillows of fried dough are one of the great breads of the world. They puff up like soufflés in the hot oil, and are simple to make.

Sopaipillas

Rancho de Chimayó, Chimayó, New Mexico

(Makes 4 dozen)

2 cups unbleached all-purpose flour
½ teaspoon baking powder
1½ teaspoons salt
½ teaspoon sugar
1½ teaspoons vegetable oil
1 tablespoon evaporated milk
⅛ cup warm water
Shortening for deep frying
Natilla, page 45, or honey for serving

Place the flour in a large mixing bowl and add the baking powder, salt, and sugar. Stir well, then add the oil, evaporated milk, and water. Using your hands, work the mixture into a dough and knead gently on a floured surface. It will remain slightly sticky.

Allow the dough to rest for 30 minutes, then divide it into 12 balls by tearing off pieces into nuggets that form balls in your hand.

On a floured surface, roll each ball into a 10-inch circle ¼ inch thick. Repeat with the remaining dough balls.

Heat the shortening in a deep-fryer to a temperature of 400°. Cut each circle into quarters and add 4 pieces at a time to the hot oil. Using a spatula or spoon, fan hot oil over the top of each triangle, which will cause it to start puffing up. After 20 seconds, turn the *sopaipillas* over and quickly brown the other side. Remove from the pan with a slotted spoon and drain on paper towels. Keep warm in a 150° oven while repeating the frying process with the remaining balls. Serve immediately with honey or topped with *natilla.*

Note: While you can make the dough up to 6 hours in advance, *sopaipillas* must be fried at the last minute, and should be made in small batches so they can be eaten hot. ■

FLORENCE AND ARTURO JARAMILLO

with daughter Laura
Rancho de Chimayó, Chimayó, New Mexico

Chimayó, nestled in the mountains twenty-five miles from Santa Fe, gets its name from the Tewa Indian word for the flaking red stone found in the nearby hills. Known for its high-quality chilies, woven fabric, and the mystical powers ascribed to its church, the village has been the home of the Jaramillo family since the 1700s. The ranch house was built in 1888, and rooms were added as the family grew.

When Hermenegildo Jaramillo died in 1959, his grandson and wife, Arturo and Florence, bought the home and restored it as Rancho de Chimayó, a restaurant specializing in the native foods Arturo ate growing up in the house.

Their cooks, Manuel Aragon, Josie Ortiz, and Kate Abeyta, all grew up in the village, and have been making a green chili sauce to top *huevos rancheros* and frying triangles of dough into pillow-like *sopaipillas* for years. They make the region's equivalent of floating island, *natilla*, and serve it by itself and as a topping for the *sopaipillas*.

The *rancho* is now a thirty-minute drive from the city, but Arturo remembers when the trip was taken only a few times a year since the roads were not paved. "It was very primitive and rural until after World War II," he says. "We had no electricity, and bedtime was at dark. We were totally self-sufficient, even to the point of grinding our own flour."

These biscuits are feathery light and sinfully delicious right from the oven, either topped with butter and jam at breakfast or used to mop up cream gravy.

Biscuits

Ray Gregg, Dallas, Texas

(Makes 12 to 14)
¼ cup shortening
2 cups self-rising flour
¾ cup milk

Preheat the oven to 450°. Cut the shortening and flour together with your hands until it has the consistency of cornmeal. Add the milk, adding more if necessary so the dough is pliable but is still wet. Turn the dough onto a heavily floured surface and knead it lightly, but do not overwork the dough.

Roll the dough to an even thickness of ¾ to 1 inch and cut out biscuits with a 2-inch round cutter (this is the diameter of a juice can), dipping the cutter into flour between biscuits so they do not stick.

Place the biscuits on an ungreased cookie sheet and bake for 12 to 15 minutes, or until golden brown. Serve immediately.

Note: The biscuits are best if baked right before serving; however, they can be kept at room temperature on the cookie sheet up to 2 hours in advance. ∎

Biscuits, Ray Gregg, Dallas, Texas

RAY GREGG

State Fair of Texas Winner
Dallas, Texas

Ray Gregg says there is "no secret to making biscuits. The recipe is right on any flour sack. But what you have to learn to do is go by the feel of the dough. If it feels heavy, you'll have heavy biscuits."

Gregg, who has been making biscuits for fifteen years, is a fifty-three-year-old North Carolina native who moved to Dallas more than thirty years ago and worked as an inhalation therapist and caterer before joining the staff of the State Fair of Texas twenty years ago.

"As a child I had a lot of good, fresh farm cooking," he says. "We raised almost everything we ate, and what we didn't raise, we'd swap with neighbors."

In addition to his biscuits, Gregg is famous for his *guacamole*, lemon pie, and cucumber sandwiches. "I like cooking for a large group of people, and what I do is read a recipe to get an idea, but it never comes into the kitchen with me. I like developing food so that it suits my taste," he says.

Aunt Chilada's uses this sauce as the basis for their Sweat-Hot Chili, page 33, as well as a topping for their justly famous Chimichangas, page 36. It has a mild spice level, and would be excellent as a sauce for any grilled meat or poultry.

Green Chili Sauce

Aunt Chilada's, Phoenix, Arizona

(Makes 2 quarts)

2 quarts beef stock
1½ yellow bell peppers, seeded and chopped
6 green onions, chopped
1 medium yellow onion, peeled and chopped
1 pound mild green chilies, such as Anaheim or *poblano*, roasted, seeded, and cut into strips (see page 10)
2 green bell peppers, seeded and chopped
¼ teaspoon dried oregano
2 garlic cloves, peeled and minced
1 tablespoon salt
3 tomatoes, peeled, seeded, and chopped
¾ cup lard
¾ cup unbleached all-purpose flour

Bring the stock to a boil and add all the ingredients except the lard and flour. Simmer the sauce, uncovered, for 1 hour, stirring occasionally.

Melt the lard in a skillet over medium heat and, when hot, whisk in the flour, a few tablespoons at a time. Stir the roux until it reaches an almond color, then whisk it into the sauce. Let the sauce simmer for a few minutes to thicken.

Note: This sauce can be kept refrigerated for up to 5 days, and will keep in the freezer for up to 3 months. ∎

GARY DARLING

Aunt Chilada's, Phoenix, Arizona

The building housing Aunt Chilada's, a restaurant within the Pointe Resort complex occupying a former mining operation on Squaw Peak, is listed on the National Register of Historic Places. The huge stone fireplaces were constructed at the turn of the century from stones quarried nearby, and Aunt Chilada's is serving the same kind of *chimichangas* and burritos that were probably served when the log building was a restaurant in its previous incarnation.

Chef Gary Darling is quick to point out, however, that Aunt Chilada's is proving that native dishes can be made with the finest ingredients. The filling for his *chimichangas*, flour tortillas rolled and fried until crispy, is filet mignon. And the *salsas* for topping them are made fresh daily in his kitchen.

Aunt Chilada's specializes in dishes native to the Phoenix area, and also uses Southwest ingredients to create more avant-garde daily specials.

He will turn swordfish into sizzling *fajitas*, and stuff filet mignons with Mexican cheese and green chilies. "The sauces of Southwestern cooking go well with any grilled item," he says.

Chef Darling, who moved to Phoenix at age six and was trained in this style of cooking at William T. Annos' Famous Old Nogales Cafe, says, "We try to cater to a broad spectrum of visitors, so I tone down the spices to moderate, and allow people to add more chilies if they wish."

This is not the case, however, with his famous Sweat-Hot Chili, fiery with *jalapeños*.

This is the basic green chili sauce used for many traditional dishes, including enchiladas verdes. The combination of green tomatoes and tomatillos gives it a fresh taste.

Salsa Verde

Ninfa's, Houston, Texas

(Makes 1 cup)

½ pound green tomatoes, cored and diced
1 medium *tomatillo*, cored and diced
2 tablespoons chopped fresh cilantro
1 *jalapeño* chili, seeded and finely chopped
1 tablespoon vegetable oil
¾ teaspoon salt
2 garlic cloves, peeled and minced
2 tablespoons chicken stock

Boil the green tomatoes and *tomatillo* in a small amount of water until soft, about 5 minutes. Drain and place in a blender or a food processor fitted with a steel blade along with the cilantro.

Sauté the *jalapeño* in the oil over medium heat until soft, about 5 minutes, and add to the blender or food processor with the remaining ingredients.

Using an on and off pulsing, chop the sauce but do not puree it to a smooth liquid.

Note: The sauce can be done up to 2 days in advance and reheated when needed. Do not allow it to come to a boil. ∎

MINNIE AND BO WAFFORD

Onion Creek Lodge, Buda, Texas

As ranch managers of Onion Creek, Minnie and Bo Wafford are part caretakers and part caterers. The ranch and its rambling stone ranch house in the hill country of Texas are owned by road construction magnate J. C. Ruby and operated by the Schreiner family, who also own the Y.O. Ranch in Mountain Home. The Waffords moved to the town four years ago, and host groups who rent the hunting lodge.

While Minnie prepares the majority of the meals, Bo specializes in barbecued brisket, both at Onion Creek and the Y.O. Ranch.

The retired Air Force pilot Bo has been barbecuing since his Mt. Vernon, Texas, childhood. His method starts with rubbing 8- to 12-pound briskets with a mixture of just salt and black pepper. He builds a fire with a mixture of mesquite and oak in the fire box and allows it to become hot, about 10 minutes.

"I place the briskets fat side up on the grill of the closed smoker, away from the direct heat of the flames. Putting them on that way keeps the meat moist," he said.

Wafford allows the meat to smoke for about 12 to 14 hours, without ever turning or basting it. He places barbecue sauce on the table to serve with the sliced meat, but allows the beef flavor of the brisket to dominate.

The lodge serves this sweet and sour barbecue sauce with its slowly smoked brisket of beef. It can be used as a condiment or as a basting sauce for almost any grilled food.

Barbecue Sauce

Onion Creek Lodge, Buda, Texas

(Makes 1 quart)

2 tablespoons butter
1 medium onion, peeled and finely chopped
1 teaspoon minced garlic
½ cup dark brown sugar
¼ teaspoon ground black pepper
½ teaspoon salt
1½ tablespoons Dijon mustard, such as Grey Poupon
1 tablespoon cider vinegar
1 tablespoon fresh lemon juice
3 tablespoons Worcestershire sauce
2 cups ketchup
2 cups water

Heat the butter in a saucepan, and when hot add the onion and garlic. Sauté over medium heat for 5 minutes, until the onion is translucent, then add the brown sugar, pepper, salt, and mustard. Stir constantly over low heat for 2 minutes, then add the remaining ingredients.

Bring to a boil over medium heat and simmer, stirring occasionally, for 15 to 20 minutes.

Note: The sauce can be stored in the refrigerator in jars with tight-fitting lids for up to 3 months. ■

Every culture has its favorite custard dessert, and flan is the crème caramel of Hispanic countries. It's velvety smooth and rich, and has a more dense texture than custards baked without condensed milk.

Flan

Ninfa's, Houston, Texas

(Serves 6)

¾ cup sugar
3 eggs
3 egg yolks
2 teaspoons vanilla extract
One 14-ounce can sweetened
    condensed milk
1¾ cups milk
2 ounces cream cheese, softened to
    room temperature

Place the sugar in a small skillet over medium-high heat and stir while it liquifies. Allow the sugar to boil and turn a walnut brown, stirring occasionally. Watch carefully so that it does not burn.

Pour the caramel into the bottom of a 9-inch flan pan or soufflé dish and, working quickly, spread it evenly with a rubber spatula over the bottom of the pan.

Preheat the oven to 350°. Place the eggs, egg yolks, vanilla, milks, and cream cheese in a blender or food processor and process for at least 5 minutes.

Pour the mixture into the flan pan and place in a baking pan in the center of the oven. Pour boiling water halfway up the sides of the pan and bake for 1 hour and 10 minutes, or until a knife inserted in the center comes out clean. Watch carefully and cover the flan with foil if the top seems to be getting too brown.

Remove from the oven, allow to cool to room temperature, then cut around the edges and invert onto a deep-sided serving plate. Serve each piece with some of the caramel syrup.

Note: The flan can be made up to 3 days before serving and kept covered with plastic wrap in the refrigerator. Leave it in the pan until ready to serve. ■

Flan, Ninfa's, Houston, Texas

This is the Southwestern version of floating island, with airy meringue topping a creamy rich custard.

Natilla

Rancho de Chimayó, Chimayó, New Mexico

(Serves 6)

2¼ cups sugar
4 cups milk
¼ teaspoon vanilla extract
8 eggs, separated
3 tablespoons cornstarch, dissolved in
    ¼ cup milk
1 teaspoon ground cinnamon

Place 2 cups of the sugar, milk, vanilla, and egg yolks in the top of a double boiler and whisk well. Stir in the cornstarch mixture and bring to a boil over simmering water, whisking constantly and beating well to get rid of any lumps. Cook until thickened, about 2 to 5 minutes, strain into a bowl or serving dish, and refrigerate until cold.

In the bowl of a mixer, beat the egg whites at medium speed until frothy. Add the remaining ¼ cup sugar, increase the speed to high, and beat until the meringue is stiff. Spread on top of the cold pudding and sprinkle with cinnamon.

Serve immediately.

Note: If making this in advance, it's best to do the egg whites at the last minute, since they tend to "weep" when refrigerated and moisture will seep out. ■

Pecan Pie, Charlotte Parks, Ben Wheeler, Texas

Pour the filling into the pie crust and bake in the center of the preheated oven for 1 hour. Check after 40 minutes and cover it loosely with foil if the top seems to be burning. Allow to cool to room temperature before serving.

Note: Part of the beauty of this pie is the creamy consistency of the filling. If made in advance, keep it refrigerated, but bring it to room temperature before serving. ■

There are orchards of peach trees in the area of Texas surrounding the Y.O. Ranch, so it's not surprising that cook Bertie Varner would concoct this dessert, in which the spices nicely balance the sweetness of the peaches, for the crowds she feeds daily. It's a quick and easy way to please a large number of sweet teeth.

Lazy Man's Peach Cobbler

Y.O. Ranch, Mountain Home, Texas

(Serves 12)

Three 29-ounce cans sliced cling
 peaches
¼ pound butter or margarine, melted
1 cup unbleached all-purpose flour
1½ cups sugar
2 teaspoons baking powder
¼ teaspoon salt
1 cup milk
1 teaspoon ground cinnamon
½ teaspoon ground nutmeg

Preheat the oven to 350° and grease a 9-by-13-inch baking pan.

Drain the peaches, reserving the juice, and set aside. Melt the butter or margarine, and pour into the bottom of the pan.

In a mixing bowl, mix the flour and 1 cup of the sugar with the baking powder and salt. Whisk in the milk and ½ cup of the reserved peach liquid. Pour into the pan on top of the melted butter.

Pour the remaining sugar over the peaches and add the cinnamon and nutmeg, mixing them together with your fingers. Pour the peaches over the batter and bake for 45 minutes to 1 hour in the center of the preheated oven.

Serve warm. ■

Pecan trees are as much a part of the landscape in Texas as they are in Georgia. This version of pecan pie is sweet, but it allows the flavor of the nuts to emerge.

Pecan Pie

Charlotte Parks, Ben Wheeler, Texas

(Serves 8)

Crust

¼ teaspoon salt
1 cup unbleached all-purpose flour
⅓ cup shortening
2 tablespoons cold water

Filling

¾ cup sugar
2 tablespoons flour
½ teaspoon salt
1 cup dark corn syrup
2 eggs, lightly beaten
½ cup evaporated milk
1 teaspoon vanilla extract
1 cup pecans

To make the crust, mix the flour and salt and cut in the shortening, using a pastry blender or 2 knives, until it resembles a coarse meal. Add the water, sprinkling in just enough to form a ball. Remove the dough from the mixing bowl, form it into a ball, wrap it in plastic wrap, and refrigerate it for at least 20 minutes.

Preheat the oven to 375°. Roll the dough into a circle on a lightly floured surface. Pat it into a 9-inch pie plate and fold a rim of dough under the lip of the pie plate to form an edge; then, using your fingers, flute the top of the edge. Prick the dough with a fork and place it back in the refrigerator while making the filling.

To make the filling, mix the sugar, flour, and salt. Mix in the corn syrup, then add the eggs, milk, and vanilla. Stir until smooth, then stir in the pecans.

Minnie Wafford has found this way of "doctoring" a cake mix to create a delicious and quick dessert with the popular Southern flavors of coconut and pecans.

Toasted Coconut Cake

Onion Creek Lodge, Buda, Texas

(Serves 10)

6 tablespoons butter
2 cups shredded sweetened coconut
1 cup finely chopped pecans
1 yellow cake mix, plus additional
    ingredients specified on the box of
    mix
One 8-ounce package cream cheese,
    softened to room temperature
2 teaspoons milk
1 teaspoon vanilla extract
3 to 3½ cups powdered sugar

Melt 3 tablespoons of the butter or margarine in a sauté pan or skillet over medium heat; allow the remaining portion to soften to room temperature. Add the coconut and pecans and stir constantly until the mixture is golden brown. Remove with a slotted spoon and drain on paper towels.

Mix the cake mix according to package directions, adding 1 cup of the toasted coconut and pecans. Divide the batter among three 8-inch-round pans and bake and cool according to package directions.

To make the frosting, cream the remaining soft butter with the cream cheese until light and fluffy. Add the milk, vanilla, and sugar, 1 cup at a time, beating well until the mixture reaches spreading consistency. Add the remaining toasted mixture, reserving ½ cup to sprinkle on the top. Fill and frost the cake with frosting, decorating with the reserved coconut and nuts. ∎

CHARLOTTE PARKS
State Fair of Texas Winner
Ben Wheeler, Texas

As a child, Charlotte Parks could make the kitchen her domain on Saturday, and she loved to bake and make candy.

The fifty-seven-year-old Dallas native, who recently retired after a career with Southwest Bell, learned to cook from her aunt and stepmother. The key to her cooking, she says, is "getting the ingredients in season." She will garner a year's supply of pecans as they are harvested in the fall, shell them, and place them in the freezer; she will buy ripe peaches in the summer and put them up for a year of cobblers, rather than having to depend on commercial canned or frozen fruit.

Her pecan pie, included in the book of prize-winning recipes published by the State Fair of Texas, calls for milk instead of butter. "It gives it a nice consistency and flavor," she says.

It was natural that Mrs. Parks would enter cooking contests, since she grew up just two miles from the fairgrounds. She won a blue ribbon for her cinnamon twist coffee cake in 1962, the first year she entered; eight years later she won another. "That first ribbon is what hooks you, and I've entered ever since," she says.

This chocolate cake is a chocoholic's dream, and the fruit flavors enhance the ultimate chocolate hit. While traditional in form, it reflects the trend towards richer chocolate flavor.

Triple Chocolate Cake

Curtis Young, Dallas, Texas

(Serves 10 to 12)

Cake

¾ cup unbleached all-purpose flour
¾ cup cocoa
1½ teaspoons baking soda
1½ teaspoons baking powder
½ teaspoon salt
1 cup milk
½ cup vegetable oil
2 eggs
2 teaspoons vanilla extract
1 ripe banana, mashed
1 cup sugar-coated chopped dates
½ cup boiling water

Topping

¼ cup sugar
1 cup chocolate chips
½ cup chopped nuts

Frosting

½ cup plus 2 tablespoons (1¼ sticks) unsalted butter, softened to room temperature
3 cups sifted powdered sugar
½ cup cocoa
¼ cup milk
1 teaspoon vanilla extract

Filling

One 4-ounce package cream cheese, softened to room temperature
¼ cup sifted powdered sugar
½ teaspoon vanilla extract
2 tablespoons cocoa
1 banana (optional)

Garnish

Nut halves

Preheat the oven to 350°. Grease two 9-inch round cake pans and dust with cocoa.

To make the cake, sift the dry ingredients together into a mixing bowl. In another bowl, mix the milk, oil, and eggs and beat into the dry ingredients. Add the vanilla, then stir

CURTIS YOUNG

State Fair of Texas Winner
Dallas, Texas

Curtis Young proves that scratch baking is still a strong part of the American tradition. While he may have started with a few mixes as a child, the thirty-one-year-old Dallas native started checking cookbooks out of the library while still in high school. He now collects old cookbooks, and considers baking his primary hobby. Since his mother was a nurse, her erratic hours meant he had to learn to cook at a young age, and he instantly enjoyed it.

Young's Triple Chocolate Cake is an example of how he likes to cook. The dates in the batter and the banana in the filling make a more textured and flavorful cake.

"I found that baby food—all those pureed fruits—are great ingredients for cakes, and I use prune and apricot in my spice cake," he says. His 7-Up cake won Best of Show at the State Fair of Texas in 1985, and that is the fifth year the Dallas Sanitation Department worker has left the fairgrounds with medals in the cake competition.

"I dream about cake combinations, and everyone tells me my specialty is baking, but I like to fool around with sauces, too," he says.

in the mashed banana and chopped dates. Pour the boiling water into the batter, mix well, and divide the batter into the two prepared pans. Mix the topping ingredients together and sprinkle over the top of the batter, pressing it in lightly.

Bake for 40 to 50 minutes, or until a toothpick inserted in the center comes out clean. Cool for 10 minutes, remove from the pans, and cool completely on wire racks.

To make the frosting, beat the butter until light and fluffy. Sift the

sugar and cocoa and beat 1 cup of this mixture into the butter. Add the remaining sugar alternately with the milk. Add the vanilla.

To make the filling, beat the cream cheese with the sugar, vanilla, and cocoa.

To assemble the cake, invert 1 layer onto a plate covered with 2 overlapping sheets of waxed paper. Spread with the filling and top with slices of banana, if desired. Place the second layer on top, then frost the sides and top with the frosting. Pull out the sheets of waxed paper and garnish with the nut halves.

Note: The cake can be prepared a day in advance and allowed to sit at room temperature. If making a day prior to serving, do not add the banana to the filling layer. ■

Certain traditions cannot be improved upon, and chef John Sedlar at Saint Estèphe still uses his grandmother's recipe for these crispy, anise-flavored cookies. Biscochitos are a Christmas cookie in the Southwest, but that should not preclude any other time of year.

Biscochitos

Eloisa Rivera, Santa Fe, New Mexico

(Makes 30 cookies)

1½ cups sugar
1 cup lard or vegetable shortening, at
    room temperature
2 eggs
1½ teaspoons anise seed
½ teaspoon vanilla extract
2½ cups unbleached all-purpose flour
1 teaspoon baking powder
Water or milk, if needed
Granulated sugar and cinnamon for
    sprinkling

In a mixer bowl or a food processor fitted with a steel blade, cream the sugar and lard together until light and fluffy. Add the eggs, one at a time, and the anise seed and vanilla.

Sift the flour with the baking powder and add to the mixture, mixing with your hands until the dough is smooth. If too thick, add a few teaspoons of water or milk, and if too thin, adjust with additional flour. Form the dough into a ball, and chill in plastic wrap in the refrigerator for a few hours.

Preheat the oven to 375°. Divide the dough into a few parts and roll each on a lightly floured surface to an even thickness of ¼ inch. Cut into decorative shapes with cookie cutters and sprinkle with granulated sugar and cinnamon.

Place the cookies on ungreased cookie sheets and bake for 7 to 10 minutes, or until lightly browned.

Note: These will keep up to a week in an airtight container, and they freeze extremely well. ■

HOME COOK

ELOISA MARTINEZ RIVERA
Santa Fe, New Mexico

As she rolls anise-flecked dough for *biscochitos*, Eloisa Martinez Rivera recalls her early teen years. "We washed with a washboard. Today people don't work, they just push buttons," she says.

But some conveniences she appreciates. When she first began baking these traditional New Mexican Christmas cookies, they had to be baked in a wood-burning stove, so regulating the heat was a delicate task.

Born to farmer parents of Spanish descent, the seventy-three-year-old native of Abiquiu, New Mexico, about fifty miles from Santa Fe, learned to cook while working as a maid, and still makes the foods of her childhood. At Christmastime, she stews *posole* with chilies and meats, rolls tamales, and always makes her own tortillas. "The ones you buy are too thin, they look like paper to me," she says.

Mrs. Rivera, whose cooking was a great influence on the decision of her grandson, John Sedlar, to become a chef, begins her tortillas by making *chicos*. These are immature ears of corn that are partially cooked and then dried in the intense New Mexican sun. The kernels are ground to make the tortilla dough.

Her style of cooking is reflective of the simple and robust foods of the region. As is true for her generation, she does not measure, but makes each recipe by judging the texture and flavor of the food. As she breaks a dried chili from a *ristra,* she smells it to gauge the level of hotness.

"These aren't things anyone can tell you, you just know from all the years you've smelled them," she says.

Assorted Meats, Kreuz Market, Lockhart, Texas

DON AND RICK SCHMIDT

Kreuz Market, Lockhart, Texas

Cooking simply with quality ingredients is hardly a modern idea. It has guaranteed the popularity of the smoked sausage at Kreuz Market and has kept the business thriving for years; the market now sells up to 5,000 links on a busy weekend.

There has been a meat market at the Lockhart location for nearly a century, and since 1900, when Charlie Kreuz, Sr., bought the business, the post oak fires have been lit at dawn each morn ing to smoke sausage and shoulder of beef.

The building, with a pressed tin ceiling and knives chained to the long wooden tables where diners eat sausage and brisket served on butcher paper, was built in 1924.

In 1948, the business was sold to the Schmidt family, and is now run by brothers Don and Rick Schmidt. They make sausages and operate a meat market in the front of the smokehouse as well as the simple dining room.

"The sausage is 85 percent beef and 15 percent pork, and we sometimes mix in some bull meat to make it even leaner," says Rick. "It is still all hand stuffed and mixed with just a little salt, pepper, and cayenne. We don't use garlic or oregano. It is then hot smoked over pure post oak, and then we chill them overnight. Like a stew, the chilling and reheating is very important, and it tastes better the next day."

New Southwest Cooking

New Southwest cooking is the much-welcomed offspring of new American cuisine, the culinary revolution of the past decade. The battle to attain validity and stature for dishes based on historic American prototypes and/or using native ingredients has been waged nightly in restaurants from coast to coast.

As recently as 1982, when the first Symposium on American Cuisine was convened in Louisville, Kentucky, my usually open-minded newspaper editor was aghast at my request to attend. "How can you possibly spend three days talking about hamburgers?" was the response.

At that time, new American cuisine was considered by many to be a peculiarity rather than a valid movement. Although Mark Miller was grilling fish over mesquite at the Fourth Street Grill in Berkeley, Bradley Ogden was updating native classics at An American Restaurant in Kansas City, and Dean Fearing's fare was arousing the curiosity of such knowledgeable American palates as Craig Claiborne's at Agnew's in Dallas, the public had not yet recognized the culinary revolution that embraced their diverse styles.

While all three chefs are now commanding other kitchens, the impact of their philosophies and those of their contemporaries has fundamentally changed the way Americans eat. Culinary leadership has moved from the food writers and cookbook authors to the chefs, who are now in a spotlight traditionally afforded creative artists working in less ephemeral media.

With a few rare exceptions, such as Jean Banchet at Le Français in Wheeling, Illinois, or Andre Soltner at New York's Lutèce, chefs in even the most heralded French restaurants never gained the recognition of the general public. This was partially due to the expense of their fare, but also to the similarity of their styles; a cheese soufflé varied little from coast to coast. Their allegiance was to the dicta of Escoffier rather than to creating dishes that reflected their convictions as chefs.

The trailblazing chefs quickly found acceptance with the critical food press and the dining public. A 1984 issue of the now-defunct *Cuisine* magazine featured Clark Gable on the cover, but the cover story depicted Wolfgang Puck and Michael Roberts as the "new stars of Los Angeles." For generations, home cooks had looked in the pages of Fannie Farmer and Irma Rombauer for inspiration, but now food editors were suddenly queuing up to print recipes of Lydia Shire's updating of New England seafood classics.

Chefs have become our most popular food writers. Paul Prudhomme's book on his native Cajun fare has sold more than 400,000 copies, and John Sedlar's *Modern Southwest Cuisine* has introduced his style of cooking to thousands. Other chefs profiled in this volume—including Ogden, Roberts, Susan Feniger, and Mary Sue Milliken—have books coming out.

No amount of publicity, however, would have overcome the economics of the restaurant business had not the American public's tastebuds been tantalized. Sophisticated diners supported the new cooking, and an important symbiosis began that has transformed the way we eat at home.

One of the tenets that united the disparate styles of cooking lumped under "new American cuisine" was the insistence on the highest-quality ingredients. This led chefs to contract with farmers to grow certain crops not available through commercial purveyors, and certainly not in supermarkets. Excess production found its way into commercial channels, as home shoppers demanded the ingredients necessary to make the recipes printed in their newspapers and food magazines.

Chicken Thighs with Black Mustard Seeds and Fermented-Rice Pancakes, Gardens,
Los Angeles, California

Mixed Grill with Cilantro Pesto Sauce, Anne Lindsay Greer, Dallas, Texas

It's now common to find a range of wild mushrooms at my local Giant Food in Washington, as well as fresh chilies and cilantro at Kroger's in Cincinnati, and the rudimentaries of Asian cookery at almost all Safeway stores nationally.

This demand for quality is one factor in the birth of new Southwest cooking. For chefs of any region, what can be grown around their city is by logic fresher than a crop imported from even a few states away. These local ingredients, of course, are the same ingredients that were the basis for traditional regional dishes. The result was the development of regional new American cuisine.

Chefs such as Lawrence Forgione at An American Place in New York had looked to the traditional foods of the country as a whole as the basis for updating dishes. Rather than being generalists, the chefs featured in this book are culinary specialists. They are more intrigued by the contrasting nuances of Texan and New Mexican cookery than by attempting to juxtapose their native foods with the dishes from other areas.

If the Bay Area of San Francisco can be credited with the creation of new American cuisine, then Dallas is the birthplace of its first child. While other chefs were working independently to develop their philosophical affinities with a region, a group of Texas chefs—including Fearing, Stephan Pyles, Anne Lindsay Greer, and Robert Del Grande—were meeting on a regular basis to share ideas and the exploration of ingredients.

I was fortunate enough to be the first guest at one of their group dinners, held at Greer's home, in 1983. The food I was served was like nothing I had ever sampled. Although involved with chronicling new American cuisine at the time, I had never tasted the likes of crunchy *jicama* with apples in a cilantro-vinaigrette dressing, tamales filled with shrimp mousse, fried cayenne pasta as a foil to the rich buttery taste of grilled foie gras, or a classic cream soup flavored with the fresh flavor of cilantro. The dishes created by the group followed the course of its parent: new Southwest cooking updated the traditional dishes of the region, and also used the native ingredients to create innovative new dishes. This section is composed of examples of the two parallel threads.

This group of chefs, the most acclaimed in their state and having national influence, soon shared their ideas with others who passed through. As their reputations justifiably grew, chefs experimenting independently joined the dialogue.

In October 1986, the Los Angeles chapter of the American Institute of Wine and Food celebrated new Southwest cooking with a symposium and dinner. Participating were not only the pioneer chefs, but also Brendan Walsh from Arizona 206, one of the new stars in New York's restaurant galaxy, and Alan Zeman from the Tucson Country Club, who had gained recognition although his restaurant is not open to the public.

Those few hundred diners who gathered at Lawry's Center in the Spanish-style courtyard that evening were the preview audience for what millions of viewers will see during the 26 episodes of "Great Chefs of the West." The freshness and depth of the flavors in new Southwest cooking harbinger the era to come.

APPETIZERS AND SOUPS

The range of recipes in this chapter is most reflective of the two threads of new Southwestern cookery: the updating of traditional dishes using unexpected ingredients in exciting ways, and the use of Southwestern ingredients in dishes that are part of the European tradition.

In the first camp, we have Gordon Naccarato of Gordon's in Aspen, Colorado, stuffing *chiles rellenos* with an herbed goat cheese before frying, and Anne Lindsay Greer filling flour tortillas with a luscious blend of Brie and papaya for *quesadillas*.

In the second school are a few pâtés made from the game now being raised in Texas, as well as Robert Del Grande's justly famous creamed mussel soup using cilantro as the dominant herb and garnished with a bright dollop of *ancho* preserves, and Jimmy Schmidt's *blini* made from blue cornmeal.

While the chefs prepare the dishes in this chapter as appetizers, many of them would be appropriate as a lunch or light supper entree if the portion size were larger. Another way to use these recipes is to combine several appetizers to make up an entire meal—the grazing phenomenon that is sweeping the country. If serving with entrees, pick dishes that offer a variety of flavors and textures, choosing some hot and some cold so that much of the preparation can be done in advance.

Scrambled Huevos Rancheros with Blue Corn Tortilla Arrows, Saint Estèphe, Manhattan Beach, California

Roasted peppers make these the most flavorful scrambled eggs you'll ever eat. The tortilla arrows are John Sedlar's characteristic dramatic touch, however, they are very easy to do.

Scrambled Huevos Rancheros with Blue Corn Tortilla Arrows

Saint Estèphe, Manhattan Beach, California

(Serves 6)

3 blue corn tortillas (see listing for sources, or yellow corn tortillas can be substituted)
1 cup vegetable oil for frying
12 eggs
2 tablespoons unsalted butter
6 tablespoons finely diced white onion
3 teaspoons finely diced roasted and seeded *jalapeño* chili (see page 10)
5 teaspoons finely diced roasted and seeded red bell pepper (see page 10)
Salt to taste

Cut each tortilla into 12 pointed arrowhead shapes with a sharp knife. Heat the oil to 375° in a heavy skillet and fry the arrowheads in small batches until crisp, about 1 minute. Remove with a slotted spoon, drain on paper towels, and continue until all are fried. Keep warm.

Using an egg cutter to carefully cut the top quarter off the narrow end of each egg, empty the contents of the shells into a bowl and wash out the shells under running water. Invert them onto paper towels to drain. Beat the eggs and set aside.

Melt the butter in a small saucepan over medium heat and sauté the onion until very lightly golden, about 2 minutes. Lower the heat and add the beaten eggs and remaining ingredients and cook, stirring frequently, for about 3 minutes. The egg should be very creamy.

To serve, spoon the scrambled eggs into the eggshells, mounding them slightly, and place each shell in an egg cup. Stand 3 tortilla arrows around one side of the inside rim of each egg and serve immediately.

Note: If you don't have an egg cutter, serve the scrambled eggs in small ramekins or custard cups, with the arrows arranged around the top. ∎

GORDON AND REBECCA NACCARATO
Gordon's, Aspen, Colorado

Rebecca and Gordon Naccarato, while not formally trained, are products of the informal apprenticeship system that has produced so many fine chefs practicing new American cuisine. Both gained their culinary knowledge in the kitchen of Michael's in Santa Monica, and have gone on to make their independent statement.

Gordon's, located on the second floor of a modern Aspen shopping complex, is a stunning post-modern restaurant with irregular glass partitions dividing the space. In the entrance foyer is a dessert table displaying Rebecca's pastries (some of which are sold at Rebecca's, her retail outlet two stories below).

The couple, both now thirty-two, were both born in the state of Washington, where they met and married. They moved to Los Angeles when Gordon enrolled in law school at Loyola University.

"I realized I wasn't going to be happy practicing law, and came upon Michael's the day before it opened. I started waiting tables, and then moved back to the kitchen to learn. When someone left, I would move into the next rung on the ladder," he says.

Rebecca started six months later, and progressed in the same way. She was born on a wheat ranch, and had always been the baker in the family. "Desserts were always the most important part of my meal, and what I am doing today is taking the French technique I learned at Michael's and giving it my American attitude. Even if I do things that are classic, like a *tarte tatin*, I don't present them in a classic way, and I am very conscious of not making things too sweet," she says.

Chef Naccarato's dishes reflect his region, but are not limited to the Southwest in their inspiration. While his signature creation is a *relleno* stuffed with creamy goat cheese and dipped in blue cornmeal before frying, he also utilizes Asian touches in some dishes.

This dish is emblematic of what the young chefs of the Southwest are doing today. The same chilies traditionally fried with American cheese are now stuffed with a creamy herbed goat cheese filling, while the method remains the same.

Goat Cheese Rellenos

Gordon's, Aspen, Colorado

(Serves 6)

Chilies

12 Anaheim or *poblano* chilies
2 garlic cloves
½ pound mild crumbled goat cheese, at room temperature
½ pound Monterey jack cheese, grated
2 tablespoons chopped shallots
2 small pieces oil-packed sun-dried tomatoes, minced
¼ cup chopped fresh cilantro
½ cup chopped fresh basil
2 tablespoons chopped fresh marjoram
2 thyme sprigs, or ¼ teaspoon dried thyme
Salt and pepper to taste
1 egg
2 tablespoons heavy cream
Blue cornmeal for dredging (yellow can be substituted)
Oil for deep-frying

Salsa

2 shallots, finely minced
¼ cup champagne vinegar
¾ cup extra-virgin olive oil
3 tomatoes, peeled, seeded, and finely chopped
1 *jalapeño* or *serrano* chili, seeded and chopped
¼ cup chopped fresh cilantro
¼ cup chopped fresh basil
2 tablespoons chopped fresh thyme
2 tablespoons chopped fresh marjoram
Salt and freshly ground pepper to taste

Garnish

3 ripe avocados
6 salad savory (purple kale) or *radicchio* leaves

To prepare the chilies, roast and peel them according to the method on page 10. Carefully slice them down one side and remove the seeds, leaving the stem attached. Set aside.

Blanch the garlic in boiling water for 5 minutes. Remove the garlic with a slotted spoon, peel, and chop finely.

In a bowl, combine the garlic with the crumbled goat cheese, Monterey jack, shallots, sun-dried tomatoes, cilantro, basil, marjoram, and thyme. Add salt and pepper to taste. Mix well and shape into 12 roll-shaped pieces about the size of the chilies. Gently insert the cheese rolls into the chilies, being careful not to overfill. Close the chilies, securing with toothpicks, and refrigerate until needed.

Beat the egg into the cream and coat the filled chilies with the mixture. Dredge the chilies in the blue cornmeal.

Heat the oil in a deep-fryer or heavy saucepan until hot, 375°. Fry the chilies until they are lightly brown. Remove them and drain well on paper towels. Remove the toothpicks.

To make the *salsa,* whisk the shallots in the vinegar. Add the oil slowly, continuing to whisk, then stir in the remaining ingredients.

To serve, peel and halve the avocados. Cut each half into a fan and set on one side of each serving plate. Place 2 chilies in the center and spoon the *salsa* into a lettuce "cup" on the other side of the plate. Serve immediately.

Note: The chilies can be roasted and stuffed up to 2 days in advance and kept covered with plastic wrap in the refrigerator. The *salsa* can be made up to 6 hours in advance. ∎

Perhaps no dish has come of age as part of new American cuisine as much as pizza. That staple Italian street food has been elevated with exotic toppings on menus from coast to coast. The cornmeal crust and spicy topping make this version a spectacular cross between pizza and an enchilada.

Cornmeal Pizza with Wild Mushrooms

Piret's, San Diego, California

(Makes 2 large or 4 individual pizzas)

Dough

3 packages (3 tablespoons) active dry yeast
1½ cups warm water (85°)
1 tablespoon sugar
2 tablespoons olive oil
2¼ cups unbleached all-purpose flour
½ cup semolina
¾ cup yellow cornmeal
½ teaspoon salt
1 tablespoon cracked black pepper
1 garlic clove, peeled and minced

Sauce

½ cup olive oil
¼ cup peeled and diced *tomatillo* (1 large)
2 tablespoons coarsely chopped fresh cilantro
1 tablespoon chopped fresh oregano or ½ teaspoon dried oregano
1 large garlic clove, peeled
2 tablespoons chopped red onion
2 egg yolks
½ cup freshly grated Parmesan cheese
Salt and freshly ground black pepper to taste

Topping

3 tablespoons olive oil
½ pound assorted wild mushrooms, such as chanterelles and *shiitakes,* cleaned and sliced
¼ cup sliced red onion
1 teaspoon minced garlic
3 tablespoons dry sherry
Salt and cracked black pepper
2 mild green chilies, such as *poblano* or Anaheim, roasted, peeled, seeded, and sliced (see page 10)
1 cup sliced cherry tomatoes
1 cup grated Mexican cheese
Cilantro leaves, roughly chopped

Cornmeal Pizza with Wild Mushrooms, Piret's, San Diego, California

To make the dough, proof the yeast in warm water with sugar until foamy. Using the dough hook of a mixer, add the remaining ingredients and knead the dough for approximately 10 minutes, or until it is elastic and forms a ball. Roll into a ball, lightly dust with flour, and place in a greased mixing bowl. Turn dough to coat with grease, and cover with a damp towel. Allow the dough to rise in a warm, draft-free place until it has doubled in bulk, approximately 1 hour. Punch the dough down, roll it out on a floured board, and allow it to rest for 10 minutes.

At this point, divide the dough into quarters or in half, depending on the size of the pizzas to be made. Roll the sections into rounds, using your hands to stretch the dough, and place on pizza pans or pizza stones that have been dusted with cornmeal.

While the dough is rising, prepare the sauce and topping. To make the sauce, heat a few tablespoons of the olive oil in a sauté pan or skillet over medium-high heat. When hot, add the *tomatillos*, cilantro, oregano, garlic, and onion. Sauté for 5 minutes, stirring frequently, then place the mixture in a blender or a food processor fitted with a steel blade. Puree, then add the egg yolks, Parmesan cheese, and remaining olive oil. Season with salt and pepper and set aside.

To make the topping, heat the olive oil in a sauté pan or skillet over medium heat. Add the mushrooms, onions, and garlic and sauté for 2 minutes over medium heat. Cover the pan, lower the heat, and allow the mixture to cook for 10 minutes, stirring occasionally. Uncover the pan, raise the heat to high, deglaze with the sherry, and reduce until only 1 tablespoon of the liquid remains. Season with salt and pepper to taste.

Preheat the oven to 500°. To assemble the pizzas, paint the dough with sauce and sprinkle with additional Parmesan cheese, if desired. Divide the cooked mushroom mixture on top of the sauce, then arrange slices of green chili, Mexican cheese, and cherry tomato over the mushrooms. Top with fresh cilantro leaves.

Bake pizzas for 12 to 15 minutes. ∎

CINDY BLACK

Piret's, San Diego, California

I n a region now famous for light food, Cindy Black, the executive chef for the Piret's restaurants, emerges as a champion of heartiness. She freely admits that "if left to my own devices, I do a braised stew or a pot roast," so it's not surprising that a long simmered coq au vin and a *boeuf à la mode* share her menu with less substantial vestiges of her French training.

Chef Black now has the responsibility for menu planning for more than ninety restaurants run by San Diego–based Vicorp Specialty Restaurants, who purchased Piret's from Piret and George Munger in 1984. She credits the well-trained palate of her father for sparking her interest in food.

It was when she was in college at Wellesley in suburban Boston that her father retired from diplomatic service and decided to hone his culinary skills with Madeleine Kamman, the famed cooking teacher whose Modern Gourmet Cooking school was nearby. Black was so impressed with Kamman that she enrolled the following year.

The first part of her training was an apprenticeship at Auberge le Cabanon in southwest France, where she learned more about the classic dishes of the region. Some of the pâtés and *terrines* learned there are still part of her repertoire, along with desserts such as an elegant chestnut mousse encased in slices of prune-stuffed roulade.

After being schooled in the classics, Black began to assimilate the second directive of Kamman's teachings. She returned from France to Boston, where she created nouvelle French dishes at Apley's in the city and at the Cranberry Moose on Cape Cod. It was in 1982 that she and her husband, Bob Brody, who was the chef at Apley's, were wooed to San Diego by Sheraton Hotels.

At Piret's, the dishes she designs also include some Southwestern touches. The dough for her pizza is based on cornmeal, and the sauce contains *tomatillos*, although the topping is the same wild mushrooms she used in France.

Tamales are a traditional Christmas food in the Southwest. In this recipe they are made with fresh corn, so their texture and flavor remain fresh and light. They make a dramatic centerpiece to a Southwestern buffet any time of year.

Green Corn Tamales with Salsa

Border Grill, Los Angeles, California

(Serves 5 to 6 as an appetizer)

Tamales

10 ears fresh corn (see note)
2 tablespoons unsalted butter
½ teaspoon salt
¼ teaspoon ground white pepper
½ teaspoon baking powder
½ cup heavy cream
½ cup hominy grits

Salsa

3 ripe tomatoes, peeled, seeded, and cut into ¼-inch cubes
1 small yellow onion, peeled and finely chopped
1 to 2 *jalapeño* chilies, seeded, deribbed, and finely diced
1 bunch cilantro, stemmed and chopped
1 tablespoon fresh lime juice
Salt to taste
Sour cream for garnish

To make the tamales, remove the husks from the corn by trimming off the ends of the cobs, trying to keep the husks from tearing. Drop the husks into boiling water and simmer for 10 minutes to soften. Remove the pan from the heat and set aside.

Run a knife between the rows of corn, then, using the back side of a knife, scrape the corn off the husks.

In a sauté pan or skillet, melt the butter over medium heat and cook the corn gently over low heat, stirring occasionally, for 5 minutes. Add the salt, pepper, baking powder, cream, and grits to the pan and continue to cook for 5 minutes, stirring frequently so the mixture does not burn. Correct seasoning.

Remove the husks from water with tongs and drain on paper towels. Make ties for the tamales by cutting strips from a few of the corn husks. Place a few tablespoons of the filling in the center of each of 10 to 12 large husks, folding the ends and then the sides over to enclose it. Tie each tamale with a strip like a small package. Do not tie it too tightly since the filling expands as it cooks.

In a steamer or a pot fitted with a rack, make a bed for the tamales with the remaining corn husks. Add the tamales and steam them over medium heat for 1 hour. Remove from the steamer and allow to rest for 10 minutes before serving.

While the tamales are steaming, mix the *salsa* ingredients together and set aside to allow the flavors to blend.

To serve, place the *salsa* and sour cream in ramekins and allot 2 tamales per serving.

Note: Frozen corn can be used for this recipe, estimating that 10 ears of fresh corn will yield 4 to 5 cups of kernels. Allow it to defrost, and break it up slightly in a food processor before continuing to cook. You will have to wrap the tamales in dried corn husks, available at Hispanic groceries, which need to be soaked overnight. ∎

Unlike some Southern corn fritters, these are savory instead of sweet. In addition to being a delicious appetizer, these fritters could be used as a side dish to enhance a simple entree, or smaller versions could be passed as hors d'oeuvres at a cocktail party.

Corn Fritters

The American Grill, Phoenix, Arizona

(Serves 8 to 10 as an appetizer)

2½ pounds whole corn kernels (either cut fresh from the cob or frozen; do not use canned)
3 eggs, lightly beaten
¼ cup finely chopped green onions, white part only
½ teaspoon finely minced garlic
2½ tablespoons finely chopped fresh cilantro
1¼ cups finely chopped onion
1¼ cups unbleached all-purpose flour
½ cup cornmeal
1 tablespoon salt
1 tablespoon sugar
1½ tablespoons baking powder
1½ tablespoons ground coriander

½ teaspoon ground black pepper
8 cups oil for deep-frying
Pineapple-Chili Sauce, page 143

Cook the corn in salted water to cover. When cooked, drain and cool, then puree in a blender or a food processor fitted with a steel blade. Beat in the eggs.

Mix the green onions, garlic, cilantro, and onion together and set aside. In another bowl, mix the dry ingredients and spices.

Beat the corn mixture and then the vegetables into the dry ingredients.

In a deep-fryer or heavy deep-sided pot, heat the oil to a temperature of 350°. Using a rubber spatula, push the batter off carefully into the hot fat, about a tablespoonful at a time. Fry the fritters until they are a deep golden brown, turning them in the hot fat to brown both sides. Drain on paper towels and keep the fritters warm in a 150° oven while frying the remaining batter.

Serve with Pineapple-Chili Sauce for dipping.

Note: The batter can be made up to 3 days in advance and kept in the refrigerator. Stir well before frying. ∎

Corn Fritters, The American Grill, Phoenix, Arizona

The fresh wild mushrooms create a flavorful variation on a French classic. It could also be a side dish to elevate a simple entree.

Wild-Mushroom Gratin

Campton Place, San Francisco, California

(Serves 6)

Herb crust

½ cup fresh white bread crumbs
½ cup freshly grated Parmesan cheese
½ cup freshly grated Gruyère cheese
3 tablespoons chopped fresh parsley
1 tablespoon chopped fresh basil
1 teaspoon chopped fresh thyme

Mushrooms

1½ cups chanterelles, cleaned, stemmed, and halved if large
2 cups fresh *shiitake* mushrooms, cleaned, stemmed, and quartered
½ cup Italian field mushrooms or oyster mushrooms, cleaned and sliced

2 tablespoons unsalted butter
3 tablespoons sliced shallots
1 teaspoon minced garlic
⅓ cup Dry Sack or other dry sherry
¼ cup Madeira
1¾ cups heavy cream
½ teaspoon cracked black pepper
1 tablespoon kosher salt

Combine all the ingredients for the herb crust and set aside.

Preheat a broiler. Combine the mushrooms and melt the butter in a sauté pan or skillet over high heat. When hot, add the mushrooms and sauté for 5 to 7 minutes, stirring frequently but gently, or until golden brown. Add the shallots and sauté 2 minutes more, then add the garlic and sauté another minute.

Add the remaining ingredients and simmer for 5 minutes over medium heat. Remove the mushrooms from the pan with a slotted spoon and reduce the sauce over low heat, stirring frequently, until it coats the

back of a wooden spoon, about 10 minutes.

Place the mushrooms back in the sauce, along with any juices that may have accumulated, and divide the mixture into buttered individual gratin dishes. Splash with a little more sherry and sprinkle with the crust mixture.

Brown under the broiler and serve immediately.

Note: The crust and mushroom mixture can be prepared 2 days in advance. Keep the crumbs in an airtight container and refrigerate the mushrooms. Heat the mushrooms in the top of a double boiler or over low heat before the final browning. ■

Wild-Mushroom Gratin, Campton Place, San Francisco, California

Quesadillas can be made from either corn or flour tortillas, and are one of the traditional appetizers of Southwestern cuisine when filled with cheese and chilies. In this updated version, they are a wonderful hors d'oeuvre for a cocktail party or a variation on cheese and fruit to end a meal.

Brie and Papaya Quesadillas

Anne Lindsay Greer, Dallas, Texas

(Makes 30 pieces)

½ cup water
½ yellow onion, thinly sliced and slices halved
10 flour tortillas
1 pound Brie or Camembert cheese, cut in ¼-inch strips
2 *poblano* chilies, roasted, peeled, and diced (see page 10)
1 ripe papaya, peeled, seeded, and diced (a mango or seedless grapes can be substituted)
4 tablespoons butter, melted, mixed with
4 tablespoons oil
Jícama Salad (see recipe for Warm Lobster Tacos, page 109), optional

Heat the water in a medium skillet over high heat. Add the onion, remove from heat, and let stand until the slices are wilted, about 12 minutes. Drain and set aside.

Heat a nonstick or well-seasoned skillet over medium heat for several minutes. When the skillet is hot, soften the tortillas by placing them in

Brie and Papaya Quesadillas, Anne Lindsay Greer, Dallas, Texas

the skillet for about 15 seconds on a side.

To make *quesadillas*, put a few strips of cheese on half of each tortilla. Add several onion strips and 1 tablespoon of the diced chilies and papaya. Fold the tortillas over and brush with the mixture of melted butter and oil.

Preheat the oven to 200°. Heat a skillet over medium heat and brown the *quesadillas* on both sides. Place

on a cookie sheet in the oven to keep warm while browning the remaining *quesadillas*.

Cut each into 3 triangular wedges and serve with Jícama Salad, if used as an appetizer.

Note: After being filled, the *quesadillas* can be refrigerated for a day, covered with plastic wrap. Bring them to room temperature before grilling and serving. ∎

ANNE LINDSAY GREER

Dallas, Texas

Anne Lindsay Greer is the original force behind the food scene in Dallas. She has influenced new Southwest cooking through her articles and books, and she was also the magnet who drew together the other chefs working in Texas, so that the developing school of cookery gained national prominence.

Greer, a Chicago native who studied art and painted before turning to cooking, taught and catered in San Antonio for a few years before moving to Dallas in 1982. She is the author of the Tastemaker Award—winning *Cuisine of the American Southwest, Creative Mexican Cookery,* and the upcoming *Foods of the Sun,* to be published by Harper & Row in the fall of 1987. In addition, she planned the Nana Grill of Loews Anatole Hotel, one of the first Texas restaurants to feature new Southwest dishes.

Greer credits her Chicago childhood with her fondness for the assertive flavors of the Southwest. "It was an ethnic city, and I grew up with a great love for all ethnic foods. I have never had the reverence for French food that most people seem to have had, although I respect the quality of the ingredients French chefs use," she says. "My goal is to prove that the comfort foods of our nation deserve being dressed up and presented with the same elegance that chefs give foreign dishes."

While Greer has influenced home cooks with her writings, she has also been a behind-the-scenes force on the Texas restaurant scene. It was Greer who first invited Dean Fearing and Stephan Pyles to dinner to discuss their mutual interests, and then broadened her list of invitees to include Houstonians Robert Del Grande and Amy Ferguson. Their joint dinners drew national attention.

"I knew that if we would all get together and support one another, then people in other places would start to take Southwest cuisine seriously," she says. "Part of what makes the whole new American cuisine movement special is that the chefs and writers share. Really creative people are not jealous of one another and don't copy one another; we give each other new ideas by the level of our conversations."

With the increasing popularity of caviar, chefs are inventing more interesting accompaniments than the traditional shot of vodka. This crispy pastry, with the surprise of the barely set egg, is innovative as well as delicious.

Ossetra Caviar with Toasted Tunisian Brik

Gardens, Los Angeles, California

(Serves 4)

2 tablespoons cumin seeds
2 tablespoons coriander seeds
½ pound *phyllo* dough, completely defrosted
2 egg yolks, lightly beaten
½ pound fresh tuna, preferably bluefin, cut into ⅓-inch dice
1 small red onion, finely diced
Salt and freshly ground black pepper
1 lemon
2 teaspoons chopped anchovies
½ cup chopped fresh cilantro
¼ cup chopped fresh parsley
4 eggs, the smallest size possible
1 quart olive oil for frying

Garnish

½ cup *crème fraîche*
4 ounces ossetra caviar (or other high-quality sturgeon caviar)
2 hard-cooked eggs, coarsely grated
4 parsley sprigs
4 bright-colored edible flowers or herb flowers

Heat a small skillet over medium heat and toast the cumin and coriander seeds until fragrant and slightly toasted. Grind them through a peppermill or in a clean coffee grinder and set aside.

To assemble the *briks,* place a sheet of *phyllo* dough lengthwise on a lightly floured board. Dip your fingers into the egg yolks and moisten the edges of the *phyllo.* Fold in half to create a rectangle.

Place one-fourth of the cubed tuna and a few teaspoons of onion in a ring halfway down the *phyllo,* and season with salt, pepper, and a squeeze of lemon juice. Sprinkle on one-fourth of the ground spices and an even portion of the chopped anchovies, cilantro, parsley, and remaining onion.

Ossetra Caviar with Toasted Tunisian Brik, Gardens, Los Angeles, California

Break an egg into the center of the tuna ring and, working as quickly as possible, fold the dough over to create a half-moon shape, sealing the pastry with the egg yolks. Repeat with the other 3 *briks*.

Heat the oil to 350° in a deep heavy pot or deep-fryer and gently slide a *brik* into the hot oil, spooning hot oil on the top to brown it. It should not cook for more than 1½ minutes, since the egg white should be set but the yolk should be runny. Gently remove from the oil with a slotted spoon and drain on paper towels, gently patting the top. Repeat to cook all the *briks*.

To serve, place on plates and squeeze a little lemon over the top. Garnish the plate with a dollop of *crème fraîche*, caviar, the remaining red onion, grated egg, a sprig of parsley, and a flower.

Note: The *briks* can be prepared up to an hour in advance, but should be fried just prior to serving. ■

This dish is becoming as common as oysters Rockefeller on a Creole menu; it has spread throughout the Southwest since Anne Lindsay Greer developed it for the Nana Grill of the Anatole Hotel. And it has become popular with good reason: the pesto topping is delicious and the perfect counterpoint to oysters.

Oysters with Cilantro Pesto

Anne Lindsay Greer, Dallas, Texas

(Serves 6)

24 large oysters in their shells
2 garlic cloves
2 *serrano* chilies, stemmed
1½ cups cilantro leaves
2 tablespoons oil
2 tablespoons freshly grated Parmesan cheese
2 tablespoons pine nuts, toasted in a 350° oven for 5 to 7 minutes
1 shallot, peeled and minced
¼ cup white wine vinegar
2 tablespoons dry white wine
½ cup (1 stick) unsalted butter
Salt and pepper to taste
Freshly squeezed lime juice to taste

Topping
4 tablespoons butter, melted
1 cup crumbs made from Jalapeño Corn Bread, page 40

Shuck the oysters and replace them on their bottom shells. Place them on a cookie sheet covered with a ½-inch layer of rock salt and refrigerate until ready to broil.

In a blender or a food processor fitted with a steel blade, chop the garlic, chilies, and cilantro leaves. Slowly add the oil with the motor running, then add the cheese and nuts, pureeing until the mixture is a smooth paste. Set aside.

In a small saucepan, combine the shallot, vinegar, and wine and boil until only a few tablespoonfuls remain. Cut the butter into small bits, remove the pan from the heat, and whisk in the butter, bit by bit, waiting until each piece is melted and incorporated before adding the next. Season with salt and pepper to taste, along with a squeeze of lime juice.

Beat the *pesto* mixture into the *beurre blanc* and spoon a tablespoonful onto each oyster. Mix the corn bread crumbs with the melted butter and sprinkle on top of the *pesto*.

Preheat the broiler and broil the oysters about 6 inches from the broiling element for about 3 minutes, or until the crumbs are brown and the oysters have curled at the edges. Serve immediately.

Note: The sauce can be prepared up to 8 hours in advance and kept at room temperature. If you cannot find oysters in their shells, jarred fresh oysters can be used. Place them in a strainer and then arrange 6 in each of 4 ovenproof gratin dishes. Top with the *pesto* sauce and crumbs. ■

The subtle nuances of flavors make this dish delicious: the slight smoke and spice of the oysters with the creamy leeks. It works equally well with medium-sized clams.

Smoked Oysters with Leeks and Curry

Grand Champions Club, Aspen, Colorado

(Serves 4)

24 fresh oysters in their shells
2 small leeks
1½ cups heavy cream
Salt and freshly ground pepper to taste
1 cup unbleached all-purpose flour
2 tablespoons curry powder
2 tablespoons unsalted butter
1 head *radicchio*
2 tablespoons chopped fresh chives

Discarding any oysters that are not firmly closed, shuck the oysters, reserving the bottom shells for presentation. Light a smoker or charcoal grill, and soak ½ cup hickory chips in water for 15 minutes.

Place the oysters in a metal pan on the rack of a smoker or in a covered grill. Sprinkle the chips over the red-hot coals and smoke the oysters for 2 to 3 minutes, or until they become opaque and their edges just start to curl. Be careful not to overcook. Remove them and set aside.

Trim both ends from the leeks, cutting away all but 1 inch of the green, and slice them open lengthwise. Wash them well under cold running water to remove all grit. Julienne the leeks and combine them with the cream in a small saucepan. Bring to a boil over medium heat and reduce, stirring occasionally, until the sauce is thick. Season with salt and pepper to taste.

Mix the flour and curry together. Dredge the oysters in the mixture to coat, shaking well in a sieve to remove any excess flour. Heat the butter in a sauté pan or skillet over high heat, add the oysters, and quickly sauté until golden brown. Remove from the heat and keep warm.

Smoked Oysters with Leeks and Curry, Grand Champions Club, Aspen, Colorado

To serve, shred the *radicchio* and arrange on 4 plates. Place 6 oyster shells on each plate and divide the leek mixture evenly among the shells. Top each shell with an oyster, sprinkle with chives, and serve immediately.

Note: The oysters can be smoked and dredged up to 4 hours in advance, and the leek mixture can be made a day in advance and reheated slowly. The oysters should be sautéed just prior to serving. ∎

The pale green of avocado paired with pink shrimp make this dish as pretty as it is easy to prepare. This recipe is a lighter and more refined version of guacamole and can be served as a lunch entree as well as an appetizer.

Avocado and Shrimp Terrine

Wine Connoisseur, Houston, Texas

(Serves 8 to 10)

Avocado mousse

8 small ripe avocados (6 should yield 7 to 8 cups of pulp)
Juice of 4 lemons
1 tablespoon Dijon mustard
Dash of Worcestershire sauce
Salt and white pepper to taste
½ cup heavy cream

Sauce

8 ripe Italian plum tomatoes, peeled, seeded, and diced
3 tablespoons heavy cream
2 teaspoons fresh lemon juice
2 tablespoons chopped fresh basil, or ½ teaspoon dried basil
Salt and freshly ground black pepper

Shrimp

1 cup dry white wine
1 cup water
Salt and pepper to taste
2 pounds fresh medium-sized shrimp, cleaned and deveined

Line a 9-by-5-inch loaf pan with parchment paper, leaving enough paper on the sides to cover the top of the mousse. Set aside.

Peel the avocados, sprinkling all cut surfaces with lemon juice. Set aside 2 and cube the remaining 6 in a large mixing bowl. Add the mustard, Worcestershire sauce, remaining lemon juice, and salt and white pepper to taste. Mash well, using an electric mixer or your hands. In a chilled bowl, whip the cream until soft peaks form.

Fold the whipped cream into the avocado mixture, adjust seasoning as needed, and pour half the mixture into the prepared mold. Take the 2 remaining avocados and halve them. Place them hollow side up in the loaf pan, tap it down on a counter to remove any holes, and fill with the remaining mousse. Refrigerate for at least 1 hour before serving, making sure the parchment is directly on the surface of the mousse to prevent discoloration.

To make the sauce, combine the tomatoes, cream, and lemon juice in a small saucepan and stew them over medium heat for 5 minutes, stirring frequently. Add the basil, season with salt and pepper, and set aside.

To cook the shrimp, bring the white wine and water to a boil, seasoning the liquid lightly with salt and pepper. Add the shrimp, and when the liquid returns to a boil remove it from the heat. Let the shrimp soak in the water for 5 minutes. Remove with a slotted spoon and drain on paper towels.

To serve, unmold the *terrine* by inverting it onto a platter. Place some of the tomato sauce on each serving plate and place a slice of *terrine* in the center. Garnish with 3 shrimp each.

Note: The *terrine* can be made up to a day in advance and kept refrigerated, and the shrimp and tomato sauce can also be done at that time. Allow the shrimp to reach room temperature, and reheat the sauce slightly before serving. ∎

Avocado and Shrimp Terrine, Wine Connoisseur, Houston, Texas

STEPHAN PYLES

Routh Street Cafe, Dallas, Texas

Stephan Pyles is one of the American chefs who has traded one art form for another. In his case, the piano was eclipsed by his love of working with pots and pans.

Chef Pyles, who owns the Routh Street Cafe with John Dayton, has spent practically all of his thirty-five years in Texas. He was born in Big Spring in the western part of the state, and started working in his parents' truck stops when he was eight.

A turning point of his life occurred during his first trip to France in 1974, a sojourn that was extended from a few weeks to two months. "I fell in love with the food, and would walk down the streets smelling freshly baked bread and thinking of the pastries as edible art," he says.

He moved to Dallas, and although still interested in pursuing his piano and voice training, he was drawn to restaurant kitchens. While chef at The Bronx, he was asked to assist the visiting French chefs at the Mondavi Cooking School in the Napa Valley, and that informal apprenticeship laid the foundation of his style. He worked with twelve different chefs, and each quarterly visit enhanced his cooking.

"The style of cooking was very nouvelle at the time, and I learned how to get the purest flavors with the least amount of altering of the ingredients," he says.

He then started a catering business, which is how he met Dayton, one of the firm's clients. The two opened Routh Street, a sleek dining room decorated in subtle tones of pink and gray, in 1983.

"I am not limiting myself to Southwestern dishes, although they play a role. I am exploring American cooking in general," he says. "What I do is use classical technique and keep the flavors refined yet aggressive; however, my presentations are as concerned with flavors as colors. I like to taste a lot of things on my plate, but nothing should jump out."

Catfish, that lowly creature of the South, is now farm-raised in many states, and chefs such as Stephan Pyles are utilizing it for its delicate flavor, which marries well with shellfish. This is an impressive dish, yet very easy to execute.

Catfish Mousse with Crayfish Sauce

Routh Street Cafe, Dallas, Texas

(Serves 4 as an appetizer, 2 as an entree)

Crayfish sauce

3 tablespoons olive oil
3 tablespoons vegetable oil
1½ to 2 pounds live crayfish
1 medium carrot, peeled and chopped
1 leek, cleaned and chopped (white part only)
1 celery stalk, chopped
1 garlic clove, crushed
3 tablespoons chopped fresh parsley
2 thyme sprigs, or ¼ teaspoon dried thyme
6 tablespoons bourbon
1 cup dry white wine
1½ tablespoons tomato paste
1½ cups heavy cream
Salt and freshly ground pepper to taste

Catfish mousse

½ pound fresh skinless catfish fillets, coarsely chopped
1 egg
1 egg yolk
¼ cup milk
½ cup heavy cream
½ teaspoon salt
Pinch of cayenne

To make the sauce, heat the oils in a 12- or 14-inch sauté pan or skillet over high heat. Add the crayfish, cover the skillet, and cook for 5 minutes, shaking the pan often. Remove the crayfish from the pan. Set aside the 4 best-looking for the garnish, and when cool enough to handle, break the bodies apart from the tails. Pinch the tails to remove the meat and set the tails aside. Place all the tail shells and bodies in a blender or a food processor fitted with a steel blade and crush.

Reheat the pan over medium heat and add the carrot, leek, celery, garlic, parsley, and thyme. Cook gently for 5 minutes, stirring occasionally. Deglaze with the bourbon and flame. Cover the pan to stop the flaming and cook over medium heat until reduced by half. Stir in the white wine, tomato paste, and crushed shells. Return to a boil and reduce by half.

Stir in the cream, reduce heat, and simmer slowly for 10 minutes. Strain into a saucepan, pressing with a wooden spoon to extract as much flavor as possible. Season with salt and pepper.

To make the mousse, grind the catfish through the finest blade of a meat grinder or puree in a blender or a food processor fitted with a steel blade. Press the fish through a fine sieve to remove any bones.

In another bowl, lightly beat the egg, egg yolk, milk, and cream. Whisk into the fish, add salt and cayenne, and stir thoroughly.

Preheat the oven to 325°. Butter eight ⅓-cup ramekins or custard cups and divide the mixture among them. Put the molds in a baking pan and pour boiling water into the pan so it comes halfway up the sides of the molds. Trim a piece of parchment paper to fit on top of the pan, then cover the entire pan with aluminum foil so no steam escapes.

Bake for 15 to 20 minutes, or until set and firm to the touch.

To serve, unmold onto plates and top with crayfish sauce. Garnish with the crayfish tails and 1 whole crayfish.

Note: The sauce and mousse mixture can be prepared a day in advance and kept refrigerated. The sauce should be reheated slowly, and the mousse should be whisked together before filling the molds. ∎

This is an updated version—with a decidedly Southwestern relish—of traditional Maryland crabcakes. The pasta takes the place of bread crumbs. The panache *is a wonderful accompaniment to any grilled or broiled food. Make it the day before you serve it.*

Deep-fried Crab Balls with Jícama-Pepper Panache

Rosalie's Restaurant, San Francisco, California

(Serves 6 to 8)

Panache

1 yellow bell pepper, seeded, deribbed, and cut into fine julienne
2 cups *jícama* julienne
1 cup thinly sliced red onions
1 cayenne or *jalapeño* chili, seeded, deribbed, and finely chopped
4 limes
1 orange
Salt to taste

Crab balls

½ pound *capellini* or vermicelli, cooked *al dente*, drained, and rinsed
1 pound fresh cooked lump or blue crab meat
3 green onions, trimmed, with entire white part and 2 inches of green part finely chopped
4 eggs, lightly beaten
¾ cup freshly grated Parmesan cheese
1 teaspoon salt
½ teaspoon freshly ground pepper
Cayenne to taste
Oil for deep-frying

Garnish

1 ripe avocado, peeled, sliced, and tossed with lemon juice to prevent discoloration
Cilantro sprigs

Make the *panache* the day before serving. Mix the pepper, *jícama*, onions, and chili in a bowl. Squeeze the juice from the limes and orange and pour over the vegetables. Toss with a little salt and allow to marinate overnight, stirring occasionally.

To make the crab balls, mix all the ingredients together in a bowl. Toss with your hands, breaking up the pasta slightly and making sure the

ingredients are well mixed. Form into 35 balls about the size of a walnut and fry in 350° fat until golden brown. Remove from the pan with a slotted spoon, drain on paper towels, and keep warm in a 150° oven while completing the frying process.

To serve, place 4 to 6 crab balls on each plate with some of the *panache* next to them. Garnish with 2 avocado slices and a few sprigs of cilantro.

Note: The crab mixture can be made the day before serving and kept refrigerated, tightly covered with plastic wrap. If the balls are fried in advance, or if there are leftovers, reheat them in a 400° oven for a few minutes to crisp. ∎

Deep-fried Crab Balls with Jícama-Pepper Panache, Rosalie's Restaurant, San Francisco, California

These nouvelle versions of the Southwestern equivalent to the grilled cheese sandwich are filled with a mixture reminiscent of deviled crab. They are a wonderful party food, since they can be cooked in small batches in minutes. If served as an appetizer, the Three-Tomato Salsa is a good contrast of flavors and textures.

Crab Quesadillas

Ann Lindsay Greer, Dallas, Texas

(Makes 64 pieces, serving 12 as an appetizer)

⅓ cup unsalted butter
¼ cup vegetable oil
1 garlic clove, minced
½ medium onion, finely chopped
1 *poblano* chili, roasted, peeled, seeded, and diced (see page 10)
1 pound fresh cooked lump crab meat, picked over to remove bones and shell
¼ cup mayonnaise (or cream cheese can be substituted)
½ teaspoon salt
1 tablespoon minced fresh cilantro
Twelve 10-inch flour tortillas
1½ cups grated *jalapeño* jack cheese
Three-Tomato Salsa, page 139 (optional)

Place the butter and oil in a medium saucepan and heat over low heat until the butter is melted. Pour all but 2 tablespoons of the mixture into a small cup and add the garlic and onion to the pan. Sauté over medium-high heat until translucent, about 3 minutes. Remove from the heat and stir in the chili, crab, mayonnaise, salt, and cilantro. Mix well.

To soften the tortillas, place them on a heated grill or skillet for about 15 seconds on one side, then turn. Brush one side with the butter-oil mixture, turn the tortilla over and spread the crab mixture on one half of the tortilla, and top with a tablespoon of grated cheese. Repeat until all the tortillas are filled.

At this point, the *quesadillas* can either be sautéed or finished in the oven. If sautéing, heat a large sauté pan or skillet over medium-high heat. Cook for about 2 minutes on a side, or until golden. Or preheat the oven to 375° and bake on a cookie sheet until the tops are golden, about 5 minutes.

Cut into quarters and serve.

Note: The *quesadillas* can be filled up to a day in advance and kept refrigerated. Bring to room temperature before cooking. ∎

These feathery light pancakes are not only the best blini I've ever tasted, but the spicy sauce and salty smoked salmon are a perfect combination. This could be a casual supper as well as the perfect brunch dish.

Blue Corn Blini with Smoked Salmon

The Rattlesnake Club, Denver, Colorado

(Serves 4)

3/8 cup milk, heated to 110°
1 tablespoon (one package) active dried yeast
2 teaspoons sugar
¼ cup unbleached all-purpose flour
¼ cup blue cornmeal (yellow can be substituted)
1 egg yolk
6 tablespoons unsalted butter, at room temperature
2 egg whites
¼ teaspoon cream of tartar
¾ cup sour cream
¼ cup mild goat cheese, softened to room temperature and crumbled
1 *jalapeño* chili, roasted, peeled, seeded, and diced (see page 10)
¼ teaspoon freshly ground white pepper
Juice of ½ lime
¼ cup red bell pepper, roasted, peeled, seeded, and finely diced (see page 10)
¼ cup yellow bell pepper, roasted, peeled, seeded, and finely diced (see page 10), or substitute an additional ¼ cup of red
¼ cup finely diced red onion
2 tablespoons chopped fresh cilantro
2 tablespoons chopped fresh chives
½ pound smoked salmon, thinly sliced

In a medium bowl, combine the milk, yeast, and sugar. Stir the mixture well and allow it to develop at room temperature until foamy, about 10 to 15 minutes. Whisk in the flour and blue cornmeal, mixing until no lumps remain. Set aside.

Whip the egg yolk and 2 tablespoons of the butter together with an electric beater until the mixture is light and fluffy. Add the yeast mixture and continue to beat until the batter does not cling to the beaters, about 10 minutes.

In another bowl, whip the egg whites with an electric beater until foamy. Add the cream of tartar and then beat on high speed until the egg whites are stiff and hold a firm peak. Fold the egg whites gently into the blue corn batter and then set the batter aside, keeping it at room temperature.

In a small bowl, mix the sour cream, goat cheese, *jalapeño* chili, lime juice, and white pepper. Refrigerate the sauce until ready to serve.

Divide the remaining 4 tablespoons of butter into equal parts. Melt one piece in a 6-inch skillet over medium-high heat. When the butter foam begins to subside, add one-fourth of the batter and fry the *blini* until golden, about 2 minutes. Turn and cook for an additional 2 minutes. Transfer the *blini* to a plate with a spatula and keep warm in a 150° oven while making the remaining *blini*.

To serve, sprinkle each *blini* with the red and yellow peppers, onion, cilantro, and chives. Form the smoked salmon into a rose-shaped cup by rolling it into a spiral and place it in the center of each *blini*. Fill the rose with the sour cream sauce and serve immediately.

Note: The sauce is actually better if made a day in advance, since the flavors then have time to meld. The *blini* batter can be made a few hours in advance; however, they should be fried just prior to serving. ∎

Blue Corn Blini with Smoked Salmon, The Rattlesnake Club, Denver, Colorado

This platter looks as pretty as a still life on a cocktail table or buffet, and the three preparations done in the kitchen are augmented by colorful and flavorful purchased items. The salmon is a variation on gravlax, the smoked trout has a slightly Oriental overtone, and the garlic is accented by sharp bleu cheese.

Assorted Hors d'Oeuvre

Wolfdale's, Lake Tahoe, California

(Serves 12)

Salmon

One 3-pound salmon fillet (an oily
    salmon such as king or Norwegian)
1 cup cilantro leaves
1 cup basil leaves
¼ cup sugar
½ cup salt
½ cup black peppercorns

Smoked trout

2 quarts water
⅓ cup salt
¾ cup honey
⅓ cup soy sauce
¼ cup freshly squeezed lemon juice
3 garlic cloves, peeled and crushed
1 tablespoon grated fresh ginger
5 pounds trout fillets

Garlic puree

3 garlic bulbs
½ cup water
6 tablespoons olive oil
½ pound Stilton or other sharp blue-
    veined cheese
Salt and pepper to taste

To serve

Garlic mayonnaise
Cornichons
Crackers
½ cup slivered blanched almonds,
    roasted in a 350° oven for 7 to 10
    minutes
Nuts
Olives

To make the salmon, mix together the marinade ingredients and place half in the bottom of a glass or stainless steel dish just large enough to hold the salmon. Wash the salmon, removing any skin if necessary and picking out any small bones. Place it on the herb bed, then place the remaining marinade on top. Cover

the salmon with plastic wrap, then place another pan on top of it containing 5 pounds of weights, such as cans or bricks wrapped in foil. Place the salmon in the refrigerator and let sit 24 hours. Turn it and pour off any juice that has accumulated, then marinate another 24 hours. Rinse the salmon and slice into thin slices on the diagonal. Roll the salmon into rosettes for the plate. The remaining salmon will keep for 2 weeks in the refrigerator, tightly covered.

To prepare the smoked trout, combine the first 7 ingredients and marinate the fillets in the brine for 6 to 8 hours. Remove them, pat dry, and allow the fillets to sit in a cool dry place, or in the refrigerator, uncovered, for 8 to 10 hours, or until they look shiny and a skin develops. Place them in a smoker using apple or cherry wood and smoke for 1 to 1½ hours. Allow to cool and chill.

To make the garlic puree, place the 3 bulbs of garlic in a baking pan with the water in the bottom. Roast in a 350° oven for 30 to 40 minutes, or until the cloves are soft. Baste with the water frequently during baking. Squeeze the cloves out of the skins and puree with the olive oil in a blender or a food processor fitted with a steel blade. Mix in the cheese and add salt and pepper to taste.

Pipe the garlic puree onto crackers and garnish with roasted almonds. For the hors d'oeuvre plate, slice a few smoked trout fillets and garnish with garlic mayonnaise and *cornichons*.

Add nuts, olives, and pickles to the hors d'oeuvre plate as desired.

Note: All of the components can be done in advance, so allow yourself time for a pretty arrangement. ∎

Assorted Hors d'Oeuvre, Wolfdale's, Lake Tahoe, California

DOUGLAS DALE
Wolfdale's, Lake Tahoe, California

Douglas Dale's fascination with Japan was sparked by an article in *National Geographic* that the thirty-four-year-old Buffalo native read in the ninth grade.

"My parents didn't believe the impression it could have, but I chose to go to Antioch College because of the exchange program with Japan," he says.

"I developed a keen interest in Japanese food, since the whole Japanese world—from flower arranging to the tea ceremony—was a synthesis of the edible and the visual," he says.

Chef Dale first studied *oshojin ryori*, a twelve-hundred-year-old Buddhist purification cuisine, and then learned *sansai ryori*, which are the mountain foods grown at the higher elevations. After returning reluctantly to this country, he finished college and then worked with Hiroshi Hayashi at the Seventh Inn restaurant in Boston, with his own authentic Japanese restaurant as his eventual goal.

In 1977 he visited Lake Tahoe, and was immediately attracted by the tranquility of the California side of the lake. A year later, he opened Wolfdale's with his brother-in-law, Jerry Wolf. For the first few years, it was a strictly Japanese restaurant, with some baked goods added to suit the American sweet tooth.

By 1981, however, he was beginning to interject his own personality into the foods, and Wolfdale's was transformed from a Japanese restaurant to a seafood restaurant with Asian overtones in the sauces and presentations. He terms it Pacific Basin Cuisine.

He uses the Japanese aesthetic format for his Assorted Hors d'Oeuvre, a combination of smoked and cured fish arranged with almost anything from nuts to olives to create a landscape on the plate. But rather than using fresh dill for what is essentially a *gravlax*, he uses a combination of basil and cilantro. "There is an affinity between the assertive flavors of Southwest cooking and Oriental. Cilantro is common to both, and the crunchiness of *jicama* is similar to *daikon*," he says.

Spicy Beef Tartare, Coyote Cafe, Santa Fe, New Mexico

Steak tartare may seem like déjà vu, along with other food fads like Swedish meatballs and lobster Thermidor, but Mark Miller has found a way to make it fresh. With his spices and condiments, it becomes a ground version of the now-popular Carpaccio—classic but updated.

Spicy Beef Tartare

Coyote Cafe, Santa Fe, New Mexico

(Serves 4)

1 pound top sirloin
2 to 4 large shallots, finely diced
2 to 4 *serrano* chilies, seeded, deribbed, and finely diced
1 cup cilantro leaves
2 *tomatillos*, finely diced
1 lime, cut into slices
3 to 4 egg yolks
1 teaspoon sea salt
Freshly ground black pepper to taste
2 tablespoons virgin olive oil
Warm tortilla chips, freshly fried in oil

Trim the meat of all fat and membrane and cut into ¾-inch cubes.

Place the meat in the bowl of a food processor fitted with a steel blade and pulse the machine on and off so the meat remains finely chopped with visible pieces rather than ground to a paste. Remove the meat, look it over, and remove any large pieces of fat. Divide the meat into small ovals on 4 plates. This should be done just prior to serving so the meat will not begin to oxidize and will keep its bright red color.

Around the meat place piles of the shallots, *serrano* chilies, cilantro leaves, *tomatillos,* and lime slices. Place an egg yolk in the center of each and sprinkle with salt, pepper, and olive oil. Serve with warm tortilla chips and let each person mix the tartare individually at the table.

Note: While this presentation works well at the table, to serve this as an hors d'oeuvre, do all the mixing in the kitchen, using 3 egg yolks and the juice from the lime. Garnish with cilantro leaves and serve immediately. ■

The richness of game marries perfectly with the woodsy taste of wild mushrooms in this terrine, *and the centerpiece of venison wrapped in green spinach makes it a stunning dish.*

Wild Game and Mushroom Terrine

Hudsons' on the Bend, Austin, Texas

(Serves 20)

4 pounds lean game meat (some combination of venison, boar, and antelope)
1 venison backstrap (about 1 pound)

Red wine reduction

40 dried morels, halved
½ bottle dry red wine
1 carrot, peeled and chopped
3 shallots, peeled and chopped
Scraps from trimming meats
1 bay leaf
6 juniper berries
1 tablespoon mixed peppercorns (green, pink, and red)

Pâté

Reserved lean game meat (above)
1 egg
2 cups heavy cream, well chilled
2½ teaspoons salt
½ teaspoon ground nutmeg
½ teaspoon paprika
½ teaspoon dried thyme, crushed
½ teaspoon dried sage, crushed
½ teaspoon ground white pepper
3 tablespoons green peppercorns in brine, drained and rinsed
Reserved venison backstrap (above)
¼ cup coarsely ground black pepper
2 tablespoons clarified butter
6 slices fatty bacon, at room temperature
1 pound spinach, stemmed and blanched (or one 10-ounce box frozen leaf spinach, defrosted), with excess water pressed out
½ cup red wine reduction, above
½ cup chopped walnuts
¼ cup chopped pecans
1½ cups fresh oyster mushrooms (*shiitakes* can be substituted)
½ cup reserved morels

Garnish

Radicchio leaves
Endive spears

Julienne of onions and carrot
Slices of star fruit (*carimbola*)

Start the recipe by trimming the fat and silver skin from the meat that will be ground for the pâté and the venison backstrap or pork tenderloin for the center. Chill the meat thoroughly and proceed with the red wine reduction.

To make the red wine reduction, soak the morels in boiling water to cover for 20 minutes. Remove the mushrooms, drain, wash them under running water to remove any remaining grit, and set them aside. Pour the soaking liquid through a strainer lined with cheesecloth or a paper coffee filter into a saucepan. Start with ¾ cup of red wine and the remaining reduction ingredients and bring to a boil over medium heat. Simmer uncovered, adding the remaining red wine in stages, and simmer until only ½ cup of liquid remains. Strain, then set aside.

To make the pâté, grind the trimmed meat through the coarse setting of a food grinder, grinding it a second time if the meat is not tender. Place the meat in a food processor fitted with a steel blade, doing it in two batches if necessary. Add the egg, then slowly add the cream while the motor is running, scraping the sides of the bowl as necessary. (Make sure to divide the cream between the two batches if necessary.) Process until it forms a smooth paste, then add the salt, nutmeg, paprika, thyme, sage, and white pepper. Process again, then scrape into a mixing bowl, stir in the green peppercorns, and set aside.

Coat the venison backstrap with pepper and heat the butter in a sauté pan or skillet over high heat. When the butter is hot, sear the pepper-coated meat on all sides to brown. Remove from the pan.

Lay the slices of bacon side by side on the counter and place the blanched spinach in the center of the bacon. Lay the tenderloin on the spinach and roll the bacon around the tenderloin lightly, trimming the excess bacon (which can be added to the red wine reduction if it is cooking at this time). Place the roll in the freezer for 30 minutes.

Stir the ¼ cup red wine reduction into the meat and cream mixture. Butter the bottom and sides of a 12-by-6½-by-4-inch loaf pan or a *terrine* pan and place some of the pâté in the bottom. Sprinkle with some of the walnuts and pecans and some of the chopped oyster mushrooms and morels reserved from making the red wine reduction, then add a layer of pâté. Place the bacon-rolled filet in the center and continue to layer with the meat, mushrooms, and nuts.

Smooth the top of the pâté and tap it on a counter to remove air pockets.

Light a charcoal smoker. Place the *terrine* in a larger pan with hot water coming halfway up the sides and place in the smoker. Cook until the center registers 125° on a meat thermometer, then remove from the smoker, pour off any liquid that has accumulated, and refrigerate until well chilled. Or bake the *terrine* in a 350° oven.

To serve, slice the *terrine* and serve with a few leaves of *radicchio* and endive spears, julienne of carrots and onions, and star fruit.

Note: The pâté can be prepared up to 2 days in advance and kept in the refrigerator, covered with plastic wrap. The red wine reduction steps can be made a few days prior to making the *terrine*. ■

Wild Game and Mushroom Terrine, Hudsons' on the Bend, Austin, Texas

Exotic-Game Pâté, Sam Houston's, Kerrville, Texas

Anyone who can make a meatloaf will have no problems dazzling guests with this game pâté, seasoned with an interesting combination of herbs and spices to add sparkle to the rich flavor of the meats.

Exotic-Game Pâté

Sam Houston's, Kerrville, Texas

(Serves 6 to 8)

Note: This recipe must be started 1 day before serving since the liver has to soak overnight and the pâté must chill after cooking.

½ pound antelope liver
1 cup milk, or enough to cover liver
1 pound lean antelope meat
1 pound Sika deer meat
½ pound pork fat
2 tablespoons minced garlic
2 eggs
2 tablespoons whiskey
2 tablespoons dry sherry
2 teaspoons dried basil
1 teaspoon salt
1 teaspoon ground black pepper
Pinch of dried rosemary
Pinch of dried thyme
Pinch of ground nutmeg
Pinch of ground ginger
12 to 15 bacon slices, blanched in
    boiling water for 5 minutes and
    drained

Garnish

Chopped Game Stock Aspic
    (optional), see recipe following
Capers
Cornichons
Toast triangles toasted with garlic
    butter, chives, and Parmesan cheese
Sliced red onion

Soak the antelope liver in milk in the refrigerator overnight, covered with plastic wrap.

Trim the antelope and deer meat of silver skin and fat and cut into 1-inch cubes. Place the cubes in batches in a food processor fitted with a steel blade and puree the meats. Puree the pork fat and drained antelope liver and add to the other purees in a large mixing bowl. Add all the remaining ingredients except the bacon to the bowl and beat well with a wooden spoon until the mixture is light and fluffy. To test seasoning, fry a tablespoon of the mixture in a small skillet and adjust seasoning as needed.

Preheat the oven to 325°. Line the bottom and sides of a *terrine* or 10-inch loaf pan with strips of blanched bacon and pour the pâté mixture into the pan, spreading it evenly and packing it down so there are no air holes. Top the pan with the remaining bacon slices, cover loosely with aluminum foil, and bake for 1 hour. Remove the foil and bake for 1½ hours more.

Pour out any liquid that has accumulated during baking, reserve for the aspic (if used), and bring the pâté to room temperature. Chill for at least 1 hour, preferably overnight, and then unmold and slice.

To serve, garnish the slices with chopped aspic (if made), capers, sliced *cornichons*, a thin slice of red onion, and 4 toast points.

Note: This recipe cannot be done successfully with meats other than wild game. Consult the page of mail-order sources at the end of this book to order it, since it is still relatively rare in supermarkets.

Chopped Game Stock Aspic

Game stock (page 19) and reserved
    pâté cooking liquid to make 2 cups
1 tablespoon (1 envelope) unflavored
    gelatin

Sprinkle the gelatin over ¼ cup of the game stock to soften for 10 minutes. Heat the remaining stock to a boil in a small saucepan over medium heat. Remove from heat, add the softened gelatin, and stir until the granules are dissolved. Pour the mixture into a jelly roll pan and chill in the refrigerator until set and firm. Chop the aspic with a sharp knife and set aside. ■

The nutty flavor of wild rice makes it a perfect vehicle for these toppings. This dish could be either an appetizer or light supper.

Wild Rice Pancakes Garnished in Two Ways

Trumps, Los Angeles, California

(Serves 4)

Pancakes

2 cups cooked wild rice
2 eggs
2 tablespoons minced shallots
2 teaspoons minced garlic
1/3 cup unbleached all-purpose flour
1/2 cup heavy cream
Salt and pepper to taste
3 tablespoons clarified butter
2 teaspoons oil

Chicken with sherry vinegar topping

4 tablespoons unsalted butter
1 teaspoon oil
1/2 pound chicken tenderloins, or 1/2 pound boned and skinned chicken breasts cut into 1-inch-wide strips
Salt and pepper to taste
1 tablespoon minced garlic
1 tablespoon minced shallots
1/4 cup sherry vinegar
8 sun-dried tomato halves, sliced
2 tablespoons minced fresh parsley

Salmon and Madeira topping

1/2 pound salmon fillet, skin removed
2 tablespoons unsalted butter
1 teaspoon oil
Salt and pepper to taste
1 teaspoon minced garlic
1 teaspoon minced shallots
2 small tomatoes, seeded and finely chopped
1/4 cup Madeira

To make the pancakes, place the wild rice, eggs, shallots, and garlic in a mixing bowl. Stir, then add the flour, cream, and salt and pepper to taste. Heat the clarified butter and oil in a skillet or sauté pan over medium-high heat and add spoonfuls of the batter to form 1 pancake. Cook for 4 to 5 minutes, or until the top begins to look dry and the bottom is golden. Turn with a spatula and cook the other side for 3 minutes. Repeat until you have made 8 pancakes. Keep warm.

To make the chicken topping, melt 1 tablespoon of the butter with the oil in a sauté pan and add the chicken. Cook for a few minutes per side over high heat, seasoning with salt and pepper, then remove the chicken from the pan and add all the remaining ingredients except for the remaining butter. Cook over medium-high heat until almost no liquid remains, then add the remaining 3 tablespoons of butter and stir. Remove from the heat, season with salt and pepper to taste, and return chicken pieces to the pan to reheat.

To make the salmon topping, slice the salmon on the diagonal into 4 thin slices. Heat 1 tablespoon of the butter and the oil in a sauté pan and add the salmon, sprinkling it with salt and pepper to taste. Cook until lightly colored on the first side, about 2 minutes, then turn and cook an additional minute. The salmon should be slightly underdone. Remove from the pan, add the garlic and shallots along with the chopped tomatoes, and deglaze with the Madeira. Reduce slightly, swirl in the remaining butter, and remove from the heat.

To serve, arrange the chicken topping on half the pancakes and salmon topping on the other half.

Note: The recipes for the toppings make 2 toppings for each diner. If you want to make only 1 topping, double the recipe for 4 servings. The pancakes can be prepared a day in advance and reheated in a warm oven; however, the toppings should be made immediately before serving. ∎

Wild Rice Pancakes Garnished in Two Ways, shown here with Chicken with Sherry Vinegar Topping, Trumps, Los Angeles, California

MICHAEL ROBERTS

Trumps, Los Angeles, California

Chef Michael Roberts is more interested in bold flavors than subtle nuances, and the ethnic mix of Southern California—Mexican, Southwest, and Asian—provides the models for his culinary improvisations.

Roberts, a New York native with a degree in music from New York University, has been a motivating force on the country's food since Trumps, where he is chef and one of the owners, opened its doors in 1980. He moved to Los Angeles the year before to become chef at a short-lived French restaurant, Le Soir, and it was there that he began his quest to bring food down to earth, with menus in English. "I am an American chef working in an American restaurant, and I couldn't stand the pretense of having menus written in French," he says.

His honesty goes beyond the printed word to the ingredients in his dishes. In a city and during an era when food was so light it barely appeared on the plate, Roberts was making hearty food to critical raves.

During the early years the influences on his style encompassed almost all ethnic groups; now he concentrates on Southwestern and Asian flavors, which he finds are compatible.

"I may end up with a new synthesis and call it Thai-Mex," he quips about his combinations of ingredients. And he employs the Japanese aesthetic when it comes to presentations, proving that hearty dishes can be as appealing visually as lighter ones. "Any artist has to stretch the definition to see old and familiar things with a new vision, and that goes for both ingredients and dishes," he says.

In his explorations of traditional Southwest cookery, he became intrigued with tamales, which are now on his lunch menu with a different filling daily. One day the filling can be seafood and the tamales will be served in a saffron sauce, and the next the filling might be chicken in a sauce of *pasilla* chilies.

Roberts creates not only for the restaurant; he has also completed a book, *Secret Ingredients*, to be published by Bantam Books in 1987.

The flavors in this dish are complex: cilantro and cheese flavor the snails, lemon and saffron scent the pasta, and the cream sauce also is aromatic with saffron. The sombreros are a new twist on the classic filled pasta, ravioli.

Escargot Sombreros in Saffron Cream Sauce

Tucson Country Club, Tucson, Arizona

(Serves 6 to 8)

Pasta

4 lemons
¼ teaspoon saffron
2 cups bread flour
2 cups semolina flour
4 eggs
2 egg yolks
1 tablespoon olive oil

Filling

30 canned snails, drained
1 cup dry white wine
¼ cup grated Monterey jack cheese
½ cup Cilantro Pesto, following
1 egg yolk
1 egg, lightly beaten

Sauce

2 tablespoons chopped shallot
1 tablespoon chopped garlic
1 tablespoon unsalted butter
1 cup fish stock or clam juice
1 cup dry white wine
1⅔ cups heavy cream
2 teaspoons chopped fresh basil, or
   ¼ teaspoon dried basil
⅛ teaspoon saffron

Garnish

¼ cup julienned sun-dried tomatoes
¼ cup pitted black olives, halved
Red Chili Paint (see recipe for
   Salmon Painted Desert, page 104)
Cumin Seed and Pepper Toasts, page
   141

To make the pasta, cut the zest off of 2 lemons using a zester or vegetable peeler and chop fine. Juice all 4 lemons and combine with the saffron and zest in a small saucepan. Reduce by half and allow to cool.

Place the flours in a mixing bowl of a mixer with a dough hook and add the eggs and egg yolks, along with the cooled lemon mixture.

Knead for several minutes, until the dough is smooth and elastic, then add the oil. If it seems crumbly and dry, add an additional egg yolk, and if too sticky, add flour. Allow the dough to sit, covered with plastic wrap, for a few hours before rolling.

To make the filling, marinate the snails in the white wine for 1 hour. Combine the cheese, *pesto*, and egg yolk and place in a pastry bag. Set aside.

To make the sombreros, roll out sheets of pasta through a pasta machine until it is set on the thinnest setting. Cut the sheets with 3-inch-round crinkle cutters. Place a snail and 1 teaspoonful of the filling to one side of the circle, brush the edges with the beaten egg, fold, and seal. Pull the sides of the edge together to form a brim shape. Set aside until ready to cook.

To make the sauce, sauté the shallot and garlic in butter for several minutes over medium heat. Add the fish stock and white wine and cook over high heat until reduced by half. Add the heavy cream, basil, and saffron and simmer for 15 minutes. Adjust seasoning.

To serve, cook the sombreros in a large amount of boiling salted water for 2 minutes, then drain. Ladle the saffron sauce onto plates, reserving a little. Toss the reserved sauce with the dried tomatoes, olives, and sombreros. Pipe Red Chili Paint on each plate and arrange 5 escargot sombreros in the center. Serve Cumin Seed and Pepper Toasts with the sombreros.

Note: Everything up to the final assembly of this dish can be done in advance. The sombreros can be made up to 6 hours in advance, as can the sauce.

Cilantro Pesto

1 tablespoon chopped garlic
¼ cup freshly grated Parmesan cheese
1 cup cilantro leaves
3 tablespoons *pepitas* (pumpkin
   seeds)
2 tablespoons olive oil
¼ teaspoon salt
Juice of ½ lime

Grind all the ingredients together in a blender or a food processor fitted with a steel blade until it becomes a paste. ■

Escargot Sombreros in Saffron Cream Sauce, Tucson Country Club, Tucson, Arizona

What a wonderful exploration of the nuances of flavors. The sweet potatoes, deep-brown caramelized onions, and roasted nuts are all slightly sweet. The flavors meld together beautifully in this delicious and innovative pasta.

Sweet Potato Tortellini in Almond-Cream Sauce with Sautéed Onions and Cilantro

Cafe Lilli, Lake Tahoe, Nevada

(Serves 4)

Tortellini

2 large sweet potatoes or yams
Salt and pepper to taste
Pinch of ground nutmeg
1½ cups unbleached pastry flour
2 large eggs, lightly beaten
Rice flour for baking sheet

Onions

2 large sweet onions, such as Maui or
   Bermuda
1 tablespoon unsalted butter
3 garlic cloves, peeled and minced
Salt and pepper to taste
1 tablespoon brandy
½ to 1 cup chicken stock

Sauce

¾ cup blanched almonds
2 cups heavy cream
1 cup chicken stock
2 shallots, peeled and chopped
1 garlic clove, peeled and smashed
2 tablespoons brandy
Pinch of freshly grated nutmeg
Salt and pepper to taste

Garnish

Salt
1 bunch cilantro, cleaned and
   stemmed
Oil for deep-frying
Skins from sweet potatoes

Preheat oven to 400°. Bake the sweet potatoes until soft but not blackened, about 45 minutes to 1 hour, depending on size. Remove from the oven and allow to sit until cool enough to handle. Then cut in half lengthwise, scoop out the pulp, reserving the shells, and season the filling with salt, pepper, and nutmeg. Set aside.

Make the pasta in the bowl of a food processor fitted with a steel

blade. Place the flour in the bowl and add the eggs and a sprinkling of salt and pepper. Pulse on and off until the dough comes together. Remove and knead by hand for a minute, then cover with plastic wrap and allow to rest 30 minutes before rolling.

Roll the pasta into sheets using a pasta machine, ending the rolling with the thinnest possible setting. Cut circles 2½ inches wide with a fluted cutter and place a little of the sweet potato filling on each. Moisten the edges with water and seal. Place on a rice flour—covered tray, cover with plastic wrap, and set aside.

Peel and thinly slice the onions. Heat the butter in a sauté pan or skillet, add the onions, and sauté for a few minutes. Add the garlic and salt and pepper to taste and sauté until well browned over medium-high heat. Add the brandy and ¼ cup of the stock and reduce until the liquid has almost evaporated. Add more stock and continue to cook over low heat until the onions are soft and well caramelized, adding more stock as necessary, about 20 minutes. Set aside and keep warm.

To make the sauce, roast the almonds in a 350° oven for 15

minutes, or until brown. Immediately chop in a food processor fitted with a steel blade and add a little cream to the work bowl. Place in a saucepan with the remaining cream, stock, shallots, garlic, brandy, and nutmeg. Bring to a boil, reduce until slightly thickened, and strain. Season with salt and pepper to taste.

In a deep heavy pan, heat the oil to a temperature of 350°. Cut the reserved potato skins into fine julienne and deep-fry the cilantro and potato skins. Remove with a slotted spoon, drain on paper towels, and sprinkle with salt while hot.

To assemble the dish, bring a large quantity of salted water to a boil. Cook the *tortellini* 3 to 5 minutes, or until tender, and drain. Place the warm onions in the bottom of a pasta bowl. Toss the *tortellini* in the sauce. Place them on top of the onions, and garnish with fried cilantro and potato skins.

Note: The *tortellini* and the sauce can be prepared a day in advance. Keep both refrigerated, and reheat the sauce slowly. The cilantro and potato skins can be fried a few hours before serving, since they do not have to be hot. ∎

Sweet Potato Tortellini in Almond-Cream Sauce with Sautéed Onions and Cilantro, Cafe Lilli, Lake Tahoe, Nevada

The contrast of the creamy soup with the fresh taste and bright green color of the cilantro and chilies makes this soup a stunning addition to any dinner.

Cream of Cilantro Soup with Mussels

Cafe Annie, Houston, Texas

(Serves 8)

Puree

2 bunches cilantro, cleaned and stemmed
1 bunch parsley, cleaned and stemmed
⅓ cup chopped onion
2 garlic cloves, peeled and chopped
2 *serrano* chilies, stemmed and seeded
1 cup fish stock or water

Soup

40 mussels
¼ cup cornmeal
2 cups fish stock
2½ cups heavy cream
1 to 1½ cups cilantro puree
For garnish: Ancho Chili Preserves, page 142

Cream of Cilantro Soup with Mussels, Cafe Annie, Houston, Texas

Place all the puree ingredients in a blender or a food processor fitted with a steel blade. Process until it is a thick, smooth puree, adding more fish stock if necessary. Set aside.

To make the soup, scrub the mussels and trim off the beards with a sharp paring knife. Soak the mussels for 1 hour in cold water in which the cornmeal is mixed. Drain and rinse them.

Place the mussels in a saucepan with the fish stock. Cover the pot and bring to a boil. Steam the mussels until the shells open, about 5 minutes, stirring a few times. Do not overcook, and discard any mussels that do not open. Remove the mussels from the pan, reserving the liquid, and remove the mussels from their shells, reserving 8 of the best for garnish. Set the mussels aside.

Boil the mussel liquid to reduce by one-third, then strain it through a cheesecloth-lined sieve and return it to the pot. Add the cream and bring to a boil, simmering for 5 minutes to reduce slightly. Stir in the cilantro puree and cook about 30 seconds; season with salt and pepper to taste.

Serve immediately, dividing the mussels among warmed soup bowls and garnishing each with a dollop of *ancho* preserves in a reserved mussel shell.

Note: The soup can be made a few hours in advance up to the addition of the cilantro puree. That should be done immediately before serving. ■

REX HALE
Brennan's, Houston, Texas

Before Rex Hale became a chef at Brennan's, he learned his craft at the stoves of some of the finest chefs in the country. The cuisines he mastered are all served at the Houston branch of the restaurant group, owned by the family who also owns Commander's Palace and Mr. B's Bistro in New Orleans.

The Creole classics on the menu, the famous name, and the gaslights and brick walls are all reminiscent of the French Quarter, but there are also dishes reflecting the Southwest locale, and some from other regions of new American cuisine.

Chef Hale, thirty, was born and raised in St. Louis, and supported himself by restaurant work while studying biology and chemistry at various universities. While enrolled at Tulane he met the Brennans.

After graduation, he returned to St. Louis and started his ad hoc apprenticeship with a year at Tony's, considered one of the best restaurants in that city. "I considered going to a school like the Culinary Institute of America, but I decided that I was already learning how to do things the right way," he says.

After working in both classic and nouvelle French restaurants, he worked at An American Restaurant in Kansas City, the showcase for new American cuisine that made Bradley Ogden a superstar. Hale became assistant chef when Ogden accepted a position at The Campton Place Hotel.

It was in Kansas City that the chef began cooking dishes like smoked pheasant with blue corn timbales, and squab with fried sweet potatoes.

After a year, he joined the staff at Commander's Palace in New Orleans, to hone his skills with lightened American classics even more finely, and after six months was given command of the Houston kitchen.

"I like to use whatever is available in Texas, and I'm developing dishes that tie Southwestern food to the present. My *fajitas* are made with tenderloin and served with red chili fettucini, and even some of the classic Brennan's egg dishes can be modified. I do poached eggs with roasted *poblanos*, and a venison sausage hash."

The smoking of the rabbit adds an earthy nuance to this gumbo, but to make the dish more rapidly, you can use commercially prepared smoked chickens.

Smoked-Rabbit Gumbo

Brennan's, Houston, Texas

(Serves 8)
Smoked rabbits

Juice of 2 limes
Juice of 2 lemons
2 cups fresh orange juice
2 garlic cloves, peeled and crushed
¼ cup olive oil
¼ cup mixed chopped fresh herbs
   (parsley, cilantro, rosemary, thyme)
4 whole rabbits

Rabbit stock

4 smoked rabbits, above (smoked
   chicken or Cornish hens can be
   substituted)
1 large yellow onion, chopped
2 medium carrots, coarsely chopped
3 celery stalks, chopped
½ cup dry white wine
10 cups brown chicken stock (see
   page 18)
1 garlic clove, peeled
1 tablespoon black peppercorns
1 bay leaf

Gumbo

3 tablespoons vegetable oil
1½ cups diced yellow onions
½ cup diced seeded and deribbed
   poblano chili
1 *serrano* chili, seeded and finely
   chopped
½ cup diced seeded and deribbed
   green bell pepper
¾ cup diced seeded and deribbed red
   bell pepper
1½ teaspoons minced garlic
¾ cup chopped peeled and seeded
   tomato
1 bay leaf
2 tablespoons minced fresh thyme, or
   1 teaspoon dried thyme
2 tablespoons gumbo filé powder
Salt to taste
½ teaspoon cayenne, or to taste
7 cups smoked rabbit stock
Reserved shredded smoked rabbit
   meat

To smoke the rabbits, mix the juices, garlic, oil, and herbs together and marinate the whole rabbits, covered, overnight in the refrigerator. Heat a hot smoker or light a covered charcoal grill and add hickory or mesquite wood chips soaked in water. Smoke the rabbits at 200° for 25 minutes.

To make the stock and rabbit meat to add to the gumbo, remove the meat from the hindquarters of the rabbit, take the loins off the carcass, and remove all silver skin from the loins. Shred the meat and set half of it aside for the gumbo; freeze the remainder to use at another time. Reserve the forequarters and all bones for the stock.

Preheat the oven to 450°. Break up all the rabbit bones and brown them, along with the vegetables, for 30 minutes, turning occasionally so they brown evenly. Deglaze the roasting pan with the white wine, and then pour the contents into a stockpot. Add the remaining ingredients, bring to a boil over medium heat, and simmer gently over low heat for 2 hours, skimming the surface as needed. Strain and refrigerate the stock, discarding the fat layer that hardens.

To make the gumbo, heat the oil in a heavy stockpot over medium heat. Add the onions, chilies, and peppers and sauté over medium-high heat, stirring frequently, until soft. Raise the heat to high, add the garlic, tomato, and herbs, and stir constantly for 5 minutes. Add the rabbit stock and bring to a boil. Allow to simmer 20 minutes, then season with the filé, salt, and cayenne. Simmer briefly and add the shredded smoked rabbit.

Note: Everything up to adding the filé powder can be done up to 3 days in advance. Do not add the filé until just prior to serving or the soup will be overly thickened.

Please note that the stock calls for the bones and forequarters from 4 rabbits and the soup the meat from 2 rabbits; the remaining meat and any additional stock can be frozen. ∎

With its creamy texture, pleasing color, and hints of sweet and sour undertastes, this is one of the most exciting soups around—and easy to make.

Sweet Potato Bisque with Avocado, Pear, and Lime

Routh Street Cafe, Dallas, Texas

(Serves 4)

Pears

2 ripe pears
2 cups dry white wine
¼ cup sugar
¼ teaspoon ground cinnamon
Juice of 1 lemon
⅓ cup pear brandy

Soup

2 pounds sweet potatoes
1 tablespoon unsalted butter
1 tablespoon minced onion
1 tablespoon chopped celery
1 tablespoon chopped carrot
½ *serrano* chili, seeded and chopped (*jalapeño* can be substituted)
1 teaspoon finely chopped fresh thyme, or ¼ teaspoon dried thyme
1¼ cups chicken stock
3 cups heavy cream
2 tablespoons pure maple syrup
½ teaspoon salt
¼ teaspoon coarsely ground black pepper
3 tablespoons freshly squeezed lime juice

Garnish

4 thin slices lime
1 ripe avocado

To cook the pears, which are used as a garnish as well as an ingredient, peel, halve, and core them. Poach the pears in the wine, sugar, cinnamon, lemon juice, and pear brandy for 10 minutes, or until the point of a knife pierces one easily. Allow to cool in syrup.

To make the soup, peel and chop the sweet potatoes, then cook in salted boiling water until soft, about 5 to 7 minutes. Drain, and place in a blender or a food processor fitted with a steel blade.

While the potatoes are cooking, melt the butter in a small sauté pan or skillet over medium heat and sauté the vegetables, chili, and thyme until the vegetables are soft, about 7 minutes. Deglaze with ¼ cup of the chicken stock and cook for 1 minute. Add to the food processor along with the remaining 1 cup of stock and 1 poached pear. Puree until smooth.

Pour the puree into a saucepan and add the cream, maple syrup, salt, pepper, and lime juice. Bring to a boil over medium heat; reduce heat and simmer for 15 minutes, stirring occasionally.

To serve, pour into warm bowls and garnish with a slice of lime, some sliced avocado, and slices from the remaining poached pear.

Note: The soup can be prepared up to 2 days in advance and reheated slowly, uncovered. Do not prepare the garnish until ready to serve. ∎

Smoked-Rabbit Gumbo, Brennan's, Houston, Texas

POULTRY AND GAME BIRD DISHES

Poultry consumption has never been higher in the United States than it is now, as people limit their weekly rations of red meat due to its relatively higher calorie and cholesterol counts. And there's no question that chicken is perhaps the most versatile of all birds, taking well to all cooking methods and a wide range of seasonings and saucings. In this chapter you will find recipes from simple grilled chicken to hearty Gypsy Stew to delicate Corn Pasta–Grilled Chicken Ravioli with Pinto Bean Sauce.

The past decade has seen the development of free-range chickens, whose flesh has more flavor than penned birds, since they are allowed to roam and forage. Chefs immediately began using these chickens, and they are now becoming more widely available.

However, poultry means much more than chicken, and histories of the Southwest detail the abundance and variety of game birds that sustained early settlers. Wild turkey, quail, squab, and pheasant were common, becoming staples in the region's larder. These native species were rendered all but extinct by the end of the nineteenth century, and it has only been during the past decade that farm-raised game birds have appeared on the market to introduce us to the rich flavors of these birds.

While they may have had access to the birds, it is doubtful that early settlers had recipes to compare with Bradley Ogden's Grilled Quail with Shoestring Sweet Potatoes or Stephan Pyles' Wild Turkey with Blue Cornmeal–Chorizo Stuffing. If your supermarket or butcher does not carry fresh game birds, consult the listing of mail-order sources, since national firms can have them at your door overnight.

Grilled California Free-Range Chicken with Smoked-Chili Butter and "Tobacco Onions," The Mansion on Turtle Creek, Dallas, Texas

What appeals to chefs such as Dean Fearing about "free range" (unpenned) chickens is their superior texture and flavor. Any frying chicken will work with this recipe, however, since the smoky-spicy flavor of the butter is such an enhancement.

Grilled California Free-Range Chicken with Smoked-Chili Butter and "Tobacco Onions"

The Mansion on Turtle Creek, Dallas, Texas

(Serves 6)
Smoked-Chili Butter, following
Three 2½ pound free-range chickens
Oil
Salt and pepper
Tobacco Onions, page 139

Butter

¼ red bell pepper
¼ yellow bell pepper
1 small garlic clove, peeled and minced
½ small shallot, peeled and minced
1 teaspoon Dijon mustard
1 teaspoon finely chopped fresh cilantro
1 *serrano* chili, seeded and finely chopped
1 tablespoon freshly squeezed lime juice
1 teaspoon freshly squeezed lemon juice
½ cup (1 stick) unsalted butter, softened to room temperature
Salt and pepper to taste

To make the butter, remove the stem, ribs, and seeds from the red and yellow peppers. In a smoker, or a covered charcoal grill used as a smoker, smoke the red and yellow pepper halves over mesquite for 15 to 20 minutes. Cool and cut into a small dice. In a bowl, add all the ingredients and mix until everything is well incorporated into the butter. Season with salt and pepper.

With a rubber spatula, scrape the butter onto a long sheet of parchment paper or waxed paper, forming a straight line. Fold the paper over the butter and roll into an even cylinder shape about the size of a half dollar. Twist each end and place in the refrigerator until solid, about 2 hours.

Partially bone the chickens. Cut down the breast bone and then, holding your knife with the blade to the carcass, scrape down the carcass, cutting through the wing and thigh joints. Remove the carcass and cut the bird into 2 halves. Leave the drumstick and wing bones attached and free the thigh bone, removing any fragments of joints, and cut off the wings. (Keep all trimmings for making stock later.)

Slice the onions for Tobacco Onions, but do not finish the dish until just prior to serving.

Light a charcoal or gas grill. Coat the skin side of the chicken halves with oil, and sprinkle both sides with salt and pepper. Place the halves skin side down over medium-hot coals and grill for 7 minutes (10 minutes on a gas grill), or until the skin is golden brown. Turn and cook an additional 6 minutes on the other side, or until the meat juices run clear.

Remove the birds from the grill and keep warm in a 150° oven while completing the coating and frying of onions.

To serve, make a nest of onions on either side of the chicken, and top the chicken with a few slices of the chili butter.

Note: The chickens can be boned and refrigerated up to a day in advance, but they must be brought to room temperature before grilling. The butter can be made up to 3 days in advance and refrigerated, or it can be frozen for up to 2 months. ■

The crunchy pasta has a slightly spicy filling with a hint of a grilled taste and the creamy sauce is a delicious addition. To do this dish quickly, use commercial wonton wrappers instead of making the corn pasta.

Corn Pasta Ravioli with Pinto Bean Sauce

Bistro Garden, Houston, Texas

(Serves 8 as an appetizer, 4 as an entree)
Filling

½ pound boned and skinned chicken breast
1 *poblano* chili, roasted, peeled, seeded, and chopped (see page 10)
1 red onion slice, 2¼ inches thick
1 ripe tomato, seeded and chopped
2½ ounces cream cheese, softened
1 garlic clove, peeled and minced
Salt and freshly ground white pepper to taste

Pasta dough

¼ cup *masa harina*
¾ cup unbleached all-purpose flour
½ teaspoon salt
2 eggs
1 teaspoon olive oil

Sauce

2 garlic cloves, peeled and minced
2 tablespoons chopped red onion
1 *jalapeño* chili, seeded and chopped
1 tablespoon clarified butter
1 cup cooked pinto beans (see Ranch Beans, page 38), drained
¼ cup milk
Salt and white pepper to taste

To finish the dish

Oil or shortening for deep-frying
Salsa for garnish (optional)

To make the filling, light a charcoal or gas grill. Grill the *poblano* over hot coals until completely charred. Place in a paper bag, close, and set aside until cool. Rub off all charred skin, seed, and chop. Grill the chicken and onion slice over medium-hot coals 2 minutes per side. Cut the chicken into chunks, dice the onion, and place all the filling ingredients in a blender or a food processor fitted with a steel blade. Process with pulsing motions to chop and combine the ingredients, but do not puree. Set aside.

To make the pasta, combine the *masa harina*, flour, and salt in a mixing bowl. Beat the eggs and olive oil together, and pour into a well in the center of the dry ingredients. Mix with a wooden spoon until all the dry ingredients are incorporated (this can also be done in a food processor). Add more flour if the dough feels sticky. Add some cold water, a few teaspoons at a time, if the dough is dry or crumbly. Let the dough rest, covered with plastic wrap, for 30 minutes, then roll it through a pasta machine to a thickness of ⅛ inch. Cut out 2-inch circles using a cookie cutter. Place 1 heaping teaspoonful of the filling in the center of a circle and moisten the edges with water. Fold the circle in half and press the edges together firmly, making sure they are securely fastened. Repeat to use all the dough.

To make the sauce, sauté the garlic, onion, and *jalapeño* in the clarified butter over medium heat until the onions are translucent. Puree with the beans, milk, and seasoning in a blender or food processor until smooth.

To cook, heat the oil in a heavy deep-sided skillet to a temperature of 350°. Add the ravioli in small batches and fry until crisp and golden brown. Remove with a slotted spoon and drain on paper towels. Warm the sauce and place a pool on each plate. Top with the fried ravioli and garnish with some *salsa*, if desired.

Note: The sauce and ravioli can be prepared a day in advance, and kept refrigerated. The sauce should be heated slowly, and may need to be thinned with a little additional milk. The ravioli can be fried directly from the refrigerator. ∎

Creamy goat cheese countered with spicy cilantro pesto adds wonderful flavor to the easy-to-prepare chicken dish. Serve it with Three-Tomato Salsa, page 139.

Chicken Breasts Stuffed with Cilantro Pesto Goat Cheese

Anne Lindsay Greer, Dallas, Texas

(Serves 4)

2 large whole chicken breasts
¼ cup finely chopped cilantro leaves
¼ cup chicken stock
2 tablespoons oil
Salt and freshly ground pepper to taste

Stuffing

2 garlic cloves, peeled
2 serrano chilies, stemmed
2 cups cilantro leaves
2 tablespoons oil
2 tablespoons freshly grated Parmesan cheese
3 ounces mild goat cheese
¼ cup ricotta cheese

ROLF JUNG
La Paloma/Atlas, San Diego, California

The career path chosen by Rolf Jung, executive chef at La Paloma/Atlas in San Diego, could be summarized by the name of his first employer in North America, The Happy Wanderer restaurant in Montreal.

The forty-six-year-old Cologne native, influenced by his grandmother, has been traveling and learning new languages since he decided to become a chef at age fourteen. After receiving certificates in cooking, he worked at various resorts in his native Germany before allowing serendipity to take control of his life.

"I was standing in the train station and reached for the map of the express routes, and my finger landed on Lyon. I arrived there at dawn and had a job a few hours later," he says.

Lyon was known as the culinary center of Europe, and Chef Jung worked, as did so many others, at La Pyramide. He moved to Paris in 1963 and worked as a saucier at Maxim's before arriving, again jobless, in Montreal a year later.

After The Happy Wanderer, he became a sous chef at the Queen Elizabeth Hotel, and then, after deciding Americans were friendlier than Canadians, he moved to Los Angeles.

But the urge to wander took hold again, and he traveled to Brazil and Colombia before joining the Marriott Hotel chain as a troubleshooter for their restaurants.

He decided he liked the resources that could be put at his disposal by hotels, as well as the constant series of challenges of opening new facilities. Seven years ago, he joined the San Diego–based Atlas Hotel chain, and now shares his time and ideas between more than two dozen restaurants in the Southwest and Mexico.

The foods of the region have influenced his classical ideas. He makes soufflés from the prickly pears native to the deserts, and uses hot chilies in marinades for simple chicken sautés. He is now more concerned than ever about restraining the calorie content of foods, and has placed his emphasis on "healthy and wholesome dishes that have a beautiful presentation so the eye eats, too."

Salt and freshly ground pepper to taste

Light a charcoal or gas grill. Remove the bones from the chicken breasts, but leave the skin attached. Cut into 4 serving pieces.

Mix the cilantro leaves with the chicken stock, oil, salt, and pepper. Marinate the breasts in the mixture for 15 minutes, then drain, reserving the marinade.

Place the breasts on the grill skin side down over red-hot coals and partially cook the breasts, brushing with the marinade, for 3 minutes on a side (2 minutes on a hot gas grill). Remove and set aside.

In a blender or a food processor fitted with a steel blade, puree the garlic, chilies, cilantro, oil, Parmesan cheese, goat cheese, and ricotta cheese. Season with salt and pepper to taste and place in a pastry bag.

Preheat the oven to 375°. Pipe the cheese mixture directly under the skin of the chicken breasts, spreading it in an even layer. Place the breasts in a baking pan and pour some of the reserved marinade over them. Bake for 12 minutes and serve immediately.

Note: The stuffing can be prepared up to 2 days in advance and kept in the refrigerator. The breasts can be taken as far as the grilling and stuffing up to 6 hours in advance of the baking; keep at room temperature. ■

The combination of a piquant cream sauce with colorful stir-fried vegetables makes this chicken entree special. It can be started ahead and takes but moments to complete.

Chicken Breast Pueblo

La Paloma/Atlas, San Diego, California

(Serves 4)

Four 6- to 8-ounce boned and skinned whole chicken breasts

Marinade

Juice of 2 grapefruit (about 1½ cups)
Juice of 1 orange (about ½ cup)
2 tablespoons olive oil
2 bay leaves
¼ red bell pepper, seeded, deribbed,

and cut into fine julienne
1 small *jalapeño* chili, seeded and chopped
2 small *poblano* chilies, seeded and cut into thin strips
1 garlic clove, peeled and minced
1 tabasco chili, seeded and chopped (1 *serrano* chili or a few drops of Tabasco sauce can be substituted)
¼ cup roughly chopped cilantro leaves
1 medium onion, peeled and sliced

Vegetable garnish

7 prickly pear cactus pads, thorns removed with tweezers, or ¾ pound fresh green beans (French-cut if large)
1 small red bell pepper, seeded, deribbed, and cut into fine julienne
2 tablespoons clarified butter
2 cups heavy cream
Salt and white pepper to taste
1 garlic clove, peeled and mashed
1 shallot, peeled and minced
1 tablespoon olive oil

Remove any fat from the chicken breasts and pound them lightly to an even thickness with a meat pounder or the back of a heavy pot. Mix all

the marinade ingredients together and add the chicken breasts. Marinate for at least 2 hours at room temperature, or overnight in the refrigerator, covered with plastic wrap.

Cut the cactus pads into a fine julienne resembling French-cut green beans and toss with the red bell pepper. Set aside.

Heat the butter in a sauté pan or skillet and, when hot, add the drained chicken breasts. Cook on both sides until golden brown, and then add one-fourth of the cactus–red pepper mixture to the pan. Sauté lightly, add the cream, and cook over high heat until the mixture is reduced by half and the chicken is cooked through, about 10 minutes. Season with salt and pepper to taste.

Heat another skillet or a wok over high heat. Mash the garlic with the shallot and oil in a small bowl or mortar. Add salt and pepper and place the mixture in the skillet. Add the remaining cactus mixture and stir-fry until cooked but still crisp.

To serve, place the chicken and sauce on plates and garnish with the stir-fried vegetables. ■

Chicken Breasts Stuffed with Cilantro Pesto Goat Cheese, Anne Lindsay Greer, Dallas, Texas

Serve this chicken sauté with wild rice, steamed asparagus, and a grilled tomato topped with hollandaise sauce.

Chicken Gonzalez

La Louisiane, San Antonio, Texas

(Serves 4)

One 3-pound frying chicken
1 cup vegetable oil
1 egg
1 cup milk
Salt and pepper to taste
Flour for dredging
4 large mushrooms, washed, stemmed, and sliced
½ cup (1 stick) unsalted butter
4 artichoke hearts, cooked and sliced
¼ cup dry white wine
1 tablespoon chopped green onions, white part only

Bone the chicken and remove the skin, reserving the skin and bones for making stock. Cut the meat into 3-inch chunks and pound them slightly so they are all a uniform thickness.

Heat the oil in a sauté pan or skillet over medium-high heat. Beat the egg with the milk and a sprinkling of salt and pepper, and dip the chicken pieces in the mixture. Then dredge in flour, shaking to remove the excess, and place the chicken in the pan, being careful not to crowd the pieces.

Cook until brown on one side, about 4 minutes, then turn with tongs and add the mushrooms to the pan. Cook for 2 minutes, then place the mushrooms on top of the chicken pieces so they will not overcook. Cook 2 minutes longer.

Pour the grease out of the pan and add the butter and artichoke hearts. Sauté gently for 2 minutes, then add the white wine and green onions and reduce slightly for 2 minutes. Turn off the heat, cover the pan, and allow the mixture to steam for 5 minutes. Adjust the seasoning.

Note: While the chef uses a whole chicken in this recipe, boned and skinned chicken breasts, 1 per person, could easily be substituted. ∎

This dish blends a United Nations of flavors, from Chinese to Mexican, with some Italian thrown in for the stuffing. The resulting delicious flavor proves that the world is truly one larder.

Marinated Grilled Chicken Breast Stuffed with Cheese and Prosciutto with Roasted Chili–Black Bean Sauce

Tila's, Houston, Texas

(Serves 4)

Roasted Chili–Black Bean Sauce, following
4 whole chicken breasts

Marinade

1 cup pineapple juice
1 cup freshly squeezed orange juice
½ cup freshly squeezed lime juice
3 tablespoons soy sauce
2 tablespoons Chinese five spice powder
¼ cup dry red wine
2 *jalapeño* chilies, seeded and finely chopped
1 tablespoon chopped fresh cilantro
3 tablespoons cracked black pepper
1 tablespoon dried basil
¼ cup olive oil

Stuffing

½ cup grated fontina cheese
½ cup grated Bel Paese cheese
¼ cup grated Parmesan cheese
2 tablespoons chopped orange mint (any fresh herb can be substituted)
2 teaspoons sesame seeds, toasted
2 large slices prosciutto, cut into slivers (about ¾ cup)

Basting sauce

½ cup chicken stock
½ cup freshly squeezed orange juice
Juice of 1 lime
1 tablespoon cracked black pepper
2 garlic cloves, peeled and crushed
½ cup (1 stick) butter, melted

Garnish

Paprika
Grated Parmesan
Chopped fresh chives
Sliced carrot and tomato
Lime wedges

Prepare the sauce and set aside.

Skin and bone the chicken breasts, keeping the breasts whole. Place the whole breasts between 2 sheets of waxed paper and pound the breasts to an even thickness. Mix all the marinade ingredients together and marinate the chicken breasts, covered with plastic wrap, in the refrigerator for at least 6 hours, or preferably overnight.

Mix the stuffing ingredients together and set aside.

Light a charcoal or gas grill and combine the ingredients for the basting sauce. Place one-fourth of the stuffing mixture on one half of each chicken breast. Gently cover with the other half, securing the breasts closed with toothpicks.

Dip the chicken gently into the basting sauce, then grill 5 minutes, brushing with the basting sauce. Turn and grill an additional 5 to 10 minutes, or until the skin is brown.

To serve, place a pool of sauce on the plate with a chicken breast on top. Sprinkle with a little paprika, Parmesan, and chopped chives, and garnish with carrot, tomato, and lime.

Roasted Chili–Black Bean Sauce

3 dried *ancho* chilies
1 dried *cascabel* chili, or other hot dried red chili
¼ cup pumpkin seeds
1 cup Refried Black Beans, page 140
¾ cup chicken stock
1 tablespoon grated fresh ginger
1 tablespoon *hoisin* sauce
1 tablespoon oyster sauce
1 teaspoon brown sugar
3 medium *tomatillos*
2 tablespoons unsalted butter
1 *poblano* chili, seeded, deribbed, and cut into fine julienne
¼ cup Marsala
1 cup light beer (lager)
¼ cup heavy cream
2 tablespoons chopped fresh basil
½ teaspoon cayenne
1 tablespoon fresh lime juice
Salt to taste

Marinated Grilled Chicken Breast Stuffed with Cheese and Prosciutto with Roasted Chili–Black Bean Sauce, Tila's, Houston, Texas

Roast the dried chilies over a medium-hot charcoal grill, and sauté the pumpkin seeds in a dry skillet until brown. Grind the chilies and seeds in a coffee grinder or in a mortar until fine. Press through a sieve and set aside.

In a blender or a food processor with a steel blade, puree the refried beans and chicken stock with the ginger, *hoisin* sauce, oyster sauce, and brown sugar. Roast the *tomatillos* over the charcoal until they are slightly burnt. Heat the butter in a sauté pan or skillet and sauté the *poblano* for 2 minutes over high heat. Deglaze the pan with the Marsala and beer and cook for 3 minutes to evaporate the alcohol. Add the *tomatillos* to the pan and mash them in.

Add the black bean mixture and simmer the sauce for 3 minutes, fold in the roasted pepper powder and remaining ingredients, and simmer an additional 3 minutes. Set aside.

Note: The sauce can be made up to 3 days in advance and refrigerated. ∎

Lydia Shire's trip to India in 1986 influenced her cooking, as did the books of noted Indian food writer Madhur Jaffrey. This dish was inspired by both. Consult your favorite Indian cookbook for your choice of vegetable garnishes; you could use one simple garnish instead of the list given here.

Chicken Thighs with Black Mustard Seeds and Fermented-Rice Pancakes

Gardens, Los Angeles, California

(Serves 4)

Pancakes

1 cup long-grain rice
¼ cup skinned *urad dal* (a skinned lentil available at Indian groceries)
1½ cups water
Salt to taste

Chicken

4 chicken thighs
1 tablespoon ground turmeric
1 tablespoon salt
Coarsely ground black pepper
½ cup olive oil
1 tablespoon black mustard seeds
1 tablespoon *urad dal*
1 tablespoon fennel seeds
½ cup diced onion
3 small dried hot red chilies, any variety, unseeded

To finish the dish

Scant amount of olive oil (enough to barely coat bottom of the pan)
2 tablespoons clarified butter

Indian vegetable garnish

Creamed spinach with black mustard seeds
Okra with yogurt, chilies, and ginger
Cauliflower with chilies, turmeric, and cilantro
Sautéed fava beans

To make the pancakes, wash the rice several times, then place in a medium bowl and add water to cover by 2 inches. Let sit at room temperature for 6 hours. Wash the *urad dal* and soak with water to cover in another bowl for 6 hours. Drain both.

Place the rice into a blender or food processor with half of the water and puree. Empty into a bowl and repeat with the *dal* and the remaining water. Combine the purees, add salt to taste, and set in a warm spot a few hours or overnight.

Remove the knobby knuckle joints from the chicken thighs, leaving the thigh bones in. Mix the turmeric and salt and rub on the chicken. Marinate for 20 to 30 minutes, then season with black pepper.

In a wok, heat the ½ cup olive oil over medium heat. When hot, add the black mustard seeds, *dal,* and fennel. When the mustard seeds begin to pop, add the onion. When the onion is soft, add the chicken, skin side down. Spoon the onion over the chicken. Turn up the heat. Add the dried red chilies, breaking them up by hand. Do not shake the pan, but if the chicken is browning too quickly, pour water into the pan a few teaspoons at a time. Turn the chicken periodically during cooking.

While the chicken is cooking, cook the pancakes. Heat a scant amount of olive oil in a 10-inch nonstick skillet over medium-high heat. Check the batter. It should be loose and crepelike in consistency. Thin with water if necessary. Pour ⅓ cup of the batter into the skillet and quickly swirl as if making a crepe. The pancake should be thin enough so that bubbles appear almost immediately. Sprinkle with clarified butter. Do not move the pan until the outside edges of the pancake are brown, then flip it and cook the other side briefly. Remove from the pan and keep warm. Repeat to make 3 more pancakes.

To serve, place 1 pancake on each plate with the brown side down and place 1 chicken thigh halfway across the middle, then surround it with Indian-style vegetables. Fold the pancake across the chicken.

Note: Any leftover pancake batter will keep for a few days in the refrigerator. The chicken can be made a few hours in advance and reheated in a 350° oven; however, the pancakes must be done at the last minute. ∎

Gypsy Stew, The Pink Adobe, Santa Fe, New Mexico

Rosalea Murphy calls this Gypsy Stew because it reminds her of a Hungarian dish from her childhood. The spicy chilies and heady sherry are a great combination in this dish. Serve with warm flour tortillas and Ranch Beans (page 38) or Guacamole (page 138).

Gypsy Stew

The Pink Adobe, Santa Fe, New Mexico

(Serves 6)

1 large frying chicken, cut into
   serving pieces
3 yellow onions, peeled and quartered
8 garlic cloves, peeled and halved
2 cups dry sherry
1 cup chicken stock
12 medium-hot green chilies, such as
   Hatch or *poblano*, roasted, peeled,
   and seeded (see page 10)
6 large ripe tomatoes
Salt to taste
½ pound Monterey jack cheese

Place the chicken, onions, garlic, 1 cup of the sherry, and the stock in a large covered saucepan or Dutch oven. If necessary, add more stock or water so the chicken is covered. Bring to a boil and simmer, covered, over low heat for 1 hour. Remove the chicken from the pot with a slotted spoon and, when cool enough to handle, pick the meat off the bones, discarding the bones and skin.

Cut the chilies into chunks. Using 2 forks, tear the tomatoes apart. Add to the chilies and set aside.

Add the chilies, tomatoes, and chicken meat to the pot along with the remaining sherry and salt to taste. Cover, bring to a boil, and simmer for 45 minutes.

To serve, cut the cheese into cubes and place them in the bottom of serving bowls. Ladle the stew over them and serve.

Note: The dish can be made 2 days in advance and slowly reheated. ■

ROSALEA MURPHY

The Pink Adobe, Santa Fe, New Mexico

Rosalea Murphy recalls Santa Fe in the 1930s, when she moved there as a bride from New Orleans. "It was a lazy, sleepy town then, and we bought wood off of burros that would wander the streets."

When she opened The Pink Adobe in 1944, it was one of the first restaurants in the city, and she introduced dishes such as French onion soup to the town. That first restaurant, basically a hamburger place where she baked her own apple pies, was named for the color it was painted when the San Antonio native leased the space.

The present Pink Adobe is housed in what was the Barrio de Analco, a three-hundred-year-old former barracks with thirty-six-inch-thick adobe walls in which the small windows were placed high as protection against arrows.

The food chef Murphy prepares is a combination of Continental dishes as filtered through her Creole sensibility, and some native specialties featuring the region's characteristic blue corn tortillas. "I changed a lot of the Mexican dishes to lighten them, but I didn't cut back on the seasonings," she says.

In addition to cooking, the sprightly seventy-two-year-old Murphy is an accomplished painter. Her illustrations decorate the pages of a cookbook of restaurant favorites titled *Cooking with a Silver Spoon*. She has studied with noted artist Richard Diebenkorn, and her style of painting is as exuberant as her cooking.

Turkey has come a long way from being viewed as the holiday bird. We know how healthful it is, and we're learning that it's versatile, too. This is a quick and masterful way of using the cutlets now available.

Grilled Turkey Breast with Vinegar and Cracked Pepper

Border Grill, Los Angeles, California

(Serves 6)

Six 4- to 6-ounce turkey breast
  cutlets, pounded thin between 2
  sheets of waxed paper (see note)
Salt and pepper to taste
½ cup unbleached all-purpose flour
1½ tablespoons black peppercorns,
  or to taste
6 tablespoons chilled unsalted butter
¾ cup finely diced red onion
⅓ cup white wine vinegar
1 cup chicken stock

Light a charcoal grill. Season the cutlets with salt and pepper and lightly dust with flour, shaking off any excess. When the coals are red-hot, grill the meat, turning it after 30 seconds for a total cooking time of 1 minute.

Coarsely crack the peppercorns with the back of a skillet or in a mortar and set aside.

Heat 4 tablespoons of the butter in a sauté pan or skillet and briefly sauté the grilled turkey just long enough to cook the flour. Remove from the pan and add the red onion, sautéing quickly. Add the black pepper, vinegar, and chicken stock. Reduce by half. Chop the remaining 2 tablespoons of butter into bits and whisk them into the sauce, incorporating each piece before the next is added. Add salt to taste and pour the sauce over the grilled turkey pieces.

Note: Most supermarkets now sell packages of turkey breast cutlets. If not, buy a half turkey breast and slice thinly across the grain. ∎

Grilled Turkey Breast with Vinegar and Cracked Pepper, Border Grill, Los Angeles, California

While the slightly gamey flavor of wild turkey is more in keeping with this spicy stuffing than the domestic variety, do not hesitate to substitute. The stuffing is also wonderful with any poultry, and will enliven a pork roast or pork chops.

Roast Wild Turkey with Blue Cornmeal–Chorizo Stuffing

Routh Street Cafe, Dallas, Texas

(Serves 10)

One 8- to 10-pound wild turkey
Salt and freshly ground black pepper

Stuffing

3 tablespoons oil
1 pound bulk chorizo sausage
4 tablespoons butter
1 cup chopped onions
¼ cup diced celery
¼ cup diced carrots
4 *serrano* chilies, seeded, deribbed,
  and finely minced
6 garlic cloves, peeled and minced
¼ cup chopped *chayote* squash
  (optional)
¼ cup bourbon
1 teaspoon minced fresh thyme, or ¼
  teaspoon dried thyme
1 teaspoon minced fresh sage, or ⅛
  teaspoon dried sage
1 tablespoon chopped fresh cilantro
8 cups coarsely crumbled corn bread
  made from blue cornmeal (see page
  141), or yellow corn bread can be
  substituted if necessary
½ cup chicken stock
Salt to taste

To finish the dish

Melted butter

Wash the turkey inside and out, sprinkle the cavity and the outside with salt and pepper, and set aside.

In a sauté pan or skillet, heat the oil over medium heat and when hot add the chorizo, breaking it up with a wooden spoon as it browns. Sauté the sausage until brown, about 5 minutes, then remove it from the pan with a slotted spoon, place it in a large mixing bowl, and pour all the grease out of the pan.

Put the butter in the pan and when it is melted add the onions, celery, carrots, chilies, garlic, and *chayote*, if used. Sauté for 4 minutes over

Roast Wild Turkey with Blue Cornmeal–Chorizo Stuffing, Routh Street Cafe, Dallas, Texas

medium heat, stirring occasionally, or until the vegetables are translucent and soft. Add the bourbon to the pan and reduce for 3 minutes.

Remove the pan from the heat and add the thyme, sage, and cilantro. Pour the mixture into the bowl with the chorizo, add the corn bread crumbs, and moisten with the chicken stock. Taste and adjust seasoning.

Preheat the oven to 350°. Stuff the turkey, placing any extra stuffing into a casserole, and truss the turkey. Place the turkey on a rack in a large roasting pan, rub generously with butter, and bake for 20 minutes per pound, basting frequently with melted butter.

Allow the turkey to rest for 15 minutes before carving.

Note: The stuffing can be prepared a day in advance and kept in the refrigerator. Bring it to room temperature before stuffing the turkey. ■

G. Scott Philip

Las Canarias, San Antonio, Texas

Las Canarias is one of the few restaurants in the San Antonio area serving the new style of Southwestern cookery. Located on the famed River Walk through the center of the city, it is an elegant dining room with traditional Mexican touches located in the Mansion del Rio Hotel.

For the past year, creating new dishes for the kitchen has been the primary task of G. Scott Philip, a twenty-five-year-old Kansas City native who graduated in 1985 from the Culinary Institute of America and won a Gold Medal in the Taste of Canada Culinary Competition while in school.

Although far younger than chefs holding equivalent jobs elsewhere, Philip had worked in hotels in his hometown, and moved to San Diego after graduation to open Ruffino's, an Italian restaurant where he created pastas nightly.

"My parents didn't want me to become a chef, but I'm talented with my hands and cooking is the way I could best express myself. From the time I entered high school I knew this was what I wanted to do," he says.

He believes that consistency is as important as creativity, and tries to elevate the basic Southern foods of his childhood as he explores the Southwestern larder. He believes that one of his favorite recipes, Smoked Barbecued Duck with Pecan Stuffing, adds texture and flavor to a traditional dish.

"I grew up on biscuits and gravy and other country foods, and think that they can be satisfying to a whole new generation if presented properly and lightened," he says.

Chef Philip believes that new Southwest cooking will take its rightful place as an offshoot of new American cuisine, and that liberties can be taken with dishes. The *jalapeño* pasta he serves with rattlesnake sausage dotted with smoked venison is a harbinger of things to come.

This dish is a Southwestern interpretation of the French classic cassoulet. The seasoning and manner of presentation are chef Michael Roberts' updatings; however, the rich flavors of confit *and hearty beans remain the stars.*

Duck and White-Bean Chili

Trumps, Los Angeles, California

(Serves 6)

Note: This dish must be started 3 days before serving to allow the duck adequate time to marinate.

Confit of duck

4 duck leg quarters (or 2 whole ducks, cut into quarters)
4 tablespoons kosher salt
1 garlic head
6 bay leaves
4 fresh thyme sprigs, or 1 teaspoon dried thyme
¼ cup black peppercorns
⅛ cup juniper berries
Duck fat to cover pieces

Beans

2 pounds dried white navy beans
1 medium onion, peeled and finely diced
1½ tablespoons chili powder
1 tablespoon ground cumin
1 carrot, peeled and finely diced
1 celery stalk, finely diced
1 tablespoon salt
1½ teaspoons cayenne
1 dried *pasilla* chili
3 quarts chicken stock
1 ham bone or smoked ham hock
Salt to taste

For presentation

¾ cup sour cream
1 to 2 fresh *pasilla* chilies, roasted, seeded, and peeled (see page 10)
2 cups shredded baby lettuces (combination of bibb, endive, romaine, etc.)
3 ripe tomatoes, seeded and finely chopped
12 warm corn or flour tortillas

To prepare the duck, start 3 days in advance by sprinkling the pieces with the salt and letting them sit, covered with plastic wrap, in the refrigerator.

Preheat the oven to 275°. Place the duck pieces in a small covered pan with the herbs and spices. Add

Duck and White-Bean Chili, Trumps, Los Angeles, California

enough oil or melted duck fat to cover the pieces entirely. Place the covered pan in the preheated oven and bake for 4 to 6 hours, or until the duck is so tender it falls off the bone. When the pieces are cool enough to handle, discard the skin and bones and shred the meat; reserve the fat. Set the meat and fat aside.

picking over them well to discard any broken beans or pebbles. Place the beans in a covered saucepan, add all the remaining bean ingredients except the salt, bring to a boil on the top of the stove, and then place them in the oven with the duck. Check from time to time to see if additional stock or water is needed, and salt the beans when they begin to become tender. The beans will take about the same amount of time as the duck, and are cooked when they are tender but not

mushy. Uncover them for the last hour, stirring occasionally.

Place the beans in a bowl and top with sour cream and strips of the roasted chili. Scatter the lettuces on a platter and top with the duck meat and chopped tomato. Pass the tortillas separately, and make soft tacos from all the ingredients.

Note: The duck and beans can be made up to 4 days in advance and reheated in a slow oven before serving. ∎

The smoky and spicy flavor of the duck combined with a slightly sweet and crunchy stuffing make this dish interesting. The barbecue sauce can also be used with any grilled or broiled meat or poultry, and the stuffing can be used for any roasted bird.

Smoked Barbecued Duck with Pecan Stuffing

Las Canarias, San Antonio, Texas

(Serves 4)

Two 5½-pound fresh ducks, preferably Long Island

Brine

1 quart orange juice
1 quart water
⅓ cup salt
2 oranges, halved, with peels on
2 limes, halved, with peels on
2 cups honey
¼ cup pickling spice

Barbecue sauce

4 bacon slices, chopped
¼ onion, chopped
¼ green bell pepper or *poblano* chili, seeded, deribbed, and chopped
¼ red bell pepper, seeded, deribbed, and chopped
1 tomato, peeled, seeded, and chopped
2 garlic cloves, peeled and chopped
¾ cup apple cider vinegar
½ cup honey
1¼ cups red chili sauce
2 tablespoons tomato paste
¼ cup brown sugar
1 tablespoon chili powder

Pecan stuffing

½ cup (1 stick) unsalted butter
8 shallots, peeled and minced
1¼ cups pecans, chopped
7/8 pound sponge cake
½ cup heated chicken stock
2 eggs, lightly beaten
3 tablespoons minced fresh parsley
Salt and pepper to taste

Cut the wings and tail sections from the ducks and remove excess fat from the necks and cavities. Combine all the ingredients for the brine and bring to a boil. Simmer 5 to 10 minutes, and allow to cool before using (this can be done a day in advance, since sitting in the refrigerator will improve the flavors).

Marinate the ducks in the brine for 4 to 6 hours in the refrigerator, then place them in a smoker, ideally at 140°, using mesquite wood. Smoke the ducks for 15 minutes, then place them in a 300° oven and roast for 30 minutes.

While the ducks are smoking, prepare the barbecue sauce. Sauté the bacon until crisp in a large saucepan, then add the onion and peppers. Sauté for 3 minutes, then add the tomato and garlic and continue to sauté until the onion is translucent. Add the vinegar and reduce by one-half. Add the remaining ingredients, stir well, and simmer over low heat, stirring occasionally, for 1 hour, or until the sauce is thickened.

Puree in small batches and place in the refrigerator until ready to use.

Allow the ducks to cool, then split them into 2 pieces, removing the backbone and freeing the carcass by severing the leg and wing joints. Remove the thighs and wing bones.

Preheat the oven to 350°. To make the stuffing, melt the butter in a sauté pan or skillet and add the shallots. Sauté until lightly brown, then add the pecans and sauté briefly. Allow to cool.

Cut the cake into small dice and combine with the nut-butter mixture. Moisten with chicken stock and add the eggs and parsley. Season to taste with salt and pepper. Place the mixture in a buttered baking dish and bake for 15 minutes, stirring a few times, or until heated through.

To finish the dish, brush the duck halves with the barbecue sauce and roast for 10 minutes in a 350° oven. Serve with the stuffing.

Note: Everything up to the finishing of the dish can be done up to 2 days in advance. Bring the stuffing and ducks to room temperature for 1 hour before finishing. A covered charcoal grill can be used for the smoking process; place some water-soaked wood chips on coals pushed to the side of the grill. ∎

Garnishing plates with refried black beans, guacamole, and salsa is part of the Southwestern tradition. Robert Del Grande utilizes these compatible flavors in a sophisticated, if somewhat time-consuming, presentation.

Grilled Squab with Black Bean Tortas and Bacon and Pumpkin Seed Sauce

Cafe Annie, Houston, Texas

(Serves 6)

Black beans

½ cup dried black beans
1 garlic clove
1 sprig *epazote*
3 bacon slices
2 tablespoons lard
½ teaspoon kosher salt
Freshly ground black pepper to taste
1 tablespoon butter
3 eggs, lightly beaten
6 squab (or 12 quail can be substituted)

Guacamole

2 large ripe avocadoes
½ cup finely chopped seeded red bell pepper
½ cup chopped onion
1 tablespoon finely minced seeded *serrano* chili
¾ cup chopped fresh cilantro
2 tablespoons fresh lime juice
2 tablespoons olive oil
Salt and black pepper to taste

To complete the tortas

12 flour tortillas
3 ounces goat cheese
4 tablespoons clarified butter

Sauce

2 *poblano* chilies, roasted, peeled, seeded, and chopped (see page 10)
½ cup pumpkin seeds, toasted in a 350° oven for 5 minutes, then chopped
4 *tomatillos*, husked and finely chopped
8 bacon slices (apple smoked is preferred)
4 tablespoons butter
2 stale French or Italian bread slices, trimmed of crusts and cubed
1½ cups chicken stock
¾ cup cilantro leaves

2 tablespoons freshly squeezed lime
 juice

Tomato salsa

6 ripe Italian plum tomatoes
½ cup chopped red onion
¾ cup chopped fresh cilantro
2 teaspoons finely minced *serrano* or
 jalapeño chili
2 tablespoons freshly squeezed lime
 juice
1 teaspoon salt
Freshly ground black pepper to taste

To finish the dish

Salt and pepper for squab
½ cup sour cream for garnish

To make the black beans, rinse the
beans in a colander, picking over
them and discarding any broken
beans or pebbles. Place them in a pot
with the garlic and *epazote* and add
enough water to cover the beans by 2
inches. Bring to a boil and simmer
until the beans are soft, adding water
as necessary. This should take about
2 hours. Let the beans cool in the
pot, then puree half of them with ½
cup of the cooking liquid. Combine
the puree with the drained whole
beans.

In a skillet, cook the bacon and
lard over medium heat until the
bacon has rendered its fat. Remove
the bacon with a slotted spoon and
add the bean mixture, stirring to
incorporate the fat. It should be a
very thick paste; if not, stir over low
heat to evaporate some of the water.
Season with salt and pepper.

In another skillet, melt the butter
over low heat and add the beans and
eggs. Scramble the eggs with the
beans until cooked, then set aside to
keep warm.

Bone the squab by removing the
wing tips at the second joint and
cutting around the wishbone. Cut
down the breastbone and, keeping the
blade of the knife towards the
carcass, free the carcass, cutting
through the leg and wing joints.
Leave only the leg and wing bones in
place, removing the thigh bone. Set
birds aside.

Make the *guacamole* by peeling the
avocadoes and dicing them into a
bowl. Add the remaining ingredients

Grilled Squab with Black Bean Tortas and Bacon and Pumpkin Seed Sauce, Cafe Annie, Houston, Texas

and mash with the back of a large
spoon, it should remain slightly
chunky. Season with salt and pepper
and set aside.

Light a charcoal or gas grill. To
finish the *tortas*, with a 4-inch cookie
cutter, or using a cup as a guide, cut
12 circles from the tortillas. Spread 2
tablespoons of black beans on one
circle and top with a slice of goat
cheese. Cover with a layer of
guacamole and a second tortilla
circle.

Heat the clarified butter in a skillet
over medium heat, and when hot fry
the *tortas* on both sides to a golden
brown. Keep warm.

To make the sauce, combine the
chopped *poblanos*, chopped pumpkin
seeds, and *tomatillos*. Cut the bacon
into small dice and sauté over
medium heat to render the fat.
Remove the bacon pieces with a
slotted spoon (reserve for another
use) and add the butter. When it is
melted add the pepper mixture and
bread cubes and sauté until the bread
is lightly brown. Add the stock,

season with salt and pepper, and
simmer until the liquid has slightly
thickened. Add the cilantro and lime
juice and adjust seasoning.

To make the *salsa*, seed and finely
chop the tomatoes, and mix with the
remaining ingredients. Set aside.

When the coals are medium-hot,
season the squabs with salt and
pepper and grill skin side down for 5
minutes. Turn and cook 1 minute on
the meat side, allowing the squab to
remain pink.

To serve, warm the *tortas* in a
250° oven and reheat the sauce
briefly. Place a *torta* on each plate,
topped with a spoonful of sour cream
and some *salsa*. Spoon the sauce onto
the plate and top with a squab.

Note: The black beans can be
prepared 2 days in advance, and the
squab can be boned at that time and
kept tightly covered in the refrigerator
(be sure to bring them to room
temperature before grilling). The
tortas can be assembled and fried up
to 6 hours in advance, and the sauce
can be made at that time. ∎

Pheasant San Xavier, The White Dove, Tucson, Arizona

Bradley Ogden likes to accompany his entrees with the vegetables and starches he feels complement them best. In this case, the crunchy sweet potatoes and bitter chard are a perfect balance to the mustard-and-herb-flavored birds.

Grilled Quail with Shoestring Sweet Potatoes and Swiss Chard with Tomato

Campton Place, San Francisco, California

(Serves 4)

Note: This dish must be started 2 days before serving.

8 fresh quail (4 ounces each)

Marinade

½ cup brandy
1 tablespoon chopped fresh garlic
½ teaspoon cracked black pepper
3 tablespoons olive oil
4 tablespoons Dijon mustard
½ cup Madeira
½ teaspoon kosher salt
12 sage leaves, chopped, or ½ teaspoon dried sage
8 rosemary sprigs, or 2 teaspoons dried rosemary
12 thyme sprigs, or ½ teaspoon dried thyme
8 savory sprigs, or ½ teaspoon dried savory

Basting sauce

2 tablespoons stone-ground mustard
5 tablespoons unsalted butter, softened
2 teaspoons white wine vinegar
Salt and pepper to taste

Garnish

8 bacon slices
4 sweet potatoes (yams cannot be substituted)
Peanut oil for deep-frying
2 bunches Swiss chard, washed and stems removed
4 tablespoons unsalted butter
½ cup water
4 tomatoes
Salt and pepper to taste

Bone the quail with a small sharp paring knife by cutting down the breastbone and carefully cutting away the carcass, keeping the blade of the knife towards the carcass so that it

Game birds and meats take well to flavoring with fruit and wine. This is an elegant and easy entree to serve with wild rice and sautéed vegetables for a last-minute dinner party.

Pheasant San Xavier

The White Dove, Tucson, Arizona

(Serves 6 as an appetizer, 3 to 4 as an entree)

3 pheasant breasts
3 tablespoons flour
Salt and pepper to taste
3 tablespoons clarified butter or oil
2 shallots, peeled and chopped
1 pint fresh raspberries (frozen unsweetened berries can be substituted)
½ cup merlot or other full-bodied red wine
1 cup pheasant stock reduced from 2 cups (made by using the pheasant carcasses) or veal *demi-glace* (see page 19)
Garnish: Whole raspberries and herb sprigs

Remove the skin from the breasts and pound them lightly to an even thickness. Dust them with flour and sprinkle with salt and pepper.

Heat the clarified butter or oil in a sauté pan or skillet over high heat. When very hot, add the pheasant breasts and sauté until golden brown. Turn the breasts over, and add the shallots, raspberries, and merlot. Stir, smashing the raspberries into the wine. Let simmer a few minutes, then add the reduced stock or *demi-glace*, simmering a few minutes more. Add salt and pepper to taste, and serve. Garnish with some whole raspberries and a sprig of fresh herb. ■

does not puncture the skin. Cut through the wing and leg joints and free the carcass, then cut the quails in half with sharp scissors.

Combine all the marinade ingredients and marinate the quail halves in the refrigerator, covered with plastic wrap, for 24 to 48 hours, turning occasionally.

Light a charcoal or gas grill. While the grill is heating, mix the basting sauce ingredients together and set aside. Sauté the bacon for garnish, drain on paper towels, and reserve the fat for basting the quail.

Peel the sweet potatoes and cut into ¼-inch slices. Cut the slices into fine julienne. Pour peanut oil into a large heavy skillet to a depth of ½ inch and heat over high heat to 375°. When hot, add the shoestring potatoes and fry until crisp. Remove with a slotted spoon and drain well on paper towels. Place on a baking sheet.

Place the chard in a covered pan with the butter and water. Cut the core and flesh from the tomatoes, reserving them for another use, and finely slice the tomato peel and meat attached to it. Add to the pan with the chard and bring to a boil, then cover and cook for 5 minutes. Season with salt and pepper to taste and set aside.

Rub the grill with oil and place the quail on the hot grill, skin side down. Grill for 3 minutes, basting occasionally with the bacon fat. Turn the halves and grill 3 minutes more, basting with the basting sauce. The quail should be medium rare.

To serve, reheat the bacon and potatoes, if needed, in a 350° oven. Place a bed of potatoes and 2 bacon slices in the center of each plate and drape 4 quail halves around one side. Place some of the chard on the other side.

Note: The quail have such a good flavor from the marinade that they do not suffer from being broiled rather than grilled. ∎

BRADLEY OGDEN
Campton Place, San Francisco, California

Chef Bradley Ogden, one of the trailblazers of new American cuisine, opened the elegant peach-toned dining room of the Campton Place Hotel in San Francisco in 1984. He has proven that food writer M.F.K. Fisher was right: there is something terribly sensual about a bowl of mashed potatoes.

The Traverse City, Michigan, native is a 1977 graduate of the Culinary Institute of America, where he received the distinguished Richard T. Keating Award.

By 1979, he was chosen to be the chef at An American Restaurant in Kansas City, the jewel of Hallmark's Crown Center. It was a natural pairing of concept and chef. Both emphasized the change of seasons with appropriate foods, and both restaurant and chef were dedicated to new American cuisine before it even had a name.

He is lightening the style of his sauces now, and is tending to move away from stock reduction sauces to vegetable purees and more light vinaigrettes. He surrounds a rich onion tart with a lightly dressed *arugola* salad, so the heartiness of the tart is balanced by the bitter greens. This is the style of cooking he will share with the home cook when his cookbook is published by Random House in 1988.

Chef Ogden has always believed that side dishes should be entree-specific, so the plate becomes a unified statement, and his combinations have become more complex. His Grilled Quail with Shoestring Sweet Potatoes and Buttered Swiss Chard with Tomatoes illustrates the direction in which his style is moving. The plate is planned around the rich, sweet, and crisp tastes of the components.

He believes that desserts should follow the format of the rest of the meal. The desire to serve "comfortable food" translates to home-style cakes with fruit sauces, and ice creams churned in the kitchen.

FISH AND SEAFOOD DISHES

While fish and seafood dishes did not play a significant role in traditional Southwest cuisine, they certainly do in new Southwest cooking as chefs adapt ideas and ingredients to please the contemporary palate and the equally contemporary appetite for more aquatic species.

The availability of fresh fish in supermarkets today has made it possible to use these interesting recipes. Modern transportation and sophisticated shipping allow fish to be sent from coast to coast in the time it used to take fishermen to bring their catch to a local market. You can find tuna steaks in Cincinnati and Chesapeake oysters in Omaha.

The chefs realize that fish is essentially delicate, and they have treated it gently in terms of spicing. Chilies form the color for the sauces in John Sedlar's Salmon Painted Desert and are a hint of flavor in Alan Zeman's Sonoran Seafood Stew, but none of these dishes will send guests running to the water tap.

Another factor uniting these concepts is an elegance of presentation. Donna Nordin's Prawns Stuffed with Goat Cheese on Tomato Coulis is a simple dish, yet the filling supported by the butterflied prawns on a vivid red sauce is as stunning as it is delicious.

Sonoran Seafood Stew, Tucson Country Club, Tucson, Arizona

Every culture and region of American cuisine has a version of a fish stew—from bouillabaisse *on the coast of the Mediterranean to* cioppino *on the Pacific Coast of California. What makes this one so delicious is the sparkle from the citrus fruit and chilies, and the Mexican touch given the seasoning.*

Sonoran Seafood Stew

Tucson Country Club, Tucson, Arizona

(Serves 6)

1 dozen clams
1 dozen mussels
1 tablespoon cornmeal or flour
12 large shrimp
Three 4- to 6-ounce lobster tails
2 garlic cloves, peeled and minced
¼ cup chopped onion
3 tablespoons olive oil
3 tomatoes, peeled, seeded, and diced
¼ cup roasted, peeled, seeded, and chopped mild green chili (*poblano* or Anaheim) (see page 6)
1 tablespoon capers, drained
¼ cup green stuffed olives, sliced
½ teaspoon dried oregano
Juice and finely chopped zest of 2 oranges
1 cup clam juice
1 cup dry white wine
¾ pound salmon, cabrilla, grouper, sea bass, or other firm-fleshed fish, cut into ¾-inch cubes
1 teaspoon Sonoran Seasoning, page xx
6 flour tortillas
1½ cups hot cooked white rice

Garnish

3 lemons
3 limes
6 cilantro sprigs
6 boiled crawfish

Since the stew cooks rapidly, start by cleaning the seafood. Scrub the clams under running water with a brush, and soak the mussels for 30 minutes in a bowl of cold water sprinkled with the cornmeal or flour. Scrub the mussels and trim off the beards with a sharp paring knife. Peel and devein the shrimp. Remove the lobster tails from their shells, devein, and split lengthwise.

In a large saucepan, sauté the garlic and onion in the olive oil for

Red Snapper George, La Louisiane, San Antonio, Texas

about 5 minutes, or until soft. Add the tomatoes, chili, capers, olives, oregano, orange juice, clam juice, and white wine and bring to a boil. Reduce for 10 minutes over medium heat, then add the salmon and shellfish, along with the Sonoran Seasoning and the lemon and orange zest.

Cover the pot, and once it returns to a boil turn the heat down and allow it to simmer, covered, for 10 minutes. Discard any clams or mussels that have not opened.

While the stew is cooking, grill the tortillas on a hot griddle or in a skillet and press 1 tortilla into each serving bowl. Top the tortilla with ¼ cup rice.

To serve, divide the fish and seafood among the bowls, then add the broth and vegetables. Top with crowns of lemon and lime, a sprig of cilantro, and a whole crawfish. ■

Mushrooms and artichoke hearts add interest to a quick sautéed fish dish.

Red Snapper George

La Louisiane, San Antonio, Texas

(Serves 4)

Four 6-ounce red snapper fillets
1 cup vegetable oil
1 egg
1 cup milk
Salt and pepper to taste
Flour for dredging
6 to 8 tablespoons unsalted butter
4 or 5 mushrooms, washed and sliced
3 artichoke hearts, cooked and sliced
Juice of 1 lemon

Wash the fillets and pat dry. Heat the oil in a sauté pan or skillet over medium-high heat. In a bowl, beat the egg, milk, and salt and pepper to taste and dip the fillets in the mixture. Dredge in flour and fry in the hot oil, turning after 2 minutes, for a total cooking time of 4 to 5 minutes. Remove the fillets with a slotted spatula and drain on paper towels.

Pour the grease out of the pan and add the butter. Add the mushrooms and artichoke hearts and sauté for 5 minutes, stirring gently. Add the lemon juice, sprinkle with salt and pepper, and divide the vegetables and sauce on top of the fillets. ■

The combination of oriental and occidental tastes is part of Douglas Dale's style of cooking, and it's a most exciting blend. His presentation is rather complex, but using just the gremolata and basting sauce with the fish will also create a memorable dinner.

Grilled Chilean Sea Bass with Dill Gremolata

Wolfdale's, Lake Tahoe, California

(Serves 8)

4 pounds Chilean sea bass fillets, cut into 8-ounce sections (striped bass, grouper, black cod, bluefish, or any other oily fish fillets can be substituted)

Gremolata

5 tablespoons chopped fresh dill
1 tablespoon grated lemon zest
2 garlic cloves, blanched in boiling water for 5 minutes, then peeled and crushed
5 tablespoons freshly grated Parmesan cheese
5 sun-dried tomato halves, boiled for 10 minutes to soften, then minced

Basting sauce

⅓ cup soybean oil
⅓ cup olive oil
⅓ cup *tamari*

Vegetable garnishes

½ cup Asian sesame oil
16 chanterelles, cleaned, stemmed, and quartered if large
1 tablespoon finely minced fresh ginger
3 tablespoons minced shallots
2 tablespoons saki
2 tablespoons *dashi* or beef stock
5 tablespoons *tamari*
16 taro potatoes (found in Asian markets)
¼ cup honey
¼ cup rice wine vinegar
12 snow peas, strings removed, blanched in boiling water for 30 seconds

Rinse the fish in cold water, pat with paper towels, and set aside. Mix all of the *gremolata* ingredients together in a small bowl and set aside.

Prepare the basting sauce, then

Grilled Chilean Sea Bass with Dill Gremolata, Wolfdale's, Lake Tahoe, California

complete the vegetable garnishes before grilling the fish.

Heat ¼ cup of the sesame oil in a sauté pan or skillet and add the chanterelles, ginger, and shallots. Sauté over low heat for 5 minutes, or until the mushrooms are tender and lightly browned, then add the saki, *dashi,* and 1 tablespoon of *tamari* and cook an additional few minutes to reduce the liquid. Set aside and keep warm.

Light a charcoal grill or preheat a broiler. Boil the taro potatoes until tender, peel, and cut into cubes. Mix the remaining 4 tablespoons *tamari,* remaining ¼ cup sesame oil,

honey, and rice wine vinegar. Pour over the hot taro potatoes and keep warm.

Place the fish in a rack. Baste with the basting liquid and grill for 4 to 5 minutes on a side over hot coals or under a hot broiler, depending on the thickness of the fillets.

To serve, garnish with the mushrooms, potatoes, *gremolata,* and a few snow peas.

Note: All the parts of the recipe except the fish can be prepared earlier on the day of service and reheated as appropriate. The fish should be grilled at the last minute. ∎

Salmon in a dill-cream sauce is a classic combination. What makes this dish exciting is the contrasting spicy pasta and the intense taste of smoked salmon paired with the fresh.

Two-Salmon Pasta

Bistro Garden, Houston, Texas

(Serves 6)

Pasta

1½ cups semolina
1½ cups unbleached all-purpose flour
4 eggs
1 tablespoon olive oil
1 teaspoon coarse-ground black pepper
⅛ teaspoon saffron
1 teaspoon salt

Topping

10 ounces smoked salmon
10 ounces fresh salmon fillet
1 cup fish stock
2 tablespoons clarified butter
¾ cup chopped peeled and seeded tomatoes
¼ cup chopped shallots
1½ teaspoons minced garlic
4 teaspoons chopped fresh dill
1 teaspoon chopped fresh rosemary
Salt and white pepper to taste
½ cup heavy cream
6 green onions, chopped, white part only

Garnish

2 tablespoons clarified butter
1 pound sugar snap beans or snow peas, cleaned
1 red bell pepper, seeded, deribbed, and cut into fine julienne
½ cup sour cream
2 ounces black caviar (preferably American black sturgeon)

To make the pasta, combine the dry ingredients in a mixing bowl or a food processor. Beat the remaining ingredients together and add to the flours, combining until the dough pulls together. Knead briefly with your hands, then allow the dough to rest for 30 minutes, covered with plastic.

Roll the dough through a pasta machine to the thinnest setting, then let the sheets dry for 5 minutes and cut into thin strips. Set aside.

Flake the smoked salmon and set aside. Poach the fresh salmon fillet in the fish stock until cooked, about 5 minutes. Remove from the stock, reserving the stock, and then flake the salmon. Set aside.

Heat the butter in a sauté pan or skillet and add the tomatoes, shallots, and garlic. Sauté for 2 minutes, then add the dill and rosemary. Season with salt and white pepper, then add the reserved fish stock and cream. Reduce the sauce by half, or until it reaches a syrupy consistency. Then stir in the onions and 2 types of salmon.

To make the vegetable garnish, heat the butter in a sauté pan or skillet and, when hot, sauté the vegetables over medium-high heat for 1 minute, until cooked but still crisp.

Cook the pasta in boiling water until just *al dente*, about 1 minute. Drain.

To serve, toss the pasta with the sauce, top with a dollop of sour cream and some caviar, and arrange some of the vegetables around the side of the plate.

Note: The pasta can be made a few days in advance and allowed to dry. Increase the cooking time if dried. The sauce can be prepared in advance to the point of adding the fish and green onions. Reheat gently to a simmer and then add the final ingredients. ∎

Two-Salmon Pasta, Bistro Garden, Houston, Texas

KATHY RUIZ

Bistro Garden, Houston, Texas

Out of all the chefs practicing new Southwest cooking, Kathy Ruiz is one of the few cooking in her own hometown. She grew up with the traditional foods she is now using as the basis for her improvisations.

The twenty-nine-year-old Houston native recalls her grandmother making tortillas, and the Mexican maids in her house rolling tamales. "I loved the food at home, and when I went away to New York for college—afraid of the horror stories about those Yankees—I couldn't wait to come home for vacations and eat pinto beans for dinner," she says.

At Bistro Garden, a charming Victorian gingerbread house with stenciled walls and white lace curtains, the tamales are likely to be filled with venison or duck, and the pinto beans appear in Corn Pasta Ravioli with Pinto Bean Sauce.

She graduated from Manhattanville College with a degree in biology. Her father is an eye surgeon in Houston, and her initial decision was to follow him into medicine. "I really wasn't that dedicated, and my real interest at the time was scuba diving. I still feel guilty when I cook fish," she says.

She always enjoyed cooking, and worked in a few kitchens in New York before moving back to Houston in 1980 for a job in a geology library. But after a year's flirtation with science, she talked her way into a job at Hilltop Herb Farm as chef. "I had to teach myself the ropes, and I knew I'd found what I wanted to do," she says.

Her next stop was Cafe Luxeford, the dining room of a newly opened hotel near the Astrodome. She changed the menu daily, and started developing the small suppliers she still counts on, moving to Bistro Garden in August of 1986. "I have local fishermen and a commune of aging hippies to grow my herbs, and I let the suppliers dictate to me. If Bob, my fisherman, shows up with a shark a few hours out of the water, that's what I'll create for dinner," she says.

Not only do the red and green feathered stripes visually glorify this dish, the chili and sorrel flavor of the sauces add to the delicacy of the shallot sauce. While it looks complex, the decoration for this poached salmon is easy to do, and once the sauces are done the dish can be completed in a very short time.

Salmon Painted Desert

Saint Estèphe, Manhattan Beach, California

(Serves 6)

Six 6-ounce salmon steaks (any pink species)
½ teaspoon kosher salt
½ teaspoon ground white pepper

Red chili Indian paint

1 tablespoon vegetable oil
2 medium garlic cloves, peeled and finely minced
½ cup red chili powder, mild to medium-hot, depending on taste
¾ cup water

Green sorrel Indian paint

¾ cup vegetable oil
2 medium garlic cloves, peeled and finely minced
¾ cup sorrel puree (available in jars, or see note)
1 teaspoon salt
1 teaspoon ground white pepper

Shallot sauce

½ cup dry white wine
1 teaspoon finely chopped shallots
2 cups heavy cream
½ teaspoon salt
½ teaspoon ground white pepper

Clean the salmon steaks, removing any bones and skin. Sprinkle with salt and white pepper and set aside, covered with plastic wrap in the refrigerator, until ready to use.

To make the red chili paint, heat the oil in a small skillet over medium heat. Add the garlic and sauté about 3 minutes, until tender but not brown. Sprinkle in the chili powder, stirring constantly, and immediately add the water. Stir until well blended, remove from the skillet, and puree in a blender. Force the mixture through a fine sieve and place in a plastic squeeze bottle. Store in the refrigerator until needed.

Salmon Painted Desert, Saint Estèphe, Manhattan Beach, California

To make the green sorrel paint, heat the oil in a small skillet over medium heat. Add the garlic and sauté until tender but not brown, about 3 minutes. Stir in the sorrel and seasonings. Puree in a blender, pass through a sieve, and place in a plastic squeeze bottle. Store in the refrigerator until needed.

To make the shallot sauce, place the wine and shallots in a saucepan and bring to a boil over medium-high heat. Reduce by half (this will take about 5 minutes), add the cream and seasonings, and continue cooking over low heat, stirring frequently with a wire whisk, until the sauce has

reduced to 1½ cups (this will take about 15 minutes). Strain through a sieve and set aside.

While the sauce is reducing, steam the salmon for 5 to 7 minutes, until it is firm to the touch but remains slightly rare. This can be done in a bamboo steamer on a wok, or on a rack in a large pot.

To serve, spoon the sauce into the middle of each warmed plate, tilting the plate to coat it evenly to the rim of the dish. Paint 5 lines of red and 5 lines of green sauce alternately onto the shallot sauce, stopping about two-thirds of the way down the plate.

With the top of a knife, draw perpendicular lines about ½ inch apart through the colored lines, as if feathering the top of a napoleon.

Place a salmon steak in the unpainted third of each plate and serve immediately.

Note: Everything up to the steaming of the salmon can be done up to 2 days in advance. Allow the paints to reach room temperature, and reheat the shallot sauce in the top of a double boiler. If sorrel puree is not available, sauté fresh sorrel leaves in a little butter; it will become a thick mixture and can then be pureed in a blender. ■

The sauce for this sautéed fish dish is an interesting variation on the classic beurre blanc, *given added richness and texture from nuts and some sparkle from cilantro.*

Speckled Trout with Cashews, Cilantro, and Lime-Butter Sauce

Jeffrey's, Austin, Texas

(Serves 4)

Four 7-ounce speckled trout fillets (see note)
Salt and freshly ground pepper
½ cup unbleached all-purpose flour
6 tablespoons clarified butter
2 to 3 limes
1 cup chicken stock
1 cup chopped cashews
8 tablespoons unsalted butter, cut into small pieces and softened
¼ cup chopped cilantro leaves
Red and green Thai chilies for decoration (optional)

Remove any skin and small bones from the fillets. Sprinkle the fillets with salt and pepper and dust lightly with flour, shaking to remove any excess.

Heat the clarified butter in a sauté pan or skillet, and add 2 fish fillets. Cook for 3 to 5 minutes, depending on the thickness of the fillets, then turn the fish gently with a slotted spatula. Cook an additional 2 to 3 minutes, remove from the pan, and drain on paper towels. Repeat with the remaining fillets, and keep the fillets warm in a 150° oven.

Pour the grease from the pan and add the juice of the limes and the chicken stock. Reduce over high heat by three-fourths, then add the cashews and turn off the heat. Beat in the unsalted butter, bit by bit, then add the cilantro. Adjust seasoning and pour the sauce over the fish.

Garnish with chilies, if desired.

Note: Other fish that can be used are swordfish, tuna, flounder, redfish, and red snapper. ∎

The rich tuna, the delicate turbot, the salty olives, and the smoky sauce make this dish a panoply of flavors and textures that excite the eye as well as the palate.

Turbot and Tuna with Crustades of Black Olives and Smoked Tomato–Butter Sauce

Gardens, Los Angeles, California

(Serves 4)

1 pound fresh tuna
¼ cup mixed fresh herbs (some combination of thyme, parsley, oregano)
2 teaspoons minced garlic
½ teaspoon crushed black pepper
2 tablespoons extra-virgin olive oil
1½ pounds fresh turbot (halibut can be substituted)
4 Italian parsley leaves

Sauce

4 large ripe tomatoes
½ cup chopped shallots
1¼ cups (2½ sticks) unsalted butter
2 cups fume blanc, or other dry white wine
2 cups fish stock
¼ cup heavy cream
2 thyme sprigs, or ½ teaspoon dried thyme
Salt, black pepper, and cayenne to taste

Olive crustades

4 rectangular *brioches* or egg bread rolls, 4 by 2 by 2 inches
20 pearl onions
¼ pound bacon slices, cut into lardons
¼ cup oil-cured olives
¼ cup niçoise olives
¼ cup Calamata olives
4 tablespoons butter, melted

Garnish

1 tablespoon unsalted butter
8 flowering purple kale leaves

Cut the tuna into 4 equal squares. Mix the herbs with the garlic, pepper, and olive oil and rub over all sides of the tuna. Allow to marinate in the refrigerator.

Divide the turbot into 4 portions and press a leaf of Italian parsley into each. Place in the refrigerator.

To make the sauce, in a smoker or covered charcoal grill, smoke the tomatoes over low heat for about 20 minutes. Seed and chop them, and set aside.

Sauté ¼ cup of the shallots in a few tablespoons of butter until soft. Deglaze with the wine and reduce to 1½ cups over high heat. Add the fish stock and reduce to 1 cup.

In another pan, sauté the remaining shallots in 2 tablespoons of the butter and cook until soft. Add the chopped smoked tomatoes and cook for 5 minutes over medium heat. Add the wine reduction and the heavy cream and reduce to 1 cup with the thyme. Whirl in the remaining butter, bit by bit, and season with salt, black pepper, and cayenne. Set aside and keep warm or pour into a thermos bottle if not to be served immediately.

To make the garnish, cut the 4 *brioches* into boxes, scooping out the center. Peel the pearl onions by blanching them in boiling water for 5 minutes, then draining and slipping off the skins; set aside. Blanch the bacon in boiling water for 3 minutes, drain, and rinse in cold water. Pit all the olives.

Preheat the oven to 350°. Brush the surfaces of the *crustades* with butter and brown in the oven for 5 minutes, or until nicely brown. Sauté the bacon in a sauté pan or skillet until crisp, remove with a slotted spoon, and brown the onions in the fat. Add the olives to warm, return the bacon to the pan, and set aside.

Sear the tuna in a sauté pan or skillet on all sides, keeping the center rare. Steam the turbot, sprinkled with salt and pepper, in a bamboo steamer

*Turbot and Tuna with Crustades of Black Olives and Smoked Tomato—Butter Sauce,
Gardens, Los Angeles, California*

for 3 to 5 minutes. Heat the butter in a wok and stir-fry the purple kale on high heat until just limp.

To assemble the dish, fill each *brioche* box with one-fourth of the olive mixture and place next to a few kale leaves on a plate. Slice the tuna pieces in half, exposing the raw

center, and place a portion of turbot next to it. Nap the sauce around the fish and sprinkle with fresh thyme leaves.

Note: The *brioche* boxes, the sauce, and the sauté of the onions and olives can be done a few hours in advance. ■

LYDIA SHIRE
Gardens, Beverly Hills, California

Chefs have traditionally created from culinary memories, and since Lydia Shire, chef at Gardens in the newly constructed Four Seasons Hotel in Beverly Hills, has been trekking to exotic places for the past few years, she has expanded the number of spices and foods she uses.

Shire was experimenting with foreign cuisines while still at Seasons, the restaurant in Boston where she established her national reputation. "I wouldn't have been tempted by anything except this job at the Four Seasons," she says. "I can't think of another woman who has had the opportunity to open a luxury hotel."

A preference for hotel kitchens has been a theme of Shire's career. While she credits Jacky Robert, the former chef at Maison Robert in Boston and her first boss, with being the most influential force on her cooking, she followed up her time there and at the Harvest Restaurant in Cambridge with a series of hotel jobs. The first one was at the Copley Plaza in Boston, which was considered the best hotel dining room in the city under her supervision. She then worked at the venerable Parker House, where she collaborated with her friend Jasper White and then, in 1981, became chef.

Seasons, the restaurant where she was executive chef for three years, is where Shire hit her culinary stride. While updating classic New England dishes, she began drawing from the ethnic pantries of Bostonians; she used Thai spices with lobster and flavored a clam and oyster bisque with curry.

The menu at Gardens reflects a United Nations of cultural influences. Her trip to China intensified Shire's use of Oriental ingredients, and while the Four Seasons was under construction she traveled to India, Spain, and Morocco. "All the cooks in Morocco were women, and while we could never say a word to one another, I so enjoyed my day watching them in the kitchen. I pitch in when I observe, and while I'm doing what I know how to do, I'm looking at the different techniques used in an ethnic group's cooking."

The combination of colors and flavors is tantalizing, and the dish is easy to do. In place of live lobsters, lobster tails or shrimp could be substituted.

Warm Lobster Tacos with Yellow Tomato Salsa and Jícama Salad

The Mansion on Turtle Creek, Dallas, Texas

(*Serves 6 as an appetizer, 4 as an entree*)

Lobster

Court bouillon or salted water
Four live 1-pound lobsters

Yellow tomato salsa

2 pints yellow cherry tomatoes (red can be substituted)
1 shallot, finely chopped
1 garlic clove, finely minced
2 tablespoons white wine vinegar
2 *serrano* chilies, seeded and finely minced
2 tablespoons fresh lime juice
Salt to taste
1 tablespoon maple syrup (optional)

Jícama salad

1 small *jícama*
1 small red bell pepper
1 small yellow bell pepper
1 carrot
1 small zucchini
6 tablespoons peanut oil
3 tablespoons fresh lime juice
Salt and cayenne to taste

To finish the dish

3 tablespoons oil
4 to 6 flour tortillas
1 cup grated *jalapeño* jack cheese
1 cup shredded spinach leaves

Bring the court bouillon or salted water to a boil in a large stockpot. Add the lobsters, cover the pot, and bring the liquid back to a boil over high heat. When it returns to a boil, cook the lobsters for 7 minutes. Remove from the water and, when cool enough to handle, remove all the meat from the lobster, cutting the tail sections into medallions and the claw meat into large dice. Set aside.

To make the yellow tomato *salsa*, grind the yellow tomatoes in a meat grinder, or chop finely in a blender or a food processor fitted with a steel blade. Mix all the ingredients except the maple syrup into the tomatoes, then add syrup if mixture needs a little sweetening. Allow to sit in the refrigerator for at least 2 hours before serving, to blend the flavors.

To make the *jícama* salad, cut the *jícama*, peppers, and carrot into fine julienne. Peel the zucchini and cut the peel into fine julienne, reserving the flesh for another use. Mix the oil, lime juice, salt, and cayenne and toss with the salad. Refrigerate until ready to serve.

Preheat the oven to 350°. To finish the dish, place the tortillas, wrapped in aluminum foil, in the oven to heat for 10 minutes, or until hot. Heat the oil in a small skillet and briefly sauté the lobster meat to heat it, about 3 minutes over medium heat.

Spoon lobster meat into the middle of a heated tortilla. Portion the cheese and spinach on top and wrap tightly into a cylinder shape. Repeat to make 4 to 6 tacos.

Place each tortilla on a warm plate, with the yellow tomato *salsa* and *jícama* salad on the sides.

Note: The lobsters can be boiled and the relishes can be made up to a day in advance and kept refrigerated. ∎

Warm Lobster Tacos with Yellow Tomato Salsa and Jícama Salad. The Mansion on Turtle Creek, Dallas, Texas

DEAN FEARING

The Mansion on Turtle Creek, Dallas, Texas

Dean Fearing, the executive chef of the elegant Mansion on Turtle Creek, dreads that his tombstone will read "The Man Who First Breaded Fish with Macadamia Nuts." Although only thirty-three years old, Fearing has been a force on the dining scene of Dallas for more than five years, and has developed a list of signature dishes that have been widely copied across the Southwest.

The Ashland, Kentucky, native is a 1978 graduate of the Culinary Institute of America. One of the earliest influences on his professional development was Harvey Colgin, who had apprenticed with Escoffier and, after retiring as executive chef for Hilton Hotels in the Pacific, had moved to Louisville, where Fearing worked for him. "He really opened my eyes to the subtleties of food, and he pushed me to go to the Institute," says Fearing.

After graduation, Fearing worked at the famed Maisonette in Cincinnati, where chef George Haidon practiced classic French technique.

He moved to Dallas in 1979 and, after a few months at the Fairmont Hotel, was hired as part of the original kitchen staff when The Mansion was first opened as a restaurant.

Tom Agnew was a captain, and he wooed chef Fearing to Agnew's, which opened to five-star reviews and was featured as the highlight of dining in Dallas in a story Craig Claiborne wrote for the *New York Times*. "It was the first time a Dallas restaurant called itself American, and it was all American kids running the place," says Fearing. "The food was not as complicated as what I am doing today, but we got the basics going with the use of *jicama*, roasted and smoked peppers, and fried pastas, one of the things I contributed."

After Agnew's closed, Fearing worked as chef at the Verandah Club at the Anatole Hotel, then came back to The Mansion two years ago as executive chef. "This is the first time I have a job where I can spend most of my time creating dishes, rather than cooking on the line," he says.

Don't be alarmed by the length of this recipe. None of the steps are difficult, and the length is due to the interesting mix of ingredients—the road that leads to an interesting mix of flavors.

Grilled Lobster Tails Stuffed with Deviled Shrimp in Brown Sauce with Tamarind and Smoked Crab

Tila's, Houston, Texas

(Serves 4 as an appetizer, 2 as an entree)

Seafood

Four 3-ounce fresh lobster tails, shelled and sliced (reserve shells)
½ pound shrimp, peeled and deveined
¼ cup chicken stock
Juice of ½ lime
2 tablespoons chopped fresh chervil
2 tablespoons olive oil
Kosher salt and white pepper to taste

Vegetables

⅓ pound lean bacon, chopped
¾ cup fresh bread cubes
1 teaspoon chopped fresh chervil, or ¼ teaspoon dried chervil
1 teaspoon chopped fresh cilantro
1 teaspoon chopped fresh applemint (or any kind of fresh mint)
¼ teaspoon freshly ground black pepper
4 tablespoons unsalted butter
1 *jalapeño* chili, seeded, deribbed, and finely chopped
1 *poblano* chili, seeded, deribbed, and cut into fine julienne
½ red bell pepper, seeded, deribbed, and cut into fine julienne
1 ear fresh corn, kernels cut from the cob
4 mushrooms, cleaned and sliced
1 garlic clove, minced
1 green onion, sliced
1 tablespoon grated fresh ginger
2 tablespoons soy sauce
¼ cup dark rum
¼ cup dry sherry
½ cup chicken stock
¼ cup light cream (half and half)
3 tablespoons sour cream
¼ cup papaya juice
Juice of 1 lime
3 tablespoons flour
Salt and black pepper to taste

4 tablespoons freshly grated
   Parmesan cheese
½ cup grated Muenster cheese
Lime juice, salt, cayenne, and white
   pepper to taste
Spicy Brown Sauce with Tamarind
   and Smoked Crab, following

Garnish

Chervil sprigs and lemon twists

Light a smoker, or a charcoal fire on
one side of a covered grill. Soak a
combination of pecan, hickory, and
mesquite wood chips in water for 15
minutes. Lightly oil a wok and add
the all the seafood ingredients. Place
the wood chips on the hot coals and
place the wok away from the coals, so
the seafood gets intense smoke
without being directly over the heat.
Cover and smoke the seafood for 10
minutes, then remove from the
smoker or grill and set aside.

Sauté the bacon in a sauté pan or
skillet until crisp, remove from the
pan with a slotted spoon, and set
aside on paper towels. Pour out most
of the bacon grease and sauté the
bread cubes with the chervil, cilantro,
applemint, and black pepper until the
cubes are toasted and dark brown.
Remove from pan, drain on paper
towels, and set aside.

Melt 2 tablespoons of the butter in
a sauté pan or skillet and, when hot,
sauté the vegetables with the garlic,
green onion, and ginger over medium-
high heat for 3 minutes, or until they
are cooked but still slightly crisp.
Deglaze the pan with the soy sauce,
rum, and sherry, boiling for 2 minutes
to cook off the alcohol, then add the
chicken stock and boil 3 minutes.
Add the light cream, sour cream,
papaya juice, and lime juice and stir.

Mix the remaining 2 tablespoons
of butter with the flour and add to
the pan, stirring to incorporate.
Simmer for 3 minutes to thicken. Add
the bacon and shellfish to the pan and
stir together. Simmer for 3 minutes
over low heat, season to taste, and
then remove from the heat and pour it
into a shallow bowl. Chill the
mixture for 15 minutes in the refrigerator, covered with plastic wrap.

Add the bread cubes and cheeses
to the stuffing. Season with lime juice,
salt, cayenne, and white pepper.
Divide the stuffing among the
reserved lobster shells. Grill for 4 or 5
minutes, until the lobster shells are
pink and the stuffing is hot.

To serve, place a bed of crab sauce
on a plate with a lobster tail and
garnish with chervil and a lemon
twist.

Note: Up to the point of grilling,
the stuffed lobster tails can be done a
day in advance, and the sauce can
also be made up to a day in advance.
Let the lobster tails sit at room
temperature for 1 hour before
grilling. ■

*Grilled Lobster Tails Stuffed with Deviled
Shrimp in Brown Sauce with Tamarind and
Smoked Crab, Tila's, Houston, Texas*

Spicy Brown Sauce with Tamarind and Smoked Crab

Smoked crab

½ pound fresh cooked crab meat
1 tablespoon olive oil
Juice of 1 lime
¼ teaspoon chopped fresh tarragon
   or basil
1 teaspoon freshly ground black
   pepper

Sauce

4 tablespoons unsalted butter
1 small *poblano* chili, seeded,
   deribbed, and cut into fine julienne
1 green onion, chopped
2 mushrooms, cleaned and sliced
1 ear fresh corn, kernels cut from the
   cob
2 tablespoons rice wine vinegar
½ cup chicken stock
1 cup *demi-glace*, page 19
1 tablespoon tamarind paste
   (available at Asian groceries)
½ cup light cream (half and half)
½ cup heavy cream
Salt and freshly ground white pepper
   to taste

To prepare the smoked crab, mix the
crab meat with the other ingredients
in a lightly oiled wok. Follow the
procedure for the lobster and shrimp
in the recipe above.

To make the sauce, melt the butter
in a saucepan, and when hot add the
poblano and sauté for 1 minute over
high heat. Add the remaining
vegetables and sauté until the
mushrooms are slightly soft, about 3
minutes. Deglaze with the vinegar
and stock and cook 30 seconds. Add
the brown sauce and bring to a boil,
then lower the heat and simmer for 3
minutes.

Puree the tamarind paste with the
creams in a blender or a food
processor fitted with a steel blade.
Add this mixture to the sauce and
fold in the crab. Simmer until the
sauce is thick enough to coat the back
of a spoon, then season with salt and
white pepper. ■

MALTE BREITLOW

The White Dove, Tucson, Arizona

C hef Malte Breitlow has always worked where others played. Born in the Black Forest region of Germany, known for its resorts, he moved to Arizona in 1962, and has centered his career around vacation areas.

"Where I grew up in Baden-Baden most people went into the tourist trade in some way, and the pace of hotels in these areas is far more relaxed and the people are much happier than in major cities where the primary customer is the business traveler," he says.

The forty-three-year-old chef trained at some of the finest hotels in his native region, including the Kurhaus, where he cooked for then Chancellor Konrad Adenauer and other dignitaries.

When he decided to move to the United States, he selected a dozen small cities and sent off letters. The first one to offer him a job was the Arizona Biltmore in Phoenix, where he started as a line cook and departed fifteen years later as the executive sous chef of the venerable resort, known for the Continental cuisine of its L'Orangerie restaurant.

During the summers, when the heat keeps most tourists away from the Arizona sun, Chef Breitlow moved from the elegance of the Biltmore to the rustic setting of a mountain camp in Wyoming's Grand Teton Mountains. The food he created there was heartier than at the Biltmore, and he could use the skills he had acquired in Germany to present buffets.

In 1982 he became executive chef at the Sheraton Conquistador resort in Tucson, and began integrating the ingredients of the Southwest into his classical approach to cooking.

"I read a lot of Indian and Mexican cookbooks, and started slowly to add some of those influences into my food. But people needed to have some reference points, so I began by smoking prime rib with mesquite and using cilantro as a seasoning for the *béarnaise* to top a filet mignon instead of tarragon," he says.

He now makes fruit tarts using the native prickly pears, and likes to create other desserts using pistachio nuts that are grown within a few miles of the hotel.

This dish is a refinement of the enchilada, using thin crepes and a seafood filling. It could be a brunch or luncheon dish as well as an appetizer.

Crepes Carmen

The White Dove, Tucson, Arizona

(Serves 6 as an appetizer, 3 as an entree)

Crepes

1 cup milk
1 cup water
4 eggs
½ teaspoon salt
2 cups unbleached all-purpose flour
4 tablespoons unsalted butter, melted
Oil for cooking crepes

Sauce and filling

2 tomatoes, peeled, seeded, and diced
1 large onion, peeled and diced
2 mild green chilies, such as *poblano* or Anaheim, seeded and diced
2 teaspoons sugar
½ teaspoon salt
½ cup dry white wine
½ cup sour cream
½ pound cooked fresh crab meat, well picked over
½ pound cooked shrimp, peeled, deveined, and diced
½ cup grated Monterey jack cheese
½ cup grated mild Cheddar cheese

Garnish (optional)

Diced tomato
Diced green bell pepper

To make the crepes, place all the ingredients except the oil in a blender jar and blend for 10 seconds. Scrape down the sides of the jar to dislodge any clinging bits of flour and blend again for 3 seconds. Allow the batter to sit in the refrigerator for at least 2 hours.

To cook the crepes, heat a crepe pan or skillet over high heat. Brush it with oil, and when the oil begins to smoke, pour ¼ cup of batter into the center of the pan. Immediately rotate it so the batter spreads to the sides of the pan, and pour out any extra. Cook for 45 seconds, then turn the crepe and cook the other side for 30 seconds more. Repeat with the remaining batter, stacking cooked crepes between sheets of waxed paper and brushing the pan with oil before cooking each crepe. You should have at least 12 crepes; any extras can be frozen.

To make the sauce, puree the tomatoes, onion, and chilies in a blender or a food processor fitted with a steel blade. Pour into a saucepan and add the sugar, salt, and white wine. Bring to a simmer and reduce over low heat, stirring occasionally, until thick, about 30 minutes. Add the sour cream and heat, but do not boil. Stir in the crab meat and shrimp, and adjust the seasoning.

Place 2 crepes on top of each other and put a few tablespoons of filling in the center. Roll and place in a baking pan. Repeat to make 6 double crepes. Top with the remaining sauce and sprinkle with the cheeses. Brown under a preheated broiler and serve. Garnish with diced tomato and green pepper, if desired.

Note: This dish can be prepared up to 2 days in advance and refrigerated. Prior to serving, heat covered in a 300° oven for 25 minutes, then brown under the broiler. ■

Crepes Carmen, The White Dove, Tucson, Arizona

The flavors in this dish are fresh and light, and it is a fast appetizer or entree to prepare. The tomatoes remain cold and crisp, and the spicy shrimp are a foil to their taste and texture. Serve with warm flour tortillas.

Spicy Blue Cornmeal Gulf Shrimp with Cold Marinated Tomatoes

Tila's, Houston, Texas

(Serves 4 as an appetizer, 2 as an entree)

Tomatoes

4 large ripe tomatoes, peeled, seeded, and diced
½ cup rice wine vinegar or distilled white vinegar
1 teaspoon brown sugar
1 green onion, chopped
1 teaspoon cracked black pepper
½ teaspoon celery salt
¼ teaspoon ground allspice
1 teaspoon Dijon mustard
½ cup olive oil

Shrimp

½ cup blue cornmeal (yellow can be substituted)
1 teaspoon cayenne
1 teaspoon Cavender's Greek seasoning or salt
2 tablespoons chopped fresh basil, or ½ teaspoon dried basil
1 pound large fresh Gulf shrimp, peeled and deveined
Flour for dredging
3 tablespoons unsalted butter
1 tablespoon grated buffalo milk mozzarella
1 tablespoon grated Parmesan
2 tablespoons grated Bel Paese
1 tablespoon grated fontina
Garnish: Chopped fresh parsley
To serve: Warm flour tortillas

Place the tomatoes in a shallow dish. Mix all the marinade ingredients except the olive oil, then slowly whisk in the olive oil. Pour the dressing over the tomatoes and allow them to marinate at room temperature for 30 minutes.

To prepare the shrimp, mix the cornmeal with the cayenne, Cavender's or salt, and basil. Dredge the shrimp in flour, then dip them in water and roll them in the spiced cornmeal. Heat the butter in a sauté pan or skillet and, when hot, add the shrimp, cooking them until golden brown. Remove from the pan and drain on paper towels.

Remove the tomatoes from the marinade with a slotted spoon and press gently on them to remove excess marinade. Place the tomatoes in ovenproof gratin dishes and divide the shrimp among them. Toss with the tomatoes.

Preheat a broiler. Combine the cheeses in a small bowl and sprinkle over the shrimp and tomatoes. Broil for 30 seconds, or until the cheeses are just melted. Garnish with chopped parsley and serve with flour tortillas.

Note: The prepping of ingredients can be done ahead; however, do not marinate the tomatoes for more than 30 minutes or the flavor will become too strong. ■

The coulis, *a pureed vegetable sauce frequently used in French cooking, is really a cooked salsa in this dish. The spices in the sauce are complemented by the creamy cheese filling, and the dish is so elegant it belies how quick and easy it is to prepare.*

Prawns Stuffed with Goat Cheese on Tomato Coulis

Cafe Terra Cotta, Tucson, Arizona

(Serves 4)

Prawns

1 pound large prawns or shrimp
¼ pound goat cheese
¼ pound natural cream cheese
1 garlic clove, peeled and minced
2 tablespoons minced fresh cilantro
2 teaspoons heavy cream
Salt and pepper to taste

Coulis

1 tablespoon olive oil
4 large tomatoes, peeled, seeded, and roughly chopped
2 tablespoons minced fresh cilantro
1 tablespoon minced seeded *jalapeño* or *serrano* chili
Juice of 1 lime
Salt and pepper to taste

Preheat oven to 350°.

Remove the shells from the prawns, leaving the tails attached. Devein the prawns and then butterfly them by slicing down the curve, but not cutting them all the way through. Flatten slightly.

Mix the goat cheese, cream cheese, garlic, cilantro, cream, and salt and pepper together. Set aside.

To make the *coulis*, heat the olive oil in a sauté pan or skillet over medium heat and cook the tomatoes, covered, for 5 minutes. Add the cilantro and chili, raise the heat to medium high, and cook uncovered until all the moisture has evaporated, stirring frequently. Add the lime juice and salt and pepper to taste and keep the *coulis* warm while finishing the prawns.

Place the prawns in the oven for 3 minutes. Remove them and raise the oven to 400°. Using a pastry bag, pipe the cheese mixture into the back of the prawns and bake an additional 3 minutes.

Prawns Stuffed with Goat Cheese on Tomato Coulis, Cafe Terra Cotta, Tucson, Arizona

To serve, spoon the *coulis* onto warmed plates and arrange the prawns on top. ∎

This rich and spicy sauté is versatile as well as delicious. It could be served for dinner, complemented by saffron rice and a green salad. The bite of green peppercorns and heady taste of Pernod balance the richness of the cream sauce.

Shrimp San Pedro

The White Dove, Tucson, Arizona

(Serves 6 as an appetizer, 3 as an entree)

18 large shrimp
3 tablespoons olive oil
3 tablespoons green peppercorns packed in brine, drained and rinsed
½ cup chopped green onions, white part only
1 large shallot, peeled and chopped (3 tablespoons chopped red onion could be substituted)
½ cup Pernod
1 cup heavy cream
½ cup sour cream
Salt and pepper to taste

Garnish (optional)

Pink peppercorns
Herb flowers

Peel and devein the shrimp, leaving the tails on. Butterfly them by cutting down the curved ridge but not all the way through the shrimp. Flatten them slightly between 2 sheets of waxed paper, and set aside.

Heat the oil in a sauté pan or skillet over medium-high heat. Add the shrimp and sauté 1 minute. Stir in the peppercorns and add the green onions and shallot, sautéing 1 minute more. Add the Pernod and reduce by half over high heat.

Remove the shrimp from the pan with a slotted spoon. Stir the cream and sour cream into the sauce and reduce over medium-high heat until thick enough to coat the back of a spoon, about 7 minutes. Return the shrimp to the pan, season with salt and pepper to taste, and serve immediately. Garnish with a sprinkling of pink peppercorns and an herb flower, if desired. ∎

MOLLY MCCALL
The White Dove, Tucson, Arizona

E ven in high school, Molly McCall, now chef at The White Dove in Tucson, derived pleasure from cooking. She cooked and hosted multi-course dinner parties for her friends, inventing such dishes as vegetable enchiladas served with different cheese sauces.

"My grandmother was a great from-scratch cook," says the thirty-one-year-old native of Boise, Idaho, "and I used to serve at their parties. I started cooking for my family when I was only ten years old, and used to experiment to try and make a dish and then try to improve on the recipe."

After two years of studying business at Boise State University and the University of Idaho, she lived in Spain for a year. After returning, she did not continue with her business studies, but moved to the West Coast to begin a culinary arts program at Spokane Community College.

"What was nice about being in a small city was that I could start out as a line cook. I didn't get stuck in the pantry the way they usually start women in professional kitchens," she says.

After a few years, she landed a job at the Sheraton Hotel in Seattle, and entered a training program where she worked in each food-related area for a few months.

In 1986, she was transferred to the Sheraton Conquistador, and has begun assimilating desert foods into her dishes for The White Dove. "The availability of fresh produce is so different; in Seattle I could get anything, and loved using edible flowers in my salads. Here, I'm learning to work with what the land can produce," she says.

MEAT AND GAME DISHES

Beef is a key factor in the economy of the Southwest as well as in the diet of the people. In Texas, cattle was king until the discovery of "black gold" on the fields, and many of the large ranchers amassed fortunes in the nineteenth century.

During the past decade, however, game has become another meat option besides the traditional beef, veal, and lamb. Selling game bagged while hunting is illegal, and venison had practically disappeared from modern restaurant menus until the development of commercial game ranches. The Y.O. Ranch in Mountain Home, Texas, and other game ranches now market venison through the Texas Wild Game Cooperative (see Mail Order Sources), and chefs have eagerly grasped the opportunity to purchase deer meat.

Despite its richer flavor, venison is far lower in calories and cholesterol than beef, since the animals are well exercised. The Sika deer are small, however, so it is as tender as veal.

Other meats gaining popularity with chefs are pork and rabbit, both of which played an important part in American regional cuisines, but were not considered "restaurant food" until elevated by the new American cuisine. Now pork, especially the very lean pork, is being prepared in such innovative ways as Pork Tenderloin with Date and Fig Chutney and Barbecued Pork with Tequila Pepper Relish. And you will find in this chapter a pair of very innovative rabbit recipes.

Enchiladas of Filet Mignon with Chanterelles and Sorrel Sauce, Saint Estèphe, Manhattan Beach, California

Exotic presentation is one of the hallmarks of John Sedlar's style, but "branding" the tortillas for this elegant and delicious dish is a simple trick to re-create.

Enchiladas of Filet Mignon with Chanterelles and Sorrel Sauce

Saint Estèphe, Manhattan Beach, California

(Serves 6)

Sorrel sauce

1 tablespoon unsalted butter
2 medium shallots, coarsely chopped
6 sorrel bunches, washed, stemmed, and coarsely chopped
½ teaspoon salt
½ teaspoon ground white pepper
1½ cups veal stock (or ¾ cup each chicken and beef broth)

Enchiladas

1 cup vegetable oil for deep-frying
12 yellow corn tortillas
Twelve 3-ounce filet mignons
1 teaspoon salt
1 teaspoon ground black pepper
2 tablespoons vegetable oil
2 tablespoons unsalted butter
1 pound chanterelle mushrooms, washed and cut into ¼-inch slices (*shiitakes* can be substituted)

To make the sorrel sauce, melt the butter in a medium saucepan over medium heat. Add the shallots and sauté them until just tender, about 2 minutes. Add the sorrel and sauté until the leaves wilt, about 3 minutes. Transfer the mixture to a blender or a food processor fitted with a steel blade and puree. Add the salt, pepper, and veal stock and puree further. Strain through a sieve and set aside.

Heat the bottom 4 inches of a metal skewer over an open flame or under a broiler until red hot. Heat the oil in a skillet to a temperature of 275°. Fry the tortillas, one at a time, holding them flat in the oil with tongs, for 10 seconds each, or until just tender. Pat dry on paper towels and continue until all the tortillas are fried.

Stack 6 tortillas and keep them warm in an oven on low heat. Using the hot skewer, make a decorative

pattern of lines and arrows on the remaining 6 tortillas, reheating the skewer as necessary.

Light a charcoal or gas grill or preheat a broiler; season the filets with a little of the salt and pepper and brush with oil. Grill or broil them 3 inches from the source of the heat, 3 minutes per side for medium-rare.

While the filets are grilling, heat the butter in a skillet over medium heat. Add the chanterelles, sprinkle with the remaining salt and pepper, and sauté about 2 minutes. Set aside.

To serve, place a plain tortilla in the center of each warmed plate and spoon the sauce on top of the tortilla, with some extending out the bottom edge. Place 2 filets on top of each tortilla and scatter the mushrooms on top. Top each with a "branded" tortilla and serve immediately.

Note: If using canned broth instead of fresh unsalted veal stock, do not add salt and pepper to the sauce until it is completed. The sauce can be made up to 2 days in advance and kept covered in the refrigerator. Reheat it slowly. ■

This is a wonderful winter supper, with a subtle spiciness balancing the heartiness of the chili. It is also a great way to use up leftover prime rib or steak, since it stretches the meat a long way.

Black Bean Chili with Sirloin and Asiago

Cafe Terra Cotta, Tucson, Arizona

(Serves 8)

1 pound dried black beans
1 tablespoon ground cumin
½ teaspoon cayenne
2 teaspoons paprika
1 tablespoon dried oregano
1 dried *pasilla* chili (*ancho* or New Mexican red can be substituted)
1 bay leaf
1 tablespoon oil
1 yellow onion, peeled and chopped
4 garlic cloves, peeled and minced
1 green bell pepper, seeded, deribbed, and finely chopped
4 large tomatoes, cored and roughly chopped
Salt and pepper to taste

3 *jalapeño* chilies, seeded, deribbed, and finely chopped
½ cup cilantro leaves
1 pound grilled sirloin steak, cut into ½-inch cubes
6 tablespoons grated Asiago cheese (fontina can be substituted)

Pour the beans into a colander and rinse under running water, sorting through them to remove any small stones. Either soak the beans in water to cover overnight, or bring them to a boil in water to cover, boil 2 minutes, and then turn off the heat, cover the pot, and allow them to soak for 1 hour. If using the latter method, the cooking should continue promptly.

Heat a dry skillet over medium heat and toast the cumin, cayenne, paprika, and oregano until they start to become fragrant. Be careful not to let them burn.

Grind the *pasilla* chili and bay leaf to a fine powder in a clean coffee or spice grinder or in a blender. Set aside.

Heat the oil in a saucepan and sauté the onion, garlic, and green pepper over medium heat until they are soft and translucent, about 5 minutes. Add the toasted spices, ground spices, tomatoes, and a sprinkling of salt and pepper, and sauté for 15 minutes, stirring occasionally.

Add the vegetable mixture to the beans, along with water to cover by 4 inches. Cook on top of the stove, covered, for 1½ to 2 hours, or until the beans are tender. Adjust seasoning, and add the chopped cilantro and the *jalapeños*, along with the cubes of sirloin, and simmer for 10 minutes.

Serve in bowls with a sprinkling of cheese on each. ■

Hill Country Mixed Grill, Austin's Courtyard, Austin, Texas

½ cup dry red wine
1 tablespoon finely chopped shallots
3 tablespoons canned lingonberries, drained
Salt and pepper to taste

Juniper berry sauce

4 tablespoons juniper berries
2 cups game stock, above
1 cup heavy cream
½ cup dry red wine
1 tablespoon finely chopped shallots
2 tablespoons chopped fresh basil
Salt and pepper to taste

To finish the dish

Salt and pepper to taste
6 tablespoons unsalted butter
4 bacon slices

Garnish

Sautéed carrots
Blanched and sautéed brussels sprouts
Jalapeño Spaetzle, page 139

In all mixed grills, the diversity of ingredients leads to a long list, and this one using Texas game is no exception. The different sauces are perfectly matched to the foods they nap, and most of the work can be done in advance.

Hill Country Mixed Grill

Austin's Courtyard, Austin, Texas

(Serves 4)

Meats

2 pheasants
4 quail
8 venison slices (about 1 ounce each)
4 rabbit tenderloins
8 wild boar slices, cut from the tender part of the leg

Game stock

Bones from quail
Back legs and bones from pheasants
Trimmings from venison, rabbit, and wild boar
2 carrots, cleaned and sliced
2 celery stalks, cleaned and sliced
2 onions, sliced
3 garlic cloves, peeled
3 thyme sprigs, or 1 teaspoon dried thyme
1 cup dry red wine
20 quarts water

Quail stuffing

4 tablespoons unsalted butter
⅓ cup finely chopped celery
4 tablespoons finely chopped shallots
4 *shiitake* mushrooms, cleaned and diced
4 oyster mushrooms, cleaned and diced
4 button mushrooms, cleaned and diced
4 rabbit or chicken livers, finely diced
¾ cup dry red wine
1½ cups crumbled corn bread
2 tablespoons chopped fresh basil
Salt and freshly ground black pepper to taste

Three-mushroom sauce

8 *shiitake* mushrooms, cleaned and diced
8 oyster mushrooms, cleaned and diced
8 *morels*, cleaned and sliced lengthwise
4 tablespoons finely minced shallots
6 tablespoons unsalted butter
½ cup dry red wine
2 cups game stock, above
1 cup heavy cream
Salt and pepper to taste

Lingonberry sauce

2 cups game stock, above

Begin one day before serving by trimming the meats and making the stock needed for the sauces. Bone off the pheasant breasts and set aside. Chop the carcass and hindquarters. Remove the breastbones from the quail by pulling them out with your fingers. Reserve the quail and chop the bones. Remove all fat, silver skin, and gristle from the other meats, carve the meat into serving slices, and set aside.

Preheat the oven to 450°. Place all the bones, trimmings, and stock vegetables and herb in a roasting pan and roast for 1½ hours, stirring occasionally. Deglaze with the wine, then pour the contents from the roasting pan into a very large stockpot. Add the water and bring to a boil. Simmer for 8 to 10 hours to reduce, strain, and refrigerate. Discard the fat layer that will rise to the surface. Simmer for another 4 or 5 hours.

To make the quail stuffing, heat the butter in a sauté pan or skillet over medium-high heat. Add the celery and shallots and sauté for 2 minutes, then add the mushrooms and sauté until cooked, about 5 minutes. Add the chopped livers and sauté for 2 minutes, until they are firm but still rare. Deglaze with the red wine, simmering briefly to cook off the alcohol, then remove from the heat. Add the corn bread crumbs and basil, and season with salt and pepper to taste.

Stuff the quail, securing them closed with toothpicks.

To make the mushroom sauce, sauté the mushrooms and shallots in butter for 5 minutes over medium heat. Add the red wine, stock, and cream, and reduce until the mixture has a syrupy consistency and coats the back of a spoon. Season with salt and pepper and set aside.

To make the lingonberry sauce, place the stock, wine, shallots, and berries in a saucepan and reduce by half. Season with salt and pepper.

To make the juniper berry sauce, crush the berries and place them in a saucepan with all the ingredients except the basil, salt, and pepper. Cook over low heat to reduce by half, then strain out the berries, add the basil, and adjust seasoning.

To finish the dish, preheat the oven to 450°. Salt and pepper the quail and brush with melted butter. Place in the preheated oven for 15 to 20 minutes. Salt and pepper the pheasant breasts and sauté in 1 tablespoon of the butter on the skin side for 2 minutes on high heat. Then wrap with bacon and place in the oven with the quail for a 12-minute cooking time.

Season the rabbit with salt and pepper and sauté for 7 minutes in a few tablespoons of butter, turning occasionally.

Heat the remaining butter in a sauté pan or skillet over high heat. Season the venison and boar with salt and pepper and sauté for just 30 seconds on a side.

To serve, cut the quail in half and arrange the meats on a plate with the lingonberry sauce over the pheasant and rabbit, the juniper berry sauce on the quail, and the mushroom sauce on the venison and boar. Serve with Jalapeño Spaetzle and vegetables.

Note: Everything up to the cooking of the meats can be done up to 2 days in advance. Do not stuff the quail until ready to cook, and reheat the sauces slowly. ∎

GERT RAUSCH
and Bernd Voll
Austin's Courtyard, Austin, Texas

Sometimes an intangible, such as the spirit of a city and its people, can lure a chef. That has been the case with Gert Rausch and Austin, Texas. The German-born forty-year-old chef arrived in the region in 1973, and decided to make it his home.

"Texans are different than other Americans; they are more flamboyant and they view life for living today. They still have a frontier spirit, and I find it makes me feel more alive," he says.

Rausch opened Austin's Courtyard in 1979. The restaurant is housed in what was a store, and rather than dividing the cavernous windowless space into small dining rooms, he painted the ceiling black and created an atmosphere of dining in an outdoor courtyard of fountains.

The chef had intended to become a hotel manager, but then became hooked on cooking. "My mother was a very good cook, and my uncle owned a fine restaurant in Munich. I used to love to watch the cooks in his kitchen when we would visit, but after a disappointing apprenticeship, I decided to become a hotel manager. Somewhere along the way I got sidetracked and have been cooking happily ever since," he says.

He was an assistant chef in a number of hotels in Switzerland, Germany, France, and Italy, including the famed George V in Paris, before moving to North America to become a saucier at the Queen Elizabeth Hotel in Montreal. The hotel, run by Hilton, sent chef Rausch to consult at the Waldorf Astoria in New York, also one of their facilities, and he determined that the United States was where he wanted to live.

His career brought him to Austin in 1973, to work as executive chef at the Lakeway Resort. "When I first came here nothing fresh was available. The advances in Texas in the past six years have been incredible," he says. "There is so much wild game now, and very good quality fish from the Gulf."

Some of that game is featured in his Hill Country Mixed Grill, an assortment of species both furred and feathered, with complementary sauces. He makes his own venison sausage, served with spicy lentils, and features a number of lamb dishes on the menu.

LOUIS AARON

Sam Houston's, Kerrville, Texas

When people visit Kerrville, they come expecting hearty ranch-style food and game. Chef Louis Aaron, who runs Sam Houston's, a stately room with red flocked wallpaper and brass chandeliers in the Y.O. Hilton Hotel, fulfills those wishes with innovative dishes utilizing the venison and antelope raised on the famous game ranch.

The twenty-five-year-old chef, who was born in Idaho and raised in Alabama, arrived in Kerrville in June 1986 to consult for the hotel and decided not to leave. "I was working in Boise, where it was Continental cuisine all the way, and I really like the country foods you can find around here—ribs, chicken-fried steak, and beans. The first few weeks I was here I just watched the Mexican cooks in the kitchen, since I knew nothing about that style of cooking," he says. "The people are so nice, and the area is involved with so much of the history of Texas, that I decided to stay."

The hotel is owned by the Schreiner family, and was built primarily to house visitors and cattlemen to the Y.O. Ranch in Mountain Home, about forty miles away. The ranch began more than a decade ago when Charles Schreiner amassed a fortune after a drive of 300,000 head of longhorns to Dodge City, Kansas. At one time the ranch was 550,000 acres; the family now retains fifty thousand acres, and sharing the land with the longhorns are Axis and Sika deer, wild boar, Black Buck antelope, and even ostriches.

Many of these species end up in chef Aaron's kitchen. He makes a Wild Game Pâté using a combination of meats but utilizing classic French spicing and cooking techniques. And for venison medallions, he advocates a quick sauté of the tender meat rather than a long marinating process.

Since guests do expect game meals, regardless of the season, he also makes venison sausage, venison chili, and a venison hash for cold mornings.

Pairing venison and other wild game with a fruit sauce is a European tradition, and the treatment works as well with domestic game. The tenderloins are one part of a deer that does not need marinating since they are so tender.

Medallions of Sika Deer

Sam Houston's, Kerrville, Texas

(Serves 4)

Eight 3-ounce medallions of Sika or Axis deer (2 tenderloins cut into ½-inch slices)
⅓ cup olive oil
Salt and pepper to taste
Flour for dredging
½ pound chanterelle mushrooms, cleaned and cut into ½-inch slices (other wild mushrooms such as *shiitakes* can be substituted)
6 thyme sprigs, or 1 teaspoon dried thyme
Pinch of freshly ground black pepper
½ cup port, warmed
1 tablespoon canned lingonberries, drained
1½ cups heavy cream
1 cup game stock made from bones of deer (see page 19), or reduced beef stock
1 carrot, peeled and sliced into thin julienne strips
20 snow peas
¼ cup dry white wine
1 cup cooked white rice
Watercress sprigs

Trim the tenderloins of any fat and silver skin and slice into 3-ounce medallions. Press the medallions flat with the bottom of a skillet or the palm of your hand.

Season the medallions with salt and pepper and dredge in flour, shaking off any excess. Pour ¼ cup of the olive oil in a sauté pan or skillet, heat the oil over medium-high heat, and add the medallions. Sauté for about 4 minutes per side, until medium rare. After turning the medallions to the second side, add the wild mushrooms and sauté.

Remove the meat from the pan and add the thyme and pepper. Flambé with the port, putting out the flames with a pot cover, then add the lingonberries, cream, and stock to the pan. Reduce over high heat by half.

While the sauce is reducing, heat the remaining oil in a small sauté pan or skillet and, when hot, add the carrot and snow peas. Sauté, stirring frequently, for 3 minutes. Add the wine and reduce until it has almost evaporated. Season with salt and pepper to taste and set aside.

To serve, place 2 medallions on each of 4 plates with some sauce spooned over them. Place some rice and some of the vegetable mixture on either side and a sprig of fresh watercress across the medallions. ∎

The fresh herbs added to the sauce at the last minute give this dish a crispness that reinforces the taste from the marinade. This is an elegant and easy company dinner.

Roasted Free-Range Veal Rack with Fresh Herbs and Natural Juices

Grand Champions Club,
Aspen, Colorado

(Serves 6)

1 whole rack of veal (7 chops)
¼ cup each chopped fresh oregano, thyme, tarragon, rosemary, and chervil (thyme is necessary, but different herbs may be substituted for the other 3)
1¼ cups olive oil
2 garlic cloves, peeled and chopped
7 tablespoons unsalted butter
Salt and black pepper to taste
Garnish of baby vegetables: ¾ pound each carrots, yellow beets, zucchini, *haricots verts*, and artichokes, cleaned and trimmed as appropriate
2 cups reserved veal stock

To prepare the veal, trim away the bones encasing the eye of the veal rack and scrape the meat from the ends of the rib bones. Reserve the bones and trimmings and roast, along with the vegetables, to make veal stock (see page 18). Using cotton string, tie the rack between the bones

Medallions of Sika Deer, Sam Houston's, Kerrville, Texas

to keep the meat in a cylindrical shape, and tie the roast together.

Chop all the herbs and mix half of the mixture with 1 cup of the olive oil and the garlic. Rub the mixture over all surfaces of the veal and marinate at room temperature for 2 hours, or in the refrigerator, covered with plastic wrap, overnight.

Preheat the oven to 400°. Heat the remaining olive oil and 2 tablespoons of the butter in a roasting pan large enough to hold the veal, and when it is hot and the butter foam has started to subside, sear the veal and brown it on all sides.

Sprinkle the veal with salt and pepper. Roast the veal for 35 to 45 minutes, turning it over once halfway through the roasting.

While the veal is roasting, blanch the vegetables in separate batches until they are cooked but still remain slightly crisp. Toss with 3 tablespoons of the butter and keep warm.

Remove the veal to a heated platter and allow it to rest for 10 minutes. Pour off the grease and deglaze the pan with the veal stock, boiling until reduced by half. Add the remaining fresh herbs, season with salt and pepper to taste, and whisk in the remaining 2 tablespoons of butter.

To serve, carve the rack into chops and place on a bed of the sauce. Garnish with a sprinkling of the vegetables and pass extra sauce separately.

Note: You can blanch the vegetables a day in advance and reheat them in the hot butter. ∎

The complex flavor of chef Mark Miller's blend of spices penetrates into each slice of meat. The rice forms a perfect, slightly sweet balance to the savory meat.

Leg of Lamb Marinated with Mexican Spices, Served with a Smoked Chili Sauce and Sweet Cinnamon Rice

Coyote Cafe, Santa Fe, New Mexico

(Serves 8 to 10)

1 whole leg of lamb (approximately 6½ pounds)
1½ tablespoons cumin seeds
3 tablespoons black peppercorns
3 tablespoons dried oregano leaves
3 tablespoons dried thyme leaves
½ teaspoon sea salt
3 to 4 dried or canned *chipotle* chilies
3 tablespoons olive oil
8 to 10 prickly pear cactus pads for garnish (optional)
Salt and pepper to taste
6 cups reserved lamb stock
Mexican Sweet Cinnamon Rice, page 141

Preheat the oven to 325°.

Trim the fell and fat from the leg of lamb and remove the hip bone with a boning knife. Re-form the lamb and tie tightly with kitchen string. Make a stock with the bones and trimmings (see page 21) and set the lamb aside, covered with plastic wrap.

In a small skillet, sauté the cumin seeds, peppercorns, oregano, and thyme over medium heat to release their flavors. Stir frequently, and remove when they turn brown and start to smoke. Add salt and one broken *chipotle* chili, and grind the mixture into a fine powder in a clean coffee grinder or by hand in a mortar.

Rub the lamb with olive oil and then with the spice mixture. Place on a rack in a shallow roasting pan and roast for about 1 hour and 15

minutes, or until the meat reaches an internal temperature of 120°. Raise the heat to 450° to brown the exterior for 5 to 10 minutes, or until the lamb has a temperature of 130°. Remove from the oven and let rest for 15 minutes before carving to allow the meat juices to be reabsorbed.

While the lamb is roasting, wash the prickly pear cactus pads in cold water, brush with olive oil, and sprinkle with salt and pepper. Grill over a low charcoal fire or under a broiler for about 5 minutes per side, or until tender. Remove any thorns.

To make the sauce, pour the fat from the roasting pan and add the lamb stock and remaining broken peppers. Reduce over high heat, stirring occasionally, until the stock is reduced by two-thirds. Adjust seasoning. Carve the lamb and serve on a platter with the rice; garnish the platter with cactus leaves and spoon the sauce over the meat.

Note: The lamb can marinate overnight in the refrigerator, covered with plastic wrap. It is important to let it sit at room temperature for 4 hours before cooking. ∎

Leg of Lamb Marinated with Mexican Spices, Served with a Smoked Chili Sauce and Sweet Cinnamon Rice, Coyote Cafe, Santa Fe, New Mexico

Turnips are one of those often forgotten vegetables; however, their delicate flavor and pale color make a delicious sauce and garnish for tender lamb loins. This is an easy recipe that can be made in less than an hour.

Lamb Loin with Turnip Sauce

Jeffrey's, Austin, Texas

(Serves 4)

8 small turnips
3 cups chicken stock
2 whole lamb loins (about 1½ pounds), created by taking the eye out of 2 racks of lamb
4 tablespoons clarified butter
1 cup *demi-glace* (see page 19)
Salt and pepper to taste

Peel the turnips. Cut 4 into 1-inch dice and cut the remaining 4 in half. Place the turnips in a saucepan with 2 cups of the chicken stock (or salted water can be substituted), and add water to cover the vegetables. Cover the saucepan, bring to a boil, and simmer until the cubed turnips are tender but not mushy, about 20 to 30 minutes. Remove the halved turnips with a slotted spoon and puree the diced turnips with their cooking liquid. Set aside.

Preheat the oven to 450°. Trim the lamb loins to remove all silver skin and cut into four serving pieces.

Melt the butter in a skillet over medium-high heat, and when it is hot, sear the lamb on all sides to brown it. Add the halved turnips to the pan and place it in the oven for 15 minutes, or until the lamb is medium rare and the turnips are lightly browned.

Remove the meat and turnips and keep warm. Pour the grease from the pan and add the remaining chicken stock. Reduce by half, add the *demi-glace*, and reduce by half again.

Add 1½ cups of the turnip puree to the pan and simmer gently for 5 minutes. Season with salt and pepper to taste.

To serve, slice lamb across the grain into medallions, spoon the sauce over them, and garnish each plate with 2 turnip halves. ∎

MARK MILLER
Coyote Cafe, Santa Fe, New Mexico

The food prepared by chef Mark Miller is the closest a diner could come to edible anthropology. Miller, a thirty-eight-year-old Boston native who moved to the Bay Area in 1967 to study at Berkeley, became intrigued with the civilizations of Mexico and Latin America, and soon was exploring the culinary side of his academic field.

This interest in non-European flavors and dishes became part of his philosophy as chef at Berkeley's famed Fourth Street Grill, where he was also one of the pioneers of California cuisine and mesquite grilling. And it is the foundation for the foods he is cooking at Coyote Cafe, where his dishes reflect the elements of New Mexican society: Indian, Spanish, and Anglo traditions.

"What I am doing is an extension and expansion of the ethnic influences of the cooking at Fourth Street. I am incorporating the traditions and histories of the other parts of the Americas that have a rich cultural tradition. Santa Fe is a primary place for me to be since it is the center of Southwest culture in the United States, and I am able to create a cuisine from the natural environment," he says.

He uses New Mexican beef and lamb, which he says have a stronger and more gamey flavor than those meats from other states, and has been experimenting with the wild herbs found in the hills. Many of his dishes feature piñon nuts, important to the Indian culture, and he has been working with local farmers to grow wild mushrooms and other crops for the restaurant.

His first job was as chef at Chez Panisse in Berkeley. He stayed there for three years, until opening Fourth Street Grill in 1979, and learned about the nature and importance of quality ingredients from Alice Waters and from Richard Olney, whom he visited in France.

While the region under examination has changed with his food at Coyote Cafe, the assertiveness of the spicing level has not. Rather than being interested in pastel nuances of European cooking, chef Miller's food is as bold and strong as the colors of New Mexico.

This is one of the best brunch or light supper dishes I've ever tasted, because it has such a variety of flavors and textures. Curry and fruit are a natural combination, and the pancakes have a rich pecan flavor.

Curried Lamb Sausage with Compote and Pecan Pancakes

The Rattlesnake Club, Denver, Colorado

(Serves 4)

Sausage

¾ pound lamb, trimmed of excess fat and cut into 1-inch cubes
¼ pound kidney suet or fat, diced
1 red onion, peeled and diced
1¼ teaspoons salt
¾ teaspoon ground black pepper
3 tablespoons curry powder, or to taste
2 egg yolks

Fruit compote

1½ cups freshly squeezed orange juice
1½ cups passion fruit juice
1 tablespoon sugar
1 papaya, peeled, seeded, and sliced into ⅛-inch slices
2 pears, peeled, cored, sliced ¼ inch thick, and tossed with lemon juice to prevent discoloration
2 teaspoons finely grated orange zest

Pancakes

2 cups peeled and coarsely grated potato
2 cups pecan pieces
1 cup diced red onion
4 eggs, beaten
1 tablespoon baking powder
1 tablespoon cornstarch
½ cup unbleached all-purpose flour
½ teaspoon salt
1 teaspoon ground white pepper
4 tablespoons unsalted butter
Herb sprigs for garnish

To make the sausage, grind the lamb, fat, and onion through the medium blade of a meat grinder. Add the salt, pepper, curry, and egg yolks and mix with your hands until well blended. Grind a second time; the texture should be pliable and not gummy. This can also be done in a food processor fitted with a steel blade

using short on and off spurts; do not puree the meats.

Form into 8 patties and refrigerate until set, covered with plastic wrap (this will take at least 2 hours).

To make the compote, combine the juices, sugar, and fruit in a stainless steel or enamel saucepan. Bring to a simmer over medium-high heat and cook until the fruit is just tender, about 10 minutes. Remove the fruit with a slotted spoon, increase the heat to high, and reduce until the mixture has thickened to coat the back of a spoon, about 10 minutes. Add the fruit and orange zest and set aside at room temperature.

Place the potatoes in a large strainer and wash under cold running water 3 times to remove the starch, stopping to press out any liquid. Dry the potatoes on paper towels and transfer to a medium bowl. Add the pecans, onion, and eggs. Mix in the baking powder, cornstarch, flour, and salt and pepper, adding additional flour if the mixture seems too loose.

Heat a heavy skillet over medium-high heat and cook the sausages until browned, about 5 minutes. Turn them over and cook the other side. Remove with a slotted spatula, drain on paper towels, and keep warm.

Heat the butter in another large skillet over medium-high heat. Spoon the potato batter into 4 large pancakes, smoothing until thin. Cook about 3 minutes, turn with a spatula, and cook an additional moment.

Reheat the compote, if needed. To serve, place the pancakes in the center of each of 4 serving plates and spoon the compote over. Arrange 2 sausages on top, and garnish with fresh herb sprigs.

Note: The sausage and compote can be done a day in advance; however, the pancake batter should not be done more than a few hours in advance, and the pancakes should be fried at the last minute. ∎

Curried Lamb Sausage with Compote and Pecan Pancakes, The Rattlesnake Club, Denver, Colorado

Anne Greer created this fresh-tasting combination to show the versatility of her basic pesto sauce, which can also serve as a basting sauce for any grilled meat or poultry as an alternative to heavier barbecue sauces. Serve this with the jícama salad accompanying the Warm Lobster Tacos, page 109.

Mixed Grill with Cilantro Pesto Sauce

Anne Lindsay Greer, Dallas, Texas

(Serves 6 as an appetizer, 4 as an entree)

12 large sea scallops
½ pound pork tenderloin, cut into 1-inch cubes
½ pound beef tenderloin or boneless sirloin, cut into 1-inch cubes
Freshly squeezed lime juice
Salt and freshly ground black pepper to taste

Basting sauce

2 garlic cloves
2 *serrano* chilies
1½ cups cilantro leaves
2 tablespoons oil
2 tablespoons melted butter
½ cup chicken stock
Salt and pepper to taste

Light a charcoal or gas grill or preheat an oven broiler, and soak 4 or 6 wooden skewers in water for 15 minutes. Thread the scallops, pork, and beef alternately onto the skewers, squeeze with lime juice, and sprinkle with salt and pepper. Set aside.

In a blender or a food processor fitted with a steel blade, puree the garlic, chilies, cilantro, oil, butter, and stock. Add salt and pepper to taste.

Coat the skewers with the basting sauce, place on the grill or under the broiler, and cook for a total of 6 minutes, basting and turning frequently. Be careful not to overcook. Serve immediately.

Note: The skewers can be assembled up to a day in advance and kept, tightly covered with plastic wrap, in the refrigerator, and the

basting sauce can also be made at that time. Let the skewers sit at room temperature 1 hour before cooking, and do not cook until immediately before serving. ∎

This dish gives new meaning to the term sweet and sour. The tangy apple chutney is a wonderful complement to the succulent pork stuffed with spicy sausage. Use any leftover sausage for breakfast, fried as patties and served with eggs.

Pork Tenderloin Stuffed with Chorizo

Hudsons' on the Bend, Austin, Texas

(Serves 4)

2 pounds pork tenderloin

Apple chutney

1¾ cups diced apple (peaches or pears can be substituted)
¼ cup white wine vinegar
½ cup raisins
½ cup brown sugar
½ cup granulated sugar
1 teaspoon mustard seeds
1 tablespoon finely chopped seeded *serrano* chili
1 tablespoon minced garlic
Juice and zest of ½ lemon

Chorizo

1 pound ground pork
Reserved scraps from trimming tenderloins
2 tablespoons oil
2 tablespoons red wine vinegar
½ teaspoon dried oregano
½ teaspoon dried basil
¼ teaspoon dried thyme
¼ teaspoon ground cloves
Pinch of ground nutmeg
1 tablespoon chili powder
½ teaspoon ground black pepper
1 teaspoon salt
¼ teaspoon ground cumin
1 teaspoon finely diced seeded *serrano* chili
¼ cup water
½ cup finely diced carrot
½ cup finely diced celery
¼ cup finely diced onion

To finish the dish

2 tablespoons clarified butter
Salt and pepper to taste

Trim the fat and silver skin from the pork tenderloins and cut them into 4 serving pieces; set aside.

To make the chutney, combine all the ingredients in an enameled or stainless steel pan and bring to a boil over medium heat. Reduce the heat to low and simmer uncovered, stirring frequently, for 45 minutes to 1 hour. Chill.

To make the chorizo, heat the oil in a sauté pan or skillet over medium-high heat. Add the ground pork and trimmings and sauté until the pork turns brown, breaking up any lumps. Add the vinegar, spices, chili, and water, and cook over low heat for 30 minutes, stirring frequently. Add the carrot, celery, and onion and cook 15 minutes. Strain the fat and allow the sausage to cool.

Preheat the oven to 400°. Using a sharp knife, cut a hole through the center of each piece of tenderloin to create a pocket and expand the width of the pocket using your fingers or the handle of a wooden spoon. Stuff the tenderloins with the cooled sausage, then skewer or sew the ends closed loosely.

Heat the butter in a sauté pan or skillet over high heat, and when it is hot, sear the tenderloins on all sides. Sprinkle with salt and pepper and place in the preheated oven. Bake for 10 to 12 minutes, then allow to rest for 5 minutes before slicing. Slice into medallions, being careful not to press on the uncut portion or the stuffing will come out. Serve immediately with the apple chutney.

Note: The chutney can be made up to a week in advance and kept refrigerated, and the chorizo can be made up to 2 days in advance and refrigerated. Allow it to reach room temperature before stuffing the tenderloins. ∎

The fruity sweet and sour chutney is a perfect foil for the pork, and the same treatment also works well with boned and skinned chicken breasts.

Pork Tenderloin with Date and Fig Chutney and Vegetable Sauté

Wine Connoisseur, Houston, Texas

(Serves 6)

2 pounds pork tenderloin (either 1 large or 2 smaller tenderloins)
4 tablespoons clarified butter
Salt and pepper to taste
1 cup cider vinegar
½ cup brown sugar
10 fresh or dried dates, halved and pitted
6 large fresh figs, quartered or sliced if large (or substitute 12 dried figs, soaked in hot water for 30 minutes)

Vegetable sauté

1 yellow bell pepper
1 red bell pepper
1 green bell pepper
½ pound mushrooms
2 tablespoons clarified butter
½ pound thin asparagus spears, blanched and cut into 2-inch sections
2 tablespoons chopped fresh purple or green basil

Additional fresh fig slices for garnish

Preheat the oven to 425°. Trim the fat and silver skin off the pork tenderloin. Tuck the tail under so that the roast is a uniform thickness, and tie with string.

Heat the clarified butter in a sauté pan or skillet over high heat and, when hot, sear the tenderloins on all sides. Season with salt and pepper and transfer to an ovenproof baking dish. Place the dish in the preheated oven and roast the smaller tenderloins for 10 minutes and the larger tenderloin for 20 minutes. Remove from the oven and keep warm.

Pour the extra grease out of the searing pan and deglaze the pan with the vinegar. Slowly add the brown sugar, stirring to dissolve well, then add the dates and figs. Simmer slowly for 4 minutes, stirring frequently but gently, and set aside.

To make the vegetable sauté, seed and derib the peppers and cut them into fine julienne. Wash and slice the mushrooms. Heat the butter in a sauté pan or skillet and add the vegetables, sautéing over medium heat until they are cooked but still retain some crispness. Add the blanched asparagus and the basil and season with salt and pepper.

To serve, slice the pork and arrange on a bed of the chutney. Garnish with additional slices of fresh fig, and serve the vegetables on a separate plate.

Note: The chutney can be made up to 4 days in advance. Reheat it in the pan in which the pork is served and roasted, after pouring off the fat. ■

Pork Tenderloin with Date and Fig Chutney and Vegetable Sauté, Wine Connoisseur, Houston, Texas

Corn Ravioli and Cinnamon-Flavored Chorizo with a Sauce of Texas Goat Cheese and Ancho Chili, Coyote Cafe, Santa Fe, New Mexico

With its spicy filling, delicate corn pasta, and creamy sauce, this dish will wow guests. If you've ever made ravioli, the recipe will be a new twist on an old procedure, and if you've not tried it before, this recipe is the time to start, since you cannot buy the pasta dough.

Corn Ravioli and Cinnamon-Flavored Chorizo with a Sauce of Texas Goat Cheese and Ancho Chili

Coyote Cafe, Santa Fe, New Mexico

(Serves 6)

Chorizo

½ pound lean pork, cut into ¾-inch cubes
¼ pound lean beef, cut into ¾-inch cubes
2 tablespoons olive oil
1 small garlic clove, peeled and minced

2 tablespoons ground *ancho* or New Mexican chili (or substitute commercial chili powder and delete ground cumin from recipe)
⅛ teaspoon ground *arbol* chili or cayenne
Pinch of ground cloves
¼ teaspoon freshly ground black pepper
½ teaspoon ground cinnamon
½ teaspoon ground cumin
1 teaspoon sea salt (or ½ teaspoon table salt)
2 to 3 cups water

Pasta

½ to ⅔ cup finely ground corn flour (not cornmeal), or ½ cup *masa harina*
1 cup unbleached all-purpose flour
Pinch of salt
2 large eggs
2 teaspoons olive oil
2 teaspoons water
Semolina

Sauce

1½ cups heavy cream
3 ounces fresh goat cheese
2 tablespoons unsalted butter

Chili puree

16 dried *ancho* chilies

Finely chop the meats in separate batches in a meat grinder or a food processor fitted with a steel blade. This can be done more easily if the cubes of meat are chilled for 30 minutes in the freezer. Use an on and off pulsing motion so the meats will be finely chopped but not puréed.

Heat the oil in a sauté pan or skillet over medium heat and add the chopped meats. Break up the mixture with a wooden spoon, but do not allow the meats to brown. Add the garlic, dried spices, and salt and stir well. Then add 1 cup of the water and bring to a simmer.

Simmer gently over very low heat for 1½ to 2 hours, adding more water as needed. At the end of the cooking time, the mixture should not be wet, and it should be simmering in its own fat. Scrape the mixture into a blender or a food processor and puree to make a smooth paste; it should yield 1¾ cups. Set aside to cool.

While the chorizo mixture is simmering, make the pasta. Combine the corn flour and flour on a board with a pinch of salt, mix well, and make a well in the center. Break the eggs into the well, add the olive oil and water, and incorporate the dry ingredients using a fork. When the dough is thick and sticky, knead for a few minutes, then cover with plastic wrap and allow to rest in the refrigerator for at least 15 minutes before rolling. Divide the dough into 4 parts and roll each through a pasta machine, ending with the lowest setting. Once the pasta sheets have been rolled through the pasta machine, dust them with semolina so they will not stick together.

Place a few teaspoons of the filling in dabs 1 inch apart on 2 sheets of the pasta. Moisten the dough with water and place the second sheet on top of the filling. Seal well by pressing down between the ravioli, then use a crinkle cutter to cut them out.

To make the sauce, place the cream in a small saucepan and bring it to a boil. Lower the heat and reduce for 5 minutes, then add the goat cheese in small lumps and remove from heat. Whisk the sauce until smooth, then add the butter, bit by bit. Keep warm until ready to use.

To make the garnish, scrub the chilies under running water and place in a saucepan with water to cover. Bring to a boil and simmer until they are tender, about 20 minutes. Remove the chilies with a slotted spoon, reserving the liquid, and puree in a blender or a food processor fitted with a steel blade. Add about ¼ cup of the cooking liquid to make a smooth paste.

To serve, bring a large quantity of salted water to a boil and add the ravioli. Cook 1½ to 2 minutes, or until the ravioli float to the surface, then drain well. Spoon some of the sauce onto a plate, arrange the ravioli on top, and garnish with the chili puree.

Note: The ravioli can be prepared up to a day in advance and kept refrigerated before cooking. The sauce should be reheated slowly in the top of a double boiler if prepared in advance, and the chili puree will last up to a week tightly covered in the refrigerator. ∎

While the dish is stellar, I find myself using the barbecue sauce on almost everything I grill or broil. The citrus adds a fresh note to the taste, and the relish is also good with other foods.

Barbecued Pork with Tequila-Chili Relish

Gordon's, Aspen, Colorado

(Serves 6)

Six 7- to 8-ounce pork tenderloins

Barbecue sauce

¼ cup olive oil
1 medium onion, peeled and sliced
1 whole garlic bulb, cut in half across the cloves
1 red bell pepper, seeded, deribbed, and diced
1 tequila sunrise chili, seeded and diced (2 small *serranos* or *jalapeños* can be substituted)
1 *jalapeño* chili, seeded and diced
2 tablespoons mixed whole peppercorns (black, green, white, and pink)
1 tablespoon whole coriander seeds
1 bay leaf
6 to 8 ripe tomatoes (depending on size), diced
½ bunch parsley, chopped
½ lemon, chopped
½ lime, chopped
½ orange, chopped
1 cup cabernet, or other dry red wine
½ cup red wine vinegar
1 bunch basil
1 bunch thyme
1 bunch marjoram
1 bunch cilantro
1 cup molasses

Pepper relish

Kernels cut from 2 ears fresh corn
1 red bell pepper, seeded, deribbed, and finely chopped
1 yellow bell pepper, seeded, deribbed, and finely chopped
2 tequila sunrise chilies, seeded, deribbed, and finely chopped
1 tablespoon finely minced shallots
1 tablespoon finely minced garlic
⅓ cup olive oil
Salt and pepper to taste
Pinch of ground coriander
1 tablespoon tequila
1 tablespoon Grand Marnier
Juice of ¼ lime
Juice of ¼ orange
1 tablespoon champagne vinegar
2 tablespoons *demi-glace*, page 19 (optional)
2 each cilantro, marjoram, basil, and thyme sprigs, chopped

Garnish

2 cups shredded lettuces (a mixture of endive, *radicchio*, and bibb)
1 cup cooked black beans
3 blue corn tortillas, cut into thin strips and crisply fried
Edible flower blossoms such as nasturtium, rose petals, sunflowers

Trim the pork tenderloins of any fat and silver skin. Cut each into 2-inch sections and place them between 2 sheets of plastic wrap. Pound with the flat side of a cleaver or with the bottom of a heavy pan until the *paillards* are ½ inch thick. Cover with plastic wrap and refrigerate until needed.

To make the sauce, heat the olive oil in a heavy saucepan over medium-high heat. Add the onion, garlic, and peppers and chilies and sauté, stirring frequently, until the peppers are soft and the onions are translucent. Add the peppercorns, coriander, bay leaf, tomatoes, parsley, lemon, lime, and orange and stir to combine. Cook over medium heat for 20 minutes, or until the fruit is soft, stirring frequently. Add the cabernet and vinegar and raise the heat to high, cooking until the liquid is reduced by half. Add the fresh herbs and cook for 5 minutes, then add the molasses and continue to cook, stirring frequently, for an additional few minutes.

Puree the sauce in small batches in a blender or a food processor fitted with a steel blade and strain. Cool to room temperature, then add the pork *paillards* and refrigerate until needed, at least 2 hours or overnight.

To make the relish, sauté the corn, minced peppers and chilies, shallots, and garlic in the olive oil over medium heat for 5 minutes, stirring frequently. Season with salt, pepper, and coriander. Remove from the heat and deglaze with tequila and Grand Marnier. Add the fruit juices and vinegar and stir in the *demi-glace*, if used. Stir in the fresh herbs and keep warm.

Light a charcoal grill. Remove the *paillards* from the marinade and place over hot coals. Cook only long enough for the marinade to brown and caramelize, about 2 minutes on a side.

To serve, cover warm plates with the shredded lettuces. Place grilled *paillards* down the center of each plate, overlapping each other slightly. Add the sautéed pepper relish around the *paillards* and decorate the plate with the tortilla strips and a "confetti" of flower petals. ∎

Barbecued Pork with Tequila-Chili Relish, Gordon's, Aspen, Colorado

The delicacy of rabbit is complemented beautifully by the sweet-hot sauce. The red chili jelly is an excellent condiment for any simple grilled or roasted meat, or as an hors d'oeuvre on crackers with cheese.

Roast Texas Rabbit with Red Chili Jelly

Brennan's, Houston, Texas

(Serves 4)

Rabbit stock

Two 2¾-pound fresh whole rabbits
1 carrot, sliced
1 medium onion, sliced
1½ celery stalks, sliced
3 black peppercorns
6 cups chicken stock

Red chili jelly

3 red bell peppers, seeded and diced
6 *jalapeño* chilies, seeded and diced
½ cup white wine vinegar
2 cups sugar
1 package Certo brand pectin

To finish the dish

2 tablespoons oil
½ cup chicken stock
3 fresh basil sprigs
1½ cups rabbit stock
4 tablespoons pine nuts
1 tablespoon clarified butter
6 tablespoons red chili jelly
1 tablespoon unsalted butter, softened
Salt and cracked black pepper to taste

Preheat the oven to 450°. Remove the hindquarters from the rabbits and bone out the upper leg. Remove the loins, and trim to remove all fat and silver skin. Set the meat aside. Break up the bones and place in a roasting pan with the vegetables. Brown in the oven for 30 minutes, turning occasionally, then deglaze the pan with some of the chicken stock and pour all contents into a stockpot. Add the remaining stock, bring to a boil over medium heat, lower the heat to a simmer, and simmer the stock for 4 hours, skimming as necessary. Strain the stock and refrigerate, discarding the fat layer that will form on the surface as it chills.

To make the red chili jelly, puree the peppers and chilies in a blender or a food processor with a steel blade.

Heat a saucepan over medium heat, and, when hot, add the pepper puree, vinegar, and sugar. Boil for 10 minutes, then add the pectin and return to a boil for 1 minute. Remove from the heat, cool to room temperature, and refrigerate.

To finish the dish, preheat the oven to 450°. Heat the oil in a large skillet. Season the rabbit meat with salt and pepper and sear the rabbit on both sides. Add the chicken stock and place in oven. Remove the loins after 2 minutes, return the pan to the oven, and bake the remaining rabbit 6 minutes more. The meat should still be slightly pink.

While the dish is cooking, prepare the sauce by infusing the basil in the reduced rabbit stock for 5 minutes; remove and discard. Toast the pine nuts in the clarified butter and add them to the stock, along with the red chili jelly. Bring to a simmer, take off the heat, and whip in the butter. Season with salt and pepper.

To serve, slice the loin meat into diagonal medallions and arrange with a hindquarter. Nap with the hot sauce.

Note: The stock and sauce can be prepared up to 2 days in advance and reheated. The red chili jelly will keep for 2 months in the refrigerator. The only part of the dish that must be done at the last minute is the cooking of the rabbit. ∎

Roast Texas Rabbit with Red Chili Jelly, Brennan's, Houston, Texas

The delicate flavor of rabbit is finally gaining in popularity, and this is one of the most delicious ways to prepare it. The apple cider imparts a fruity taste, and the mustard seed adds some spice.

Rabbit with Apple Cider and Mustard Seeds

Cafe Lilli, Lake Tahoe, Nevada

(Serves 2)

One 1¾- to 2-pound fresh rabbit

Marinade

2 cups buttermilk
½ cup hard (alcoholic) apple cider
Pinch of cracked black pepper

Rabbit glaze

Reserved rabbit carcass and
 trimmings
2 leeks, white part only, washed and
 chopped

Turnovers

1 apple such as Jonathan or Pippin,
 peeled, cored, and cut into small
 dice
¾ cup hard (alcoholic) apple cider
1½ teaspoons unsalted butter
Two 4-inch puff pastry circles, ¼ inch
 thick
1 egg white, at room temperature

Rabbit sauce

3 tablespoons clarified unsalted
 butter
Reserved marinated rabbit
Salt and pepper to taste
2 shallots
¼ cup hard (alcoholic) cider
½ to 1 cup rabbit glaze, above
½ cup heavy cream
¾ teaspoon mustard seeds
1 tablespoon butter

Greens

1 to 2 bunches mustard greens,
 washed and stemmed
2 teaspoons unsalted butter
Pinch of salt and white pepper

Bone the rabbit by slicing the front and hind legs off and removing the fillets from both sides, reserving the carcass and all the trimmings for the stock. Trim the side flaps off the fillets and pull off the silver skin. Cut the fillets into sections and sever the second leg bones from the thigh bones. Remove the meat from the thigh bones and leave the bones in the legs.

Mix the marinade ingredients and add the rabbit pieces. Marinate at room temperature for 3 hours or overnight in the refrigerator, covered with plastic wrap.

To make the glaze, chop the carcass and trimmings and brown in a 500° oven. Place in a stockpot and add water to cover. Bring to a boil and skim to remove the scum that rises to the surface. Add the chopped leeks and simmer over low heat for 2 to 3 hours. Strain and reduce 2 cups of stock to make ½ to 1 cup of glaze; set aside.

To prepare the turnovers, simmer the apple in the cider, partially covered, over medium heat until the apple is tender and the liquid has almost evaporated. Remove the apple chunks to a small bowl and toss with the butter. Allow to cool to room temperature.

Place the cooled apple on one side of the puff pastry circles and brush the edges with egg white. Press together to seal and make decorative slits with a sharp knife in the top.

Chill the turnovers in the freezer for 30 minutes. Preheat the oven to 450°. Sprinkle the baking sheet with water and bake the turnovers for 8 to 10 minutes, or until golden brown.

To prepare the rabbit sauce, heat the clarified butter in a sauté pan or skillet. Remove the rabbit from the marinade and pat dry. Sprinkle with salt and pepper. Place the portions with bones in the pan first and the fillets last, giving more cooking time to the larger pieces. Use tongs to turn the rabbit and cook until medium rare.

Remove the rabbit pieces and pour the grease out of the pan. Add the shallots and sauté lightly and then deglaze with the cider. Add the rabbit glaze, cream, and mustard seeds and reduce slightly. Whisk in the butter, add the rabbit and any juices that have accumulated, and set aside to keep warm.

Prepare the greens by cutting them into ¹⁄₁₆-inch slices. Blanch in boiling salted water and remove immediately. Drain, pressing out any water, and toss with the butter, salt, and pepper.

To serve, reheat the rabbit if necessary, and arrange on plates with a turnover and some greens.

Note: The rabbit does not suffer from reheating, so that part of the dish can be done up to 2 days in advance. The turnovers can be kept in the freezer until just before baking; however, the greens should be done at the last minute. ∎

The texture and flavor of roasted apples are the perfect complement to delicate rabbit livers, and raspberry vinegar adds a complex, almost sweet and sour flavor to this dish.

Rabbit Livers with Roasted Apples

Jeffrey's, Austin, Texas

(Serves 4)

2 Granny Smith apples, peeled, cut in
 half, and cored
1 cup port
½ cup raspberry vinegar
½ cup Calvados, or apple brandy
10 tablespoons butter
4 rabbit livers (see note)
Salt and pepper to taste
Flour for dredging
8 tablespoons clarified butter
1⅓ cups *demi-glace* (see page 19)

Preheat the oven to 350°. Place the apples cut side down in a baking pan, and pour half the port, raspberry vinegar, and Calvados over them. Dot the pan with 4 tablespoons of the butter and bake the apples uncovered, basting frequently with the pan juices, for 20 minutes, or until they can easily be pierced with the point of a knife but are still slightly firm. Remove and keep warm.

Season the rabbit livers with salt and pepper and dredge with flour, shaking them in a sieve to remove any excess. Heat the clarified butter in a sauté pan or skillet over medium-high heat and, when hot, add the livers and sauté them on one side until brown, about 2 minutes. Turn and cook the other side until medium rare, about 3 minutes. Remove the livers from the pan with a slotted spoon and keep them hot in the turned-off oven.

Pour the grease from the pan and deglaze with the remaining port, vinegar, and brandy. Reduce by half, add the *demi-glace,* and reduce until as thick as heavy cream.

Whip the remaining butter into the sauce, pour the sauce over the livers, and arrange the apples on the serving plates.

Note: While the chef likes the texture and mild flavor of rabbit livers, duck or chicken livers can be substituted. The cooking time will be shorter for smaller livers, however. ∎

Rabbit with Apple Cider and Mustard Seeds, Cafe Lilli, Lake Tahoe, Nevada

Don't be alarmed by the sound of it; rattlesnake is really a very delicate meat—and also not readily available on the market. You can use any game meat, or even a combination of pork and veal, and the savory sausage is really enhanced by the spicy pasta. This could be a casual supper as well as an appetizer.

Jalapeño Pasta with Rattlesnake Sausage

Las Canarias, San Antonio, Texas

(Serves 6 as an appetizer, 4 as an entree.)

Red pepper vinaigrette

4 tablespoons freshly squeezed lime juice
6 tablespoons hot pepper vinegar (see note, following)
1 teaspoon salt
1 teaspoon ground white pepper
4 cups olive oil
¾ cup chopped red bell pepper, roasted, peeled, and seeded (see page 10)
¼ cup chopped green bell pepper, roasted, peeled, and seeded (see page 10)
2 tablespoons chopped fresh cilantro

Sausage

½ pound rattlesnake meat (venison, veal, or any wild game can be substituted)
¼ pound lean pork shoulder
3/8 pound fatback
1 tablespoon brandy
2 teaspoons cumin seed, ground
2 teaspoons salt
1 teaspoon ground white pepper
½ pound smoked venison, cut into a small dice
2 tablespoons diced roasted and peeled red pepper (see page 10)
2 tablespoons tarragon leaves
Sausage casing
1 gallon chicken stock for poaching

Pasta

15 *jalapeño* chilies
6 tablespoons olive oil
3 to 4 cups unbleached all-purpose flour

4 eggs
Pinch of salt

For garnish: prickly pear cactus pads

Note: The hot pepper vinegar for the vinaigrette must be made 1 week before serving the dish, and the sausage must be made 1 day before serving.

To make the vinaigrette, place the lime juice, vinegar, salt, and pepper in a blender or a food processor fitted with a steel blade. With the motor running, slowly add the olive oil through the feed tube and beat until emulsified. Stir in the diced peppers and cilantro and adjust seasoning.

To make the sausage, debone the rattlesnake and scrape off the silver skin encasing the fillets. Cut the rattlesnake, pork, and fatback into small cubes, and place all the meats on a baking sheet in the freezer for 30 minutes to partially freeze (this will make grinding easier). Grind meats and fat separately through the small die of a meat grinder, then freeze each again for 30 minutes. Dissolve the cumin seed, salt, and pepper in the brandy.

Place the rattlesnake, pork, and brandy mixture in the bowl of a food processor fitted with a steel blade and work until smooth. Add the fatback and process again. Place the mixture in a bowl and fold in the smoked venison, red pepper, and tarragon leaves.

Wash the sausage casing well and cut off a 1½-foot section. Using a #9 tip on a pastry bag, fill the casing with the sausage mixture, making sure not to stuff it too full. Tie the ends securely.

Bring the chicken stock to a simmer and poach the sausage until it reaches an internal temperature of 160°, about 10 to 15 minutes. Remove from the stock, cool at room temperature, and then chill overnight.

To make the pasta, make a *jalapeño* puree by boiling the chilies to soften them for 15 minutes. Destem and place the chilies with 1 to 2 tablespoons of the olive oil in a blender or a food processor fitted with a steel blade. Puree for 3

Jalapeño Pasta with Rattlesnake Sausage, Las Canarias, San Antonio, Texas

minutes, then push the puree through a fine sieve to remove the seeds. Set aside.

Sift the flour into a mound on a work surface and make a well in the center. Break in the eggs and add the remaining olive oil, 5 tablespoons of the *jalapeño* puree, and the salt. Using a fork, mix the eggs and then start to incorporate the flour. Once the dough has started to form and as much flour is incorporated as possible, work the dough by hand and knead it for 10 minutes, or until it is dry and elastic. Add more flour if necessary.

Form the dough into a ball, dust with flour, and wrap in plastic wrap. Allow to rest for 1 hour in the refrigerator before rolling.

Divide the dough into 4 parts, and form 1 part into a ball. Flatten the ball with a rolling pin until thin enough to pass through the largest setting on a pasta machine, then begin rolling the pasta, dusting it with flour between rollings. Keep closing the setting on the rollers until the pasta is rolled through the thinnest setting. Then cut the pasta for *fettuccine*, toss with flour, and allow it to dry for at least 15 minutes before cooking. Repeat with the remaining parts of dough.

Bring a large quantity of salted water to a boil and add the fresh pasta just before serving. Cook for 30 seconds once the water returns to a boil, then drain and place in cool water for 10 minutes. Do not rinse.

To make the garnish, pull the eyes out of the cactus pads with a tweezers and blanch the pads in boiling salted water until tender, about 10 minutes. Peel off the outer layer of the pads.

To serve, place medallions of sausage on a plate with some of the cooled pasta and a cactus pad. Drizzle the vinaigrette on the plate.

Note: To make hot pepper vinegar, combine 1 quart of white wine vinegar with 1 *poblano*, 2 Anaheim, and 4 *jalapeño* chilies, 3 sprigs of tarragon, and 4 bay leaves, all chopped. Bring to a boil and simmer 10 minutes. Place in glass jars and allow to sit for at least a week before using. ∎

RAYMOND TATUM
Jeffrey's, Austin, Texas

Raymond Tatum, who has been the chef at Jeffrey's in Austin, is an example of an intuitive cook. While not acknowledging any influences on his style, he has been cooking for the past seven years, changing the menu on a daily basis.

Tatum, a thirty-five-year-old Austin native, has worked in the city since he decided to cook more than ten years ago. His first job was at Pelican's Wharf, an Austin private club; then he worked at Bloom's, a restaurant known for simple grilled fish and steak and some Continental specialties. After cooking Creole food at the Buffalo Grill for a few months, he became chef at Jeffrey's.

"The ideas for dishes are in my head, and I look at the refrigerator and decide what to do with what I see," he says. "My rule is to cook the best food I possibly can, and I don't want to follow any one style."

He says some dishes evolve from discussions among the kitchen staff of the sixty-seat restaurant, which is decorated with contemporary art hung on white walls. A wine rack divides the space into two dining rooms, each containing a blackboard on which the night's menu is written.

The influences in those dishes can be Southwestern, such as Speckled Trout with Cashews, Cilantro, and Lime Butter Sauce; they can be decidedly Asian, such as a roast duck done in either a Hunanese or Szechwanese manner; or they can revert to European models, such as Lamb Loin with Turnip Sauce.

"I never make a dish exactly the same way twice, even though one dish may have come from one I have already done," he says.

LITTLE TOUCHES

Chefs have known for years that even if a diner orders a steak medium rare or a simple sautéd fish fillet, the accompaniments can make a meal memorable. A basket of freshly baked bread or a special vegetable can be as important to the success of a dinner as the main event.

Part of the popularity of new American cuisine, with new Southwest cooking as one of its subsets, results from the care that chefs take with even the small touches. Although tortillas, *salsas,* and *guacamole* are used extensively, they are always used in innovative ways.

Most of the recipes in this chapter started out as parts of entree presentations by the chefs; however, I thought they were special enough to stand on their own. Dean Fearing's Tobacco Onions, for example, were piled high on a plate with grilled chicken at The Mansion on Turtle Creek. They were so delicious and light they could eclipse the fried onion ring forever. The same was true when Clive DuVal's Refried Black Beans were brought to the table. While he uses them as the basis for a sauce elsewhere in this volume, their depth of flavor and richness made them a new standard all on their own.

In this chapter you will also find some tequila-based drinks that are the perfect additions to the bar for a Southwestern meal. In addition to the traditional Margarita, we encountered the Killer Margarita at Tila's in Houston, and a cocktail made from the delicate cider pressed in Chimayó, New Mexico.

Herb Sorbet, Hudsons' on the Bend, Austin, Texas

This fresh herb and citrus sorbet is intended as an intermezzo and not a dessert. It has an attractive green color, and the wine adds sparkle.

Herb Sorbet

Hudsons' on the Bend, Austin, Texas

(Serves 12)

1¼ cups sugar
1 cup water
2 limes
1 egg white
¾ cup dry white wine
½ cup dry vermouth
Salt, nutmeg, and white pepper to
   taste
Some combination of the following
   chopped fresh herbs, to make ½ to
   ¾ cup total: peppermint, lemon
   balm, lemon thyme, dill, rosemary,
   tarragon, parsley, oregano, sorrel,
   or basil
½ cup champagne

Mix the sugar and water in a saucepan and stir over medium heat until the sugar is dissolved. Take off the heat and cool. Cut the zest off the limes with a zester or vegetable peeler and chop fine, then squeeze the limes.

In a mixing bowl, combine the sugar syrup, lime zest and juice, egg white, white wine, and vermouth. Chop all the herbs finely in a blender or a food processor and add to the mixture. Mix well and place in an ice cream freezer, processing according to the manufacturer's instructions.

To serve, spoon a small scoop into each of 12 cups and drizzle with champagne.

Note: The *sorbet* will lose its freshness after a few days in the freezer. ∎

JEFF BLANK
Hudsons' on the Bend, Austin, Texas

Hot smoking is part of the cooking tradition in Texas, and Jeff Blank, the chef and owner of Hudsons' on the Bend, is updating the tradition in his sophisticated dishes. He smokes a Wild Game and Mushroom Terrine to add a nuance of flavor, and he also smokes everything from oysters for tossing with pasta, to ducks and all meats.

Chef Blank's intention is to blend the light style of California cuisine with the cooking traditions of Texas. He stuffs a pork tenderloin with chorizo in the Southwestern mode, then accompanies it with fruit chutney, a condiment popular on the West Coast.

Cooking was not Blank's first career. The thirty-six-year-old Pittsburgh native was raised in Houston and graduated from Oklahoma State University with a degree in hotel and restaurant management. It was while he was working as food and beverage director at the Lakeway Resort in Austin that he met Gert Rausch, now the chef and owner of Austin's Courtyard, and a partner of Blank's at Hudsons'.

The pair opened the Wineskin Restaurant in Snowmass, Colorado, in 1973, and closed it four years later when one winter produced no snow and, therefore, no diners. "The lesson was to never own a restaurant dependent on the weather," says Blank.

After three years in San Antonio managing restaurants, he moved back to Austin and opened Hudsons', this time as the chef. "What I know about cooking I really learned watching Gert; he is my mentor and working with him was my schooling," he says.

The light style of cooking Blank creates at Hudsons' is different from the more European tradition at Austin's Courtyard. Blank started using mesquite in his smoker, a converted oil drum, and now uses pecan since "it gives food a rounder and smoother flavor." His technique is to smoke all foods to medium rare, and then complete the cooking on indoor grills. "The smoked flavor of foods is part of Texas, but it also adds interest to even Maine lobster," he says.

SUSAN FENIGER AND MARY SUE MILLIKEN

Border Grill, Los Angeles, California

Susan Feniger and Mary Sue Milliken, the co-chefs and co-owners of the Border Grill and the City Cafe in Los Angeles, credit their similarity in cooking styles to their compatible backgrounds and natures. The two work side by side, alternating between their two restaurants but devising the contemporary California dishes for City Cafe and the Mexican and Southwest specialties of the Border Grill together.

The two met while working at Le Perroquet in Chicago in 1979. Susan, who graduated from the Culinary Institute of America in 1975, went on to work at Ma Maison in Los Angeles before starting the City Cafe, now housing the Border Grill, in 1982. When she began the first restaurant, Mary Sue went to work for her, and the two became partners.

"It's amazing to meet someone who thinks the same way you do, and we base our philosophy on cooking what we like to eat. We are both drawn to simple cultures of a simple life. We started out liking country French food, and then became influenced by Indian after Susan visited there for a month, and then Mexican," says Mary Sue.

The two view themselves as a creative unit. They have been honored as a team by both *Cook's Magazine,* who included them in the prestigious "Who's Who of Cooking in America," and by *Food and Wine* magazine on their Honor Roll of American Chefs.

"We both like eating Mexican food, and had only had Americanized versions in restaurants. We had a lot of Mexican help in the kitchen, and the food we were eating out wasn't as good as the dishes the cooks were making for themselves in our kitchens," says Susan.

They started by traveling to Mexico for a few weeks to work with the families of their kitchen help, and spent a few hours of each day visiting the markets. In interpreting the dishes they learned there, they choose only the finest ingredients and handle them as lightly as possible.

While this stellar version of a Mexican and Southwestern classic can be a delicious appetizer by itself, it's also traditionally served as an accompaniment to almost all tortilla specialties.

Guacamole

Border Grill, Los Angeles, California

(Serves 8)

5 ripe avocados
1 small red onion, peeled and finely diced
2 *jalapeño* chilies, seeded, deribbed, and finely diced (see page 10)
½ cup cilantro leaves
¼ teaspoon ground white pepper
½ to 1 teaspoon salt
2 tablespoons fresh lime juice, or to taste

To serve

Shredded lettuce
Tomato wedges

Halve the avocados and remove the pits. Cut into quarters and peel, then cut into chunks. Place the avocado in a bowl with the red onion and *jalapeño* chilies and, using a table fork, mash the mixture together, leaving some of the avocado in chunks.

Add the cilantro, white pepper, and salt to the mixture along with the lime juice and mix well.

To serve, place some shredded lettuce on a plate and garnish the *guacamole* with tomato wedges.

Note: All dishes made with avocado will darken when exposed to air. You can make this dish up to 8 hours in advance if you push a piece of plastic wrap directly into the surface, and then store it in the refrigerator. ∎

This alternative to a green salad is as pretty as a bowl of confetti, and the individual flavors of the vegetables remain crisp.

Three-Tomato Salsa

Anne Lindsay Greer, Dallas, Texas

(Serves 6 to 8)

3 tablespoons olive oil
½ small red onion, peeled and diced
⅓ cup dry white wine
8 *tomatillos*, husked, cored, and diced (3 unripe green tomatoes, seeded and diced, can be substituted)
4 ripe tomatoes, seeded and diced
1 pint yellow cherry tomatoes, seeded and diced
Salt and white pepper to taste
6 fresh basil sprigs, minced

Heat the oil in a sauté pan or skillet over medium-high heat. Add the onion and sauté 2 minutes. Add the white wine and *tomatillos*, stir to combine, and remove from heat.

Add the red and yellow tomatoes to the pan while the mixture is still warm. Season to taste with salt and pepper, add the basil, and allow to stand at least 20 minutes before serving for the flavors to blend.

Drain the juices from the relish before serving.

Note: The relish can be prepared up to a day in advance and refrigerated. Bring to room temperature before serving to achieve the best flavor. ∎

Chef Dean Fearing dubbed these crispy and spicy rings of fried onion "tobacco onions" because they look like shredded tobacco when cooked. He serves them with Grilled Free-Range Chicken, page 85, but they are delicious with any grilled meat or poultry.

Tobacco Onions

The Mansion on Turtle Creek, Dallas, Texas

(Serves 6)

1 large red onion
1 large yellow Spanish onion
3 cups unbleached all-purpose flour
1 tablespoon cayenne
1 tablespoon paprika
Salt and black pepper to taste
5 cups vegetable oil for frying

Peel the onions and slice them thinly. Separate into rings and set aside.

Mix the flour and seasonings in a bowl, and heat the oil in a deep-fryer or heavy saucepan to a temperature of 350°.

Dredge some of the onion rings in the flour, shaking off any excess, and fry until golden brown, making sure the rings do not stick together. Remove from the oil with a slotted spoon, drain on paper towels, and keep warm while frying the remaining onions.

Serve immediately.

Note: Do not dredge the onions until just prior to frying or they will give off too much moisture. ∎

The slight spice of these traditional German dropped noodles is an interesting touch. They are an alternative to other starches with any meal.

Jalapeño Spaetzle

Austin's Courtyard, Austin, Texas

(Serves 10)

5 *jalapeño* chilies
1 cup water
4 cups unbleached all-purpose flour
12 eggs
Salt, nutmeg, and freshly ground black pepper to taste
2 tablespoons unsalted butter

Place the *jalapeños* and the water in a small saucepan and bring to a boil over medium heat. Simmer, uncovered, for 10 minutes. Drain, and when cool enough to handle, remove the stems from the chilies and puree them in a blender or a food processor fitted with a steel blade. Force the puree through a sieve and set aside.

Place the flour and 6 of the eggs in a mixer bowl and beat to combine well. Add the remaining eggs, 2 to 4 tablespoons of the *jalapeño* puree, and the seasonings and beat the mixture for 7 to 10 minutes, or until enough air is incorporated that air pockets begin to appear.

Bring a large amount of salted water to a boil. Using a potato ricer or a grater placed over the pot, drop the *spaetzle* into the water. Boil for 2 minutes, then remove with a slotted spoon and place in ice water to cool. Drain, pat dry on paper towels, and sauté in the butter to warm before serving.

Note: The *spaetzle* can be made a few hours in advance. They will reheat in the butter. ∎

CLIVE DuVAL

Tila's, Houston, Texas

Most of the items on the menu at Clive DuVal's Tila's Cantina and Taqueria are stalwarts of Mexican food found in many places in Houston: refried beans, *fajitas,* tacos. But when the refried beans arrive, they are black beans flavored with smoky bacon and green onions. And the *fajitas* are sirloin, with hints of Szechwan peppers and soy sauce.

"Asian and South American flavors have a lot in common, and of all the world's foods that I use in my dishes, I turn to Asia more often than Europe," he says.

DuVal terms his style of cooking "eclectic Latin," although some reviewers have termed it "nouvelle Mexican." The thirty-seven-year-old New York native interprets traditional foods in an innovative and constantly changing fashion. Tila's is as modern in approach as its appearance: black and white tiles and neon make it a beacon from the outside, and bright chili *ristras* and stylized colored tile murals decorate the interior.

He gave up his entrepreneurial efforts in 1976, and signed up for a course at the Philadelphia Restaurant School. "I went there because it was the shortest course I could find, and it reinforced that I liked cooking food and wanted a restaurant," he says.

After working for a year for a restaurant chain in Chattanooga, Tennessee, he moved to Houston. Tila's is named for a former girlfriend who introduced DuVal to the flavors of the authentic cuisine of Mexico City.

When he opened in 1979, the menu featured some of the same dishes he offers today; however, the nature of the dishes is now entirely different. He infuses black bean soup with mint, tarragon, and basil, and with dark beer in lieu of sherry.

As important as his quest for innovation is his dedication to freshness. The kitchen at Tila's runs round the clock, so food is prepared in batches three times a day.

These are the best refried beans I've ever tasted, with the smoky bacon and the jalapeño *chilies giving them zest.*

Refried Black Beans

Tila's, Houston, Texas

(Serves 8)

1 pound dried black beans
¼ large white onion, chopped
2 garlic cloves
2 cups chicken stock
½ pound bacon, minced
3 *jalapeño* chilies, chopped
3 green onions, white and green part chopped
3 tablespoons vegetable oil
Salt and white pepper to taste
¾ pound white cheese such as Monterey jack or *feta,* grated

Wash the black beans in a colander, picking over them well to remove any pebbles or broken beans. Place in a stockpot with water to cover by at least 3 inches and bring to a boil. Reduce heat and simmer the beans, partially covered, for 1 hour.

Add half of the onion and the 2 garlic cloves along with the chicken stock and simmer another 30 minutes, or until the beans are very tender, skimming the foam as it rises to the surface.

In a sauté pan or skillet, sauté the bacon until it is almost burnt. Remove the bacon with a slotted spoon, and pour off the rendered fat, reserving 4 tablespoons. Sauté the remaining onion with the *jalapeños* and green onions in the reserved fat over medium heat until the onions are translucent.

Drain the cooked beans, reserving the bean broth. Place the beans, bacon, and *jalapeño* mixture in a blender or a food processor along with 3 cups of the bean broth. This will have to be done in batches. Process until the mixture is pureed but the consistency is still chunky. Stir to combine the batches of puree.

Heat the oil in a deep heavy skillet and add the beans. Cook over low heat, stirring constantly, until the beans are thick and some of the liquid has evaporated, about 10 minutes. Season with salt and pepper to taste.

Serve sprinkled with grated cheese.

Note: The starch in the beans will thicken the mixture when it cools. The beans can be cooked and pureed up to 6 hours in advance; however, do not refry them until just prior to serving. ■

This rice is as pretty as it is good. The vegetables and zesty dried currants make it look like confetti, and cinnamon augments the other flavors. This is a perfect side dish with any roasted or broiled food.

Mexican Sweet Cinnamon Rice

Coyote Cafe, Santa Fe, New Mexico

(Serves 8 to 10)

4 tablespoons unsalted butter
½ cup carrots, cut into small dice
½ cup celery, cut into small dice
½ cup white onion, cut into small dice
2 cups long-grain rice
½ to 1 teaspoon salt
4 sticks Mexican cinnamon, or 1 tablespoon ground cinnamon
⅓ cup dried currants
6 cups water

Melt 2 tablespoons of the butter in a deep saucepan over medium heat. Add the carrots, celery, and onion, cover the pan, and cook the vegetables over low heat, stirring occasionally, for 10 minutes. Add the rice, salt, cinnamon, currants, and water to the pan and bring to a boil over high heat. When the water has reduced down to the level of the rice, turn the heat to low, cover, and cook for 15 to 20 minutes, stirring occasionally.

Remove the cinnamon sticks, add the remaining butter, and adjust the seasoning. ■

Flecks of peppers and cilantro enliven this corn bread. If making the stuffing for Roast Wild Turkey (page 92) you might want to cut back on the number of chilies in the bread, since additional ones are sautéed for the stuffing.

Serrano Chili Blue Corn Bread

Routh Street Cafe, Dallas, Texas

(Serves 12)

1 cup unbleached all-purpose flour
1¼ cups blue cornmeal (substitute yellow if necessary)
2 tablespoons sugar
1 teaspoon salt
1 tablespoon baking powder
2 tablespoons unsalted butter
3 *serrano* chilies, seeded and diced (*jalapeños* can be substituted)
1 medium red bell pepper, seeded and diced
1 medium green bell pepper, seeded and diced
3 garlic cloves, minced
2 eggs
6 tablespoons shortening, melted and cooled
6 tablespoons butter, melted and cooled
⅛ teaspoon baking soda
1 cup buttermilk, at room temperature
3 tablespoons chopped fresh cilantro

Preheat the oven to 400°.

Sift together the flour, cornmeal, sugar, salt, and baking powder. Heat the butter in a medium sauté pan or skillet over medium heat and when hot, sauté the *serrano* chilies, red and green peppers, and garlic for 4 minutes, or until the vegetables are soft. Set aside.

In a large bowl, whisk the eggs lightly and add the melted shortening and butter. Stir the baking soda into the buttermilk and add it to the mixture. Add the dry ingredients, beating until the batter is just smooth; do not overmix. Fold in the vegetable mixture and cilantro.

Pour the batter into a buttered 9 by-13-inch pan and bake in the center of the preheated oven for 25 to 30 minutes, or until the top is golden brown.

Note: The corn bread is best right from the oven; however, it freezes well, too. Reheat before serving. ■

These spicy toasts are a wonderful alternative to garlic bread in the bread basket.

Cumin Seed and Pepper Toasts

Tucson Country Club, Tucson, Arizona

(Makes 14 slices)

2 eggs, lightly beaten
1 tablespoon olive oil
12 to 14 diagonal slices of French bread, about ½ inch thick
¾ teaspoon ground cumin
¾ teaspoon coarsely ground pepper
¼ teaspoon whole cumin seeds
2 tablespoons soft butter

Preheat the oven to 400°. Beat the eggs and oil together and dip the bread slices in the mixture, coating both sides and shaking off the excess. Mix the spices together and sprinkle on both sides of the toasts.

Use the soft butter to heavily butter a baking sheet and place the toasts in a single layer. Bake for 10 to 15 minutes, turning once, or until golden brown.

Note: These toasts keep very well in a canister, and can be reheated. ■

Nancy Weiss
The American Grill, Phoenix, Arizona

Chef Nancy Weiss calls herself a "culinary conservative." Rather than charting new courses for the menu at The American Grill, her third restaurant in Phoenix since moving there in 1981, she is "creating variations on something that is understood."

Chef Weiss, now thirty-three, attended the Culinary Institute of America after spending two years in liberal arts studies at Boston University. "I always liked to eat, and that's how I got into the business—for the wrong reason. I should have liked to work instead," she says.

After graduating from the Institute in 1975, she worked for five years for the Lettuce Entertain You group in Chicago, the owners of the Pump Room, Ambria, and such casual spots as Lawrence of Oregano and Ed Debivic's. At various restaurants, she alternated between the kitchen and working as a captain in the dining room, so she learned both sides of the house.

It was a partner of the company, Steven Stone, who lured her to Phoenix to become head chef at Steven. "It was the first restaurant in Phoenix not serving Veal Oscar," she recalls. "We were doing dishes that made sense for our region and creating a modern interpretation of Continental cuisine."

After Steven, she opened Pop's, which was an upscale pizza and pasta operation, and then began working at The American Grill, which opened in 1984.

The American Grill specializes in seafood, which she has flown in from all over the country. "A grill means different things in different parts of the country. In San Francisco it means simple treatments of fish, while in the East it is usually a very masculine place with large cuts of beef," she says, noting that she took the former route.

Asian influences balance the Southwestern touches in her cooking. Grilled salmon is served with a ginger and scallion butter, while her catfish is fried in the Southern tradition, and grilled hens are marinated in *jalapeño* jelly and lime juice.

Chef Robert Del Grande uses this bright red condiment as a garnish for his cream of cilantro soup, but it can also be used with any hot or cold meats or poultry to spark the flavor.

Ancho Chili Preserves

Cafe Annie, Houston, Texas

(Makes 2 cups)

2 pounds dried *ancho* chilies
¾ cup red currant jelly
1 small shallot, peeled
1 garlic clove, peeled
¼ cup honey
3 tablespoons white wine vinegar

Wash the *ancho* chilies and soak them in hot water until soft, about 15 minutes. Discard the stems and puree the chilies with the remaining ingredients in a blender or a food processor fitted with a steel blade, scraping the sides of the jar as necessary.

Pass the puree through a sieve.

Note: The puree can be kept up to 2 months in the refrigerator. ∎

Chef Nancy Weiss credits Mark Miller of Coyote Cafe with developing this sauce, which she uses as a dip for corn fritters, page 61. It's a wonderful relish to serve with any grilled poultry or seafood.

Pineapple-Chili Sauce

The American Grill, Phoenix, Arizona

(Makes 3 cups)

1 ripe pineapple
½ cup brown sugar
1½ teaspoons unseeded *jalapeño* chili
1 cup water
1½ tablespoons chopped fresh cilantro
1 tablespoon freshly squeezed lime juice

Cut the skin off the pineapple and remove any eyes with a sharp knife. Cut the pineapple in quarters and cut out the core, then roughly dice the flesh. Combine the pineapple, brown sugar, *jalapeño*, and water in a saucepan and bring to a boil. Simmer over low heat, stirring occasionally, for 25 minutes.

Let the mixture cool, then puree it in a blender or a food processor fitted with a steel blade. Stir in the cilantro and lime juice and refrigerate until served.

Note: The sauce will keep for 1 week refrigerated. ■

The small red Chimayó apples grown within sight of the restaurant form the basis for this drink, which is a great switch from a Margarita, but just as lethal.

Chimayó Cocktail

Rancho de Chimayó, Chimayó, New Mexico

(Serves 4)

Ice cubes
5 ounces gold tequila
1 tablespoon *crème de cassis*
½ cup apple cider
2 tablespoons freshly squeezed lemon juice
4 apple wedges for garnish

Margarita, Rancho de Chimayó, Chimayó, New Mexico

Fill a cocktail shaker or quart jar with the ice cubes. Add the tequila, *crème de cassis*, cider, and lemon juice. Shake well and strain into 4 glasses. Add the ice cubes and garnish the rim of each glass with an apple wedge.

Note: This is a terrific punch for a brunch or party, but do increase the percentage of cider to maintain the sobriety of your guests. ■

The lemon, rather than lime, juice is a refreshing change in this drink, which is as much a part of the Southwest as a tamale.

Margarita

Rancho de Chimayó, Chimayó, New Mexico

(Serves 4)

5 ounces white tequila
4 ounces Triple Sec
Juice of 2 lemons
Salt
Ice

Place the tequila, Triple Sec, and lemon juice in a cocktail shaker and add ice. Shake well. Rub the rim of 4 glasses with the cut lemon and dip into a plate of salt. Strain the mixture into the glasses and add ice, if desired. ■

Oysters with Cilantro Pesto, Anne Lindsay Greer, Dallas, Texas

It's not only the size of this drink that makes it a "killer," albeit a delicious one. It's also the reinforcement of the tequila with even more potent potables not found in the traditional drink.

Killer Margarita

Tila's, Houston, Texas

(Makes 2 "killer" drinks, or 4 regular cocktails)

Juice from 5 limes (about ¾ cup)
Juice from 2 oranges (about 1 cup)
2 tablespoons sugar
2½ ounces Cointreau
2½ ounces Grand Marnier
5 ounces Cuervo Gold tequila
Salt
Thin slices of orange and lime for garnish

Shake the juices, sugar, and liquors with crushed ice in a cocktail shaker, and serve in a glass rimmed with salt. Garnish with a slice of orange and lime. ∎

This seasoning mix, which lasts for months if kept in tightly closed jars, is excellent on grilled meats, seafood, and poultry.

Sonoran Seasoning

Tucson Country Club, Tucson, Arizona

(Makes 24 ounces)

1 pound salt
4 tablespoons roasted chili powder
5 tablespoons cumin seed
4 tablespoons chamomile
3 tablespoons dried orange rind
6 tablespoons black peppercorns
2 tablespoons paprika
4 tablespoons granulated onion
5 tablespoons granulated garlic
3 pieces star anise

Mix the ingredients in a blender to combine. ∎

JUDY YOVIN
Tucson Country Club, Tucson, Arizona

The vivid colors and intense flavors of the fruits of the Southwest have intrigued Judy Yovin, the pastry chef at the Tucson Country Club for the past five years, since she ventured to the desert region. "When you've been born and educated in the east, the variety of food we now have to work with and the high quality of all the ingredients begins a process of innovation," says the twenty-five-year-old Florida native.

Yovin met Alan Zeman, executive chef of the posh private club, when they were both students at the Culinary Institute of America, where she graduated second in her class in 1982. She became hooked on cooking when she started working in restaurants after high school, because she wanted to earn money to buy a car. After the CIA foundation, she took cake decorating courses in New York and learned the fine art of elaborate sugar-pulling in Detroit. She then studied in Switzerland at the famed Fachschule Richemont, and her work has been featured in *Bon Appetit* and on television in Tucson.

In her tenure as pastry chef at the club, such desserts as Arizona Pecan Torte, crunchy with nuts grown in the region, and a rich mousse torte she calls Ebony and Ivory, with layers of white and dark chocolate mousse, have become signature items.

Yovin decorates her desserts with clues to the flavors contained inside. For her Sonoran Sunrise cake, desert fruits such as prickly pears and carimbola (star fruit), are displayed across the top; in the European mode, she fashions pumpkins from almond paste to signify the flavors of the Pumpkin Chocolate Cheesecake.

While her training was in the classics, she now looks to restaurants such as Spago and Chez Panisse for her inspiration.

"The desserts in California are so light and eye-appealing, and that's the direction my work is taking," she says.

DESSERTS

Everyone has friends to whom dessert is synonymous with chocolate, but even confirmed chocoholics appreciate a light fruit dessert after a rich and heavy meal. Selection of a dessert is part of menu planning, which should keep the meal in balance while it takes into account the weather and the seasonal availability of fruits.

You should also decide if the dessert should be a departure from what has come before it, or whether it should continue in the spirit of the menu. If dinner has been composed of elegant foods served in a formal manner, you might want to serve an elaborate dessert like Rebecca Naccarato's Poppy Seed Cake, or the finale could be less dramatic, such as Bradley Ogden's Lemon Pound Cake with Fruit Sauce.

Some of the desserts in this chapter are perfect endings for a meal of other updated Southwest foods. Anne Lindsay Greer's Cookie Tacos and Michael Roberts' Dessert Tostadas are whimsical as well as being stellar combinations of textures and flavors, while the Red Yam Flan from the Border Grill adds color and flavor to a traditional form.

Many of these pastries are far easier to make than their elegant appearance will lead guests to believe. Cindy Black's Chestnut Royal, with spirals of jelly roll covering a decadent chestnut mousse, is really quite simple to assemble, as is Rick O'Connell's Chocolate Roulade with Bittersweet Sauce and Hazelnut Filling.

Dessert Tostadas, Trumps, Los Angeles, California

As polenta is just another name for American johnnycake, so flour tortillas, when fried crispy into a basket shape, are similar to puff pastry. Chef Michael Roberts' concept of using them as holders for a delicious and easy-to-construct dessert is now being copied around the country with good reason—they are fun to serve and take little time to create.

Dessert Tostadas

Trumps, Los Angeles, California

(Serves 4)

Oil for deep-frying
4 flour tortillas

Custard

4 egg yolks
½ cup sugar
½ cup *crème fraîche*
1 cup heavy cream
¼ teaspoon vanilla extract
4 ounces bittersweet chocolate, melted
2 cups assorted fresh fruit, sliced (any mix of strawberries, bananas, raspberries, etc.)
4 tablespoons dark brown sugar, or 4 tablespoons chocolate syrup

In a deep heavy saucepan, heat the oil to a temperature of 375°; a drop of water should explode when it hits the oil. Using a strainer, or a tortilla basket-maker made for this purpose, hold a flour tortilla down in the oil until it forms a cup shape. Remove the strainer and keep it submerged in the oil using tongs. Fry until golden brown and remove with the tongs. Drain upside down on paper towels, and repeat with remaining tortillas.

To make the custard, beat the egg yolks until light and lemon colored. Add the sugar and continue to beat until thick. Add the *crème fraîche*, heavy cream, and vanilla and beat in the top of a double boiler until the mixture is thickened and coats the back of a wooden spoon. Do not allow it to boil or the egg yolks will curdle. Press a sheet of plastic wrap into the surface so no skin will form, allow to cool, and refrigerate until needed.

To assemble the dessert, paint the outside of the cups with melted chocolate and allow it to harden.

Divide the fruit among the cups, top with custard, and sprinkle with brown sugar. Using a salamander iron heated under a broiler, "brand" the brown sugar so it caramelizes. If you do not have a salamander, drizzle the custard with chocolate syrup, but do not place the tostadas under the broiler or the chocolate will melt.

Note: The baskets can be fried and the custard can be made up to a day in advance. Keep the baskets in a dry place or in an airtight container. ∎

Crispy cookies, with an interesting contrast of lemon and anise, form elegant and edible bowls for fresh berries in this springtime dessert.

Fresh-Berry Mousse in Pizzelle-Cookie Bowls

Wolfdale's, Lake Tahoe, California

(Serves 12)

Cookie bowls

2 eggs
⅓ cup sugar
¾ teaspoon vanilla extract
1 tablespoon grated lemon zest
Pinch of salt
⅓ cup all-purpose unbleached flour
½ cup pastry flour
1 teaspoon star anise powder
⅓ cup vegetable oil

Mousse

1 cup heavy cream
1 teaspoon vanilla extract
½ pint raspberries
½ pint elderberries or blackberries
½ cup sugar
Juice of ½ lemon

Garnish

Mint sprigs
Additional whipped cream

To make the cookie bowls, mix the eggs, sugar, vanilla, and lemon zest together, beating until light and fluffy. Add the dry ingredients, beating well, then fold in the oil.

Heat a *pizzelle* iron and coat it with oil. Spread 2 tablespoons of the batter on the iron and press to cook. Remove from the press and push into an oiled bowl while hot to make a cup. Trim while hot and repeat with the remaining batter, oiling the grill between each cup or as needed.

To make the mousse, whip the cream with the vanilla and set aside. Wash the berries by floating them in cold water, then drain them on paper towels. Puree the berries with the sugar and lemon juice; additional sugar may be needed depending on the sweetness of the fruit. Fold half the puree into the whipped cream and chill the mousse.

To serve, place some of the puree on serving plates and a dollop of the mousse in the cups. Garnish with mint sprigs.

Note: The cookies can be made up to 4 days in advance and kept in an airtight container. ∎

JOHN SEDLAR

Saint Estèphe, Manhattan Beach, California

The controversy rages as to how to define the artfully presented dishes at John Sedlar's Saint Estèphe: Is he doing nouvelle French food with some ingredients from his New Mexican childhood, or is he crafting an elegant level of Southwest cuisine utilizing French techniques?

Sedlar believes the two are not mutually exclusive. His menu is written in French, although there is a painting of a Pueblo village and the words "Modern Southwest Cuisine" on its cover. The interior of the restaurant has been transformed along with its food, so even though the chairs may be in the nouvelle style, the artworks have been collected on Sedlar's trips back to his native Santa Fe.

"My goal is to take traditional dishes and concepts and metamorphose them to the 1980s. I use the vernacular of the Southwest, but present things in the most elegant fashion I can."

That means lines of red chili and green sorrel sauce are feathered through a shallot sauce for his Salmon Painted Desert, and that the top tortilla for his Enchilada of Filet Mignon with Sorrel Sauce is seared into a linear pattern with a branding iron.

The food at Saint Estèphe is a reflection of Sedlar's past. While the formative influence was his grandmother, Eloisa Rivera, his training was in French kitchens. "The strongest influence on my style was the years I spent at L'Ermitage working with Jean Bertranou. My first meal there is still part of my life, and part of it was pigeon with corncakes," he says.

He worked for Bertranou for four years, and then decided to open his own French restaurant with fellow Santa Fe native Steve Garcia as his partner.

Two years after chef Sedlar began doing nouvelle French food, he brought a few bushels of Chimayó chilies back from a trip to New Mexico. The dishes resulting from his experimentations were listed on a a menu card inside the French menu, and by 1983, the entire restaurant had become new Southwest cooking.

Crisp, delicate shells, a creamy sauce with a hint of white chocolate, and luscious ripe fruits—the components of this dazzling trompe l'oeil dessert—are individually wonderful and spectacular when combined.

Cookie Tacos

Anne Lindsay Greer, Dallas, Texas

(Serves 8)

Cookie tacos

1 cup sugar
¾ cup blanched almonds (or ¼ cup pine nuts and ½ cup blanched almonds)
¼ cup water

Custard sauce

6 egg yolks
2 teaspoons cornstarch
2 cups heavy cream
½ cup sugar
2 cups half and half
2 teaspoons vanilla extract
3 ounces white chocolate, chopped

Assembly

2 pints raspberries
1 ripe papaya
1 pint strawberries
1 cup chocolate sauce (homemade or commercial)
2 ounces white chocolate, grated

To make the cookies, place the sugar and almonds in a blender or a food processor fitted with a steel blade. Grind very fine, then add the water and mix well. It should be a paste. Let stand for 10 minutes.

Preheat the oven to 375°. Line cookie sheets with parchment paper and place the dough in a pastry bag without a tip. Pipe small half-dollar-sized rounds onto the paper, leaving about 4 inches between the cookies since they spread.

Bake for 10 to 13 minutes, or until evenly browned, in the top half of the oven, 1 tray at a time.

Cut with scissors between the cookies and gently fold the edges of the paper to make 1 cookie a taco shape. Place it between 2 boxes of kitchen wrap until set, about 30 seconds. Shape the remaining cookies, working as quickly as

Cookie Tacos, Anne Lindsay Greer, Dallas, Texas

possible since once the cookies cool they cannot be bent without breaking.

Bake and shape the second tray of cookies.

To make the custard sauce, combine the egg yolks with the cornstarch, 1½ cups of the cream, and the sugar in a mixing bowl. Heat the half and half in a saucepan and bring to a boil. Reduce the heat to low and cook 5 minutes. Remove from the heat.

In the top of a double boiler, heat the remaining ½ cup cream and the white chocolate until the chocolate melts. Whisk until smooth and keep warm.

Whisk ½ cup of the hot cream into the yolk mixture, then slowly stir the egg yolks into the remaining hot cream, along with the white chocolate cream.

Cook over medium-low heat, stirring constantly, until the custard is thickened and coats a spoon, about 8 minutes. Strain into a bowl.

Fill another bowl with cracked ice and place the bowl of custard on top. Let cool 1 to 2 hours, stirring occasionally.

To assemble, wash the raspberries; peel and remove the seeds from the

papaya, then dice; wash and slice the strawberries. Gently place an assortment of the fruit into each cookie, spooning the custard sauce on one side and the chocolate sauce on the other. Sprinkle with grated white chocolate to simulate the "cheese."

Note: Any assortment of colorful ripe fruit can be substituted for those specified above. The cookies can be made up to a week in advance and kept in a tightly covered tin; the custard can be made up to 3 days in advance and kept refrigerated. Do not assemble, however, until just before serving. ■

Neon Tumbleweed with Biscochitos, Saint Estèphe, Manhattan Beach, California

This dessert is as light as it is colorful and dramatic. While John Sedlar has cookie cutters in the shape of a cactus, stars or any standard cookie shape will make attractive biscochitos. *The dessert is such fun to make; it brings out the artist in us all.*

Neon Tumbleweed with Biscochitos

Saint Estèphe, Manhattan Beach, California

(Serves 6)

6 ripe kiwi fruit, peeled and sliced
1 ripe papaya, peeled and seeded
4 cups fresh raspberries
4 cups fresh blackberries
4 tablespoons fresh lemon juice
4 tablespoons sugar
1 banana
1 pineapple, peeled and cored
1 recipe *biscochitos*, cut in decorative
    shapes (page 49)

In a blender or a food processor fitted with a steel blade, separately puree 2 cups each of the blackberries and raspberries, all the kiwis, and the papaya, adding 1 tablespoon of the lemon juice and 1 tablespoon of the sugar to each fruit near the end of the puree process. If you begin with the kiwi, then the papaya, and end with the blackberries, you will merely have to scrape the bowl rather than washing it out.

With a spoon, press each of the purees through a fine sieve to remove the seeds, place each in a separate plastic squeeze bottle, and chill at least 1 hour in the refrigerator.

Squeeze the purees onto chilled serving plates in a free-form pattern. Cut the banana and pineapple into geometric pieces and randomly place them with the reserved blackberries and raspberries on each plate. Serve with *biscochitos*.

Note: The cookies and purees can be prepared up to 2 days in advance. ■

This is a lighter variation on the traditional Italian zabaglione, *and the pairing of Grand Marnier with Marsala is a delicious one.*

Orange Zabaglione in Orange Cups

The White Dove, Tucson, Arizona

(Serves 6)

6 medium navel oranges
8 egg yolks
¼ cup sugar
½ cup Grand Marnier
½ cup Marsala
1 tablespoon ice water
Candied violets or orange sections for
    garnish

Cut a slice off the bottom of each orange so it will stand upright on a plate, then cut off the top third and scrape out all the pulp. Set aside.

Whisk the egg yolks and sugar together in the top of a double boiler until thick, then place the pan over simmering water. Add the Grand Marnier and Marsala. Beat until the mixture thickens and coats the back of a spoon. Remove from the heat, beat in the ice water, then return to the heat and continue to whisk until it has the consistency of a hollandaise. Spoon into the orange shells, and serve either hot or cold. Garnish with candied violets or orange sections.

Note: If served cold, the dessert can be prepared a day in advance, and if a lighter taste is desired, some orange juice can be substituted for some of the liquors. ■

Orange Zabaglione in Orange Cups, The White Dove, Tucson, Arizona

Southwestern Fruit Flan with Prickly Pear Glaze, The White Dove, Tucson, Arizona

Preheat the oven to 425°. Roll the puff pastry to a thickness of ¼ inch and, using a cake pan as a guide, cut out two 9-inch circles. Prick with a fork and bake on a cookie sheet for 10 to 15 minutes in the center of the oven, or until brown.

While the pastry is baking, grind the nuts in a nut grinder or a food processor. Mix all the nut mixture ingredients together and prepare all the fruit for the topping. Set aside.

Turn the heat down to 375° and toast the nut mixture on a baking sheet for 3 minutes.

Whip the cream with the vanilla and sugar until stiff, and melt the marmalade over low heat in a saucepan. Stir in the liquor.

To assemble, place one pastry circle on a cake stand and spread with whipped cream. Top with more cream and the remaining circle. Spread with more cream on the top and sides. Place the grapefruit around the outer edge of the top, then arrange the other fruit on top in a decorative pattern. Brush the glaze over the fruit, pat the nut mixture around the sides of the cake, and serve.

Note: Any combination of fruits can be used, using color and flavor contrasts as guides. The dessert should not be assembled more than a few hours prior to serving. ■

Using frozen puff pastry, this dessert is deceptively easy to assemble, and the finished dish will make you feel like a professional pastry chef.

Southwestern Fruit Flan with Prickly Pear Glaze

The White Dove, Tucson, Arizona

(Serves 6 to 8)

½ pound puff pastry

Nut mixture

¾ cup blanched almonds
¾ cup hazelnuts
½ cup sugar
1 egg white

Fruit topping

¼ honeydew melon, sliced
¼ cantaloupe, sliced
2 grapefruit, peeled and sectioned
   with white membrane removed
1 orange, peeled and sectioned with
   white membrane removed
5 strawberries, hulled and sliced
12 raspberries

Flavored cream

1 quart heavy cream
1 teaspoon vanilla extract
¼ cup sugar

Prickly pear glaze

1 jar prickly pear marmalade (apricot
   jam can be substituted)
2 tablespoons brandy or kirsch

Like many of chef Bradley Ogden's creations, this elegant dessert is an updating of an American classic. The pound cake, scented with lemon, is paired with a sophisticated fruit sauce flavored with kirsch.

Lemon Pound Cake with Fruit Sauce

Campton Place, San Francisco, California

(*Serves 10 to 12*)

Cake

1 cup (2 sticks) unsalted butter, softened
2⅔ cups sugar
6 eggs, at room temperature
3 cups unbleached all-purpose flour, sifted
½ teaspoon salt
¼ teaspoon baking soda
1 cup sour cream or *crème fraîche*
1 teaspoon vanilla extract
Grated zest of 2 lemons

Sauce

1½ cups mixed fresh berries, such as grapes, raspberries, and strawberries
3 tablespoons honey
1 tablespoon kirsch
1 tablespoon freshly squeezed lemon juice
½ teaspoon vanilla extract
2 tablespoons cold water
12 fresh figs, halved
2 ripe peaches, peeled and sliced
2 nectarines, peeled and sliced
1½ cups strawberries, washed and hulled
1½ cups raspberries, washed
(*Note:* Fruits such as apricots, blueberries, and blackberries can be substituted for the mix above)
6 tablespoons water
6 tablespoons sugar
4 lemons
6 tablespoons kirsch
Whipped cream for garnish

Preheat the oven to 350°. Line the bottom of a 9-inch tube pan with parchment, then butter and flour the paper and the sides of the pan.

In a mixer bowl, cream the butter and sugar together until light and fluffy, scraping the sides of the bowl occasionally. Add the eggs, one at a time, and continue to beat until the mixture is silky and smooth. Sift the dry ingredients together and add alternatively with the sour cream to the mixture. Beat until smooth. Add the vanilla and lemon zest, and pour the batter into the prepared pan. Bake for 1 hour, or until a toothpick inserted in the center comes out clean. Let stand for 5 minutes, then turn out of the pan and cool on a rack.

To make the sauce, puree the first 6 ingredients in a blender or a food processor fitted with a steel blade. Strain and pour over the sliced fruit. In a small heavy saucepan, combine the water, sugar, lemon juice and zest, and kirsch. Bring to a boil and simmer for 3 minutes. Remove from heat and let cool slightly. Add to the fruit-puree mixture.

To serve, place a slice of cake on each plate, top with whipped cream, and spoon the fruit sauce around the cake.

Note: Both the cake and the sauce can be prepared up to 2 days in advance. Keep the cake tightly covered and refrigerate the sauce. Heat the sauce slightly before serving. ∎

Lemon Pound Cake with Fruit Sauce, Campton Place, San Francisco, California

CARLA SUMMER AND DENNIS CORRADI

Cafe Lilli, Lake Tahoe, Nevada

At Cafe Lilli, perched on a hillside near the shimmering waters of Lake Tahoe, there is a meshing of the talents and interests of chefs Carla Summer and Dennis Corradi. The husband-and-wife team work side by side in the kitchen, but Carla is responsible for creating the dishes for the changing monthly menus and the breads and desserts made daily, and Dennis organizes the logistics of the restaurant kitchen.

"I'm more interested in the chemistry of things, and if I have a philosophy for the dishes I create it's that I like foods that feel good to me and that I've had a relationship with. I don't like trendy foods that are just used for shock value," says Carla.

The restaurant, named for Carla's heroine, playwright Lillian Hellman, opened in 1985. The chefs met while both were students at the California Culinary Academy in San Francisco, after diverse careers up to that time.

After they teamed up and spent some months exploring the foods of France and Italy, Carla worked for Jeremiah Tower at the Santa Fe Bar and Grill in Berkeley, while Dennis, who had learned French cooking at L'Omellette in Palo Alto, became assistant to noted author and cooking teacher Ken Hom.

The menu at Cafe Lilli, a twenty-four-seat restaurant, features only seasonal foods. They have game shipped in from the Napa Valley and use the lamb from nearby Reno, where there is a large Basque community. "If I don't like the looks of the lettuces, then we won't have a salad that night, and it's hard to explain to people that if the ingredients aren't up to my specifications I won't use them," Carla says.

There is a sense of whimsy about some of their creations. The Sweet Potato Tortellini are placed on a bed of creamy caramelized onions, then topped with sprigs of fried cilantro and fried sweet potato skins. "Not everything should be serious, even in a serious restaurant," says Dennis. "There is a place for lighthearted food, as there is for lighthearted music."

The mousse is really a velvety cheese topping for the luscious figs. The flavors of the two meld together perfectly.

Pahska Mousse Lilli with Fruit

Cafe Lilli, Lake Tahoe, Nevada

(Serves 8 to 10)

Mousse

½ cup ricotta cheese
1½ pounds natural cream cheese, at room temperature
1½ cups superfine sugar
3 egg yolks
Grated zest of 1 lemon
4 teaspoons vanilla extract
6 egg whites
2 cups heavy cream

Compote

2 cups water
1 cup sugar
1 vanilla bean (or 1 teaspoon vanilla extract)
1 tablespoon honey
½ cup zinfandel or another fruity red wine
32 fresh black mission figs, quartered (leave stems on 1 quarter of each fig)
4 cups fresh raspberries
Crème fraîche for garnish (optional)

The day before serving, line a strainer with a double layer of damp cheesecloth and place the ricotta in the strainer. Set the strainer over a bowl and let sit in the refrigerator overnight to drain.

In a blender or a food processor fitted with a steel blade, puree the ricotta and set aside. Cook the cream cheese with half of the sugar over low heat until warm, beating with a wooden spoon. Add the egg yolks, one at a time, beating well after each addition, then add the lemon zest, 2 teaspoons of the vanilla, and the ricotta. Beat well, strain through a fine sieve, and cover with plastic wrap pressed directly onto the surface so no skin forms. Cool to room temperature.

Place the egg whites in a bowl and beat at medium speed until frothy. Increase the speed to high and slowly add the remaining sugar. Whip until stiff and shiny, then add the remaining vanilla. In another bowl, beat the cream into soft peaks and set aside.

Fold the egg whites and then the whipped cream into the cheese mixture and turn into a bowl, pressing plastic wrap directly into the surface. Refrigerate at least a few hours, or overnight, until chilled through.

To make the compote, combine the water, sugar, vanilla, honey, and wine in a saucepan. Bring to a boil and reduce over low heat for a few minutes. Reduce the heat and add the figs with stems on. Simmer 2 minutes and remove from the heat. With a slotted spoon, transfer the figs to a cool bowl. Add the raspberries and strain the warm syrup over the figs. Cool and chill well.

To serve, stir the mousse gently until smooth. Spoon the compote into serving bowls and top with a spoonful of mousse and a touch of *crème fraîche* or whipping cream, if desired.

Note: Both mousse and compote can be prepared up to 3 days in advance and kept refrigerated. ■

This is a stunning dessert: luscious warm peaches stuffed with crunchy macadamia nuts, in an apricot sauce scented with allspice.

Baked Peaches with Macadamia Nuts and Apricot Coulis

Grand Champions Club, Aspen, Colorado

(Serves 4)

1 pound apricots, pitted and halved
2 cups water
1¼ cups superfine sugar
4 large ripe peaches
½ cup coarsely chopped unsalted macadamia nuts
5 allspice berries
2 tablespoons soft butter

Garnish

4 rosemary sprigs
12 raspberries

Preheat the oven to 400°.

In a saucepan, combine the apricots, water, and 1 cup of the sugar. Bring to a boil and simmer, uncovered, for 8 minutes; set aside.

Blanch the peaches for 2 minutes in boiling water, then plunge them into ice water. Slip off the skins, and cut off the top of each peach at the top of the pit. Using a sharp knife, remove the pits.

Heat a sauté pan or skillet over medium heat, and toast the macadamia nuts with the allspice. Stir constantly until the nuts are golden brown. Discard the allspice and stuff the nuts into the cores of each peach.

Use the soft butter to butter a metal baking dish and arrange the peaches in it. Place the apricots around them, using a slotted spoon; discard their poaching liquid. Sprinkle with the remaining sugar and bake 10 to 15 minutes.

Arrange the peaches on 4 serving plates. Place the baking dish over medium heat and reduce the juices slightly. Puree the apricot mixture in a blender or a food processor fitted with a steel blade, and push the puree through a sieve. Spoon the sauce around the peaches, and garnish each with a sprig of rosemary and 3 raspberries.

Note: The dish can be prepared a day in advance and reheated in a 250° oven before serving. ■

Baked Peaches with Macadamia Nuts and Apricot Coulis, Grand Champions Club, Aspen, Colorado

BERNARD DERVIEUX

Grand Champions Club, Aspen, Colorado

In other parts of the Southwest the climate does not vary greatly, but chef Bernard Dervieux must create radically different seasonal menus for the dining room of the Grand Champions Club in Aspen. The private sports club is nestled at the bottom of a mountain, with ski slopes visible from the bar and the tennis courts full constantly.

The thirty-four-year-old chef was born in France and trained in the kitchens of some of the luminaries of French cooking, including Paul Bocuse and Roger Verge, before moving to the United States in 1975, when he took a position as saucier at Jean Banchet's famed Le Français in Wheeling, Illinois.

"You still have to know the classics to do any good cooking, and I learned a great deal from these men, as well as putting in many long hours of work," he says.

His next job was as executive chef at The Pump Room, before moving to California in 1980 to become executive chef at the Beverly Hills Hotel.

"It was an exciting time to be in California, since that was when the whole California cuisine movement with the pizzas and pastas was just beginning," he says.

He still spends much of his time in California, since the kitchen of the Grand Champions Club in Indian Wells, near Palm Springs, is also under his command.

During the winter months, his menu features meats and game, and he makes venison sausage in the kitchen. The summer is much lighter, with the menu relying on fish. What unites the two seasons is his use of a combination of mesquite and hickory woods in his grill. He even uses woods to flavor delicate mollusks such as oysters, which he then sauces with creamed leeks and sautés with a hint of curry.

Since the membership of the club is health-minded, many of his desserts feature seasonal fruits. He churns his own sorbets during the summer, and one of his favorite dishes is Baked Peaches with Macadamia Nuts and Apricot Coulis, a combination of fruit tastes with the crunchy texture of nuts.

The pale peach mousse and vivid red raspberries are a beautiful and delicious combination. This mousse is quick to make since it uses canned fruit.

Peach Mousse with Raspberry Coulis

Austin's Courtyard, Austin, Texas

(Serves 6)

Peach mousse

One 22-ounce can peach slices, drained
2 envelopes unflavored gelatin
¼ cup cold water
5 egg yolks
3 tablespoons sugar
¼ cup dry white wine
2 cups heavy cream, whipped

Raspberry coulis

2 pints fresh raspberries
1 tablespoon sugar
¼ cup dry red wine

Puree the peaches in a blender or a food processor fitted with a steel blade, and sprinkle the gelatin over the water to soften for 10 minutes.

Beat the egg yolks until light and lemon colored, then beat in the sugar and wine. Place over simmering water in the top of a double boiler and stir constantly until the custard is thickened and coats the back of a spoon. Do not allow it to boil or the eggs will curdle. Stir the gelatin into the hot custard and stir to dissolve.

Cool the custard and then beat in one-third of the whipped cream. Quickly fold in the remaining cream and pour into glasses. Chill until set, at least 3 hours, in the refrigerator.

To make the *coulis*, boil the ingredients together for 3 minutes over medium heat, then push the mixture through a fine sieve and chill.

To serve, place some of the *coulis* on top of each mousse.

Note: The mousse and sauce can be prepared up to 2 days in advance and kept tightly wrapped with plastic wrap in the refrigerator. ∎

Do not be put off by the length of this recipe; none of the steps are difficult, and it's the combination of flavors and textures that makes it so special. The crunchy poppy seeds, creamy filling, and succulent fresh peaches make this cake well worth the effort.

Poppy Seed Cake

Gordon's, Aspen, Colorado

(Serves 10 to 12)
Cake

1 orange
⅓ cup poppy seeds
1 cup buttermilk
1¾ sticks unsalted butter, softened
1 cup granulated sugar
1 cup powdered sugar
3 extra-large eggs, separated
1 teaspoon vanilla extract
2 cups unbleached all-purpose flour
1 teaspoon baking soda
½ teaspoon salt
1 teaspoon ground cinnamon

Orange buttercream

½ cup granulated sugar
½ cup water
8 egg yolks
1½ cups (3 sticks) unsalted butter, softened
Grated zest of 2 oranges

Crème fraîche

1 cup heavy cream
1 cup sour cream

For assembly

6 ripe peaches, peeled, pitted, and thinly sliced
4 tablespoons plus 1 teaspoon poppy seeds
12 ounces white chocolate, melted

Garnish

Additional peach slices
1 teaspoon poppy seeds

Grate the zest from the orange, and soak it, along with the poppy seeds, in the buttermilk for 15 minutes.

Preheat the oven to 350°. Place the butter in the bowl of a mixer and add the sugars. Start beating on low speed to incorporate, then raise the speed to high and beat, scraping the sides of the bowl occasionally, until the mixture is light and fluffy. Add the egg yolks one at a time, beating well between each addition, then add the vanilla.

Sift the flour with the baking powder and salt and add alternately to the batter with the buttermilk mixture. In another bowl, beat the egg whites until stiff peaks form. Beat one-fourth of the meringue into the batter to lighten it, then gently fold in the remaining whites.

Line a 12½ by 17½ inch jelly roll pan with parchment paper. Butter and flour the paper. Gently spread the batter evenly in the pan and sprinkle the top with the cinnamon. Bake in the preheated oven for 25 to 30 minutes, or until the top is lightly brown and springs back when touched. Remove from the oven and cool on a rack.

To make the buttercream, combine the sugar and water in a heavy saucepan and bring to a boil over high heat. Cook to the small-crack stage (290°). While the sugar syrup is cooking, beat the egg yolks at high speed in a mixer bowl until light and lemon colored. With the mixer running, slowly pour the syrup into the yolks. Continue beating until the mixture is cool, about 3 to 5 minutes. Add the softened butter bit by bit and continue beating until the frosting has a shiny look to it. Add the orange zest and set aside.

To make the *crème fraîche*, whisk together the heavy cream and sour cream, cover with plastic wrap, and allow to stand at room temperature for 24 hours. Refrigerate at least 12 hours before using.

To assemble, butter and line a 13-by-4½-inch loaf pan with parchment paper. Using the bottom of the loaf pan as a guide, cut 2 pieces of cake the same size. Slice the layers in half lengthwise to create 4 thin layers.

Place 1 layer at the bottom of the loaf pan, and spread one-half of the *crème fraîche* over it. Top with sliced peaches, and place a second cake layer in the pan. Spread with one-half of the buttercream and top with peaches. Repeat with the third and fourth layers, ending with buttercream. Chill the cake 1 hour.

Run a knife along the sides of the loaf pan. Invert the cake onto a serving platter, wrapping the pan in hot towels to facilitate loosening it. Lift the pan off the cake.

Cut 2 pieces of waxed paper into 20-by-3-inch strips. Sprinkle with 2 tablespoons of poppy seeds, then spread melted white chocolate

Poppy Seed Cake, Gordon's, Aspen, Colorado

over the poppy seeds with a spatula. Place the ribbons on a chilled marble slab, or in the refrigerator on a cookie sheet, and when firm but pliable, press against the long sides of the cake. Trim the ends and use the trimmed pieces for the ends of the cake. Return the cake to the refrigerator and allow the chocolate to chill hard. Then remove the waxed paper.

Decorate the top of the cake with additional peach slices, and sprinkle with 1 teaspoon of poppy seeds.

Note: This cake can be made up to a day before serving and kept in the refrigerator. Allow it to sit at room temperature for 1 hour before serving. ■

Soufflés are one of those magical desserts that are sure to draw raves, are not difficult to make, and require very little advance planning. The succulent taste and vivid pink color of prickly pears enhance this soufflé, and the cornstarch is a trick to make it more stable and less prone to deflation.

Prickly Pear Soufflé

La Paloma/Atlas, San Diego, California

(*Serves 8*)

Prickly pear puree

11 ripe prickly pears
¾ cup unsweetened coconut milk
¼ cup sugar, melted in ¼ cup boiling water
1 ounce tequila

Soufflé

1½ cups milk
6 tablespoons unsalted butter
1½ cups sugar
¾ cup unbleached all-purpose flour
9 eggs, separated and at room temperature
1 ounce tequila
¼ cup prickly pear puree
Pinch of salt
2 tablespoons cornstarch

Garnish

Prickly pear slices
Remaining prickly pear puree

Prickly Pear Soufflé, La Paloma/Atlas, San Diego, California

To make the prickly pear puree, peel all the prickly pears and coarsely chop 6 of them. Place the chopped fruit in a blender or a food processor fitted with a steel blade along with the coconut milk, sugar syrup, and tequila. Puree the mixture. Slice the remaining prickly pears, place the slices flat in a pan, and pour the puree over them. Allow to stand 1 hour before continuing.

Prepare a 2-quart soufflé dish. Chill the dish well, butter it heavily, coat the inside with sugar, and return the dish to the refrigerator. Preheat the oven to 375°.

To make the soufflé, pour the milk into a heavy saucepan and bring it to a boil with the butter and 1 cup of the sugar, stirring constantly. When it comes to a brisk boil, add the flour all at once and whisk to remove any lumps. Reduce the heat to low and whisk until the mixture pulls away from the sides of the pan.

Transfer the mixture to another bowl and allow it to cool slightly.

Beat the egg yolks into the cooled mixture a few at a time, beating well after each addition. Add the tequila and ¼ cup of the prickly pear puree, beat well, and set aside.

Beat the egg whites with a pinch of salt until soft peaks form, then slowly add the remaining ½ cup sugar, beating until the whites are stiff and glossy. Sift the cornstarch over the egg whites and beat briefly to incorporate.

Beat one-third of the egg whites into the yolk mixture, then quickly fold the remaining whites in. Pour half the batter into the prepared mold, then layer with some of the sliced prickly pears. Top with the remaining batter and place in the center of the preheated oven.

Bake 40 to 45 minutes, turning the heat down to 350° after 30 minutes. The soufflé will be brown and puffy.

Serve immediately, garnishing the portions with slices of prickly pear and some of the puree. ■

This dessert is delicious, with a marvelous blending of flavors and textures united by a hint of liquor, and it looks far more difficult than it is. The pinwheels of roulade around a creamy chestnut mousse are a real showstopper.

Chestnut Royal

Piret's, San Diego, California

(Serves 10)

Note: This cake must be started 2 days in advance of serving, since the prunes have to marinate overnight and the completed cake should chill overnight.

Filling

½ pound pitted prunes
½ cup Jack Daniels whiskey (bourbon can be substituted)
¼ cup freshly squeezed lemon juice

Cake

5 eggs, separated and at room temperature
½ cup sugar
1½ teaspoons vanilla extract
1 cup sifted cake flour
Pinch of salt

Chestnut mousse

4 eggs, separated and at room temperature
1½ cups canned sweetened chestnut puree
¾ cup (1½ sticks) unsalted butter, softened
¼ cup Jack Daniels whiskey or bourbon
2 tablespoons freshly squeezed lemon juice
½ teaspoon vanilla extract
1½ cups heavy cream
Pinch of salt

To make the prune filling, marinate the prunes in the liquor and lemon juice overnight. Drain the prunes and place in a blender or food processor, add a few tablespoons of the marinade, and puree until smooth, adding liquid as needed to make a smooth puree. Set aside.

Preheat the oven to 325°. Prepare a 10-by-15-inch jelly roll pan by buttering it, lining it with parchment paper, and buttering the paper.

To make the cake, beat the egg yolks with an electric mixer until light and lemon colored. Slowly add the sugar and continue to beat until the mixture is thick and forms a ribbon on itself when the beater is lifted, about 5 to 7 minutes. Add the vanilla to the yolks and beat an additional minute, then sift the cake flour over the yolks and beat to incorporate. Set aside.

Beat the egg whites at medium speed until foamy, adding a pinch of salt, and then beat to the soft peak stage. Beat one-fourth of the egg whites into the yolk mixture and then quickly fold in the remaining whites.

Pour the batter into the prepared pan, rap it on the counter to even it out, and bake in the center of the preheated oven for 20 to 25 minutes. When done, invert onto a sheet of oiled plastic wrap and, when slightly cool, remove the parchment paper. Spread the warm cake with the prune filling, roll it lengthwise into a roll, wrap it in oiled plastic wrap, and freeze it to facilitate slicing.

To make the chestnut mousse, beat the egg yolks at medium speed until light and lemon colored. Continue to beat until thick. Set aside. In another bowl, beat the chestnut puree and butter until light and fluffy. Add the whiskey, lemon juice, and vanilla and continue to beat. Add the egg yolk mixture and set aside.

Beat the cream until lightly whipped and store in the refrigerator. Beat the egg whites to the soft peak stage, adding a pinch of salt when foamy, then fold first the cream and then the egg whites into the chestnut mixture.

To assemble the cake, line a 10-inch springform pan with oiled plastic. Slice the roulade into ⅓-inch slices and line the bottom and sides of the pan with the slices, putting them as closely together as possible. Fill the pan with the chestnut mousse, placing any leftover slices of roulade on top. Cover the cake and chill overnight.

To serve, invert onto a serving platter and remove the pan and plastic. ∎

Chestnut Royal, Piret's, San Diego, California

Strawberry shortcake, a favorite American dessert since the mid-nineteenth century, has been described in poetry and prose. These rich biscuits with a hint of Grand Marnier flavoring the luscious berries show why it's an ageless treat.

Strawberry Shortcake

Brennan's, Houston, Texas

(Serves 6)

Shortcakes

3 cups cake flour
1 cup sugar
1½ tablespoons baking powder
1 teaspoon salt
¾ cup shortening
3 eggs, lightly beaten
½ cup milk
2 tablespoons vanilla extract

To assemble

3½ pints strawberries
1¼ cups sugar
2 tablespoons Grand Marnier
2 cups heavy cream
Mint sprig for garnish (optional)

Preheat the oven to 350°. In a mixer, blend the dry ingredients. Add the shortening and mix until it forms uniform crumbs, scraping the bowl as needed, then add the egg, milk, and vanilla. Blend until it is a smooth thick dough. Refrigerate at least 30 minutes, then roll into a ¾-inch-thick rectangle on a floured surface. Cut 6 shortcakes with a 4-inch-round cutter and place on a greased cookie sheet.

Slice 2½ pints of the strawberries and set aside. Puree the remaining pint with 1 cup of the sugar and the Grand Marnier. Pour over the sliced strawberries and set aside. Beat the cream with the remaining ¼ cup sugar until stiff. Set aside in the refrigerator.

Bake the shortcakes for 12 minutes, or until the tops are brown. Slice in half while hot, spoon equal portions of the strawberry filling on each, and cover with a dollop of whipped cream. Replace the top of the shortcakes and top with more berries and cream. Garnish with a mint sprig, if desired.

Note: The shortcakes are best if baked immediately before serving;

however, the dough can be made and formed up to 6 hours in advance with the cookie sheet kept refrigerated. The berries can also be done in advance. ■

What could be more Southwestern than the combination of citrus and tequila? This pastel sorbet tastes like a frozen Margarita, and the blush of red from the pomegranate juice adds to the visual appeal.

Texas Fruit Sorbet

Las Canarias, San Antonio, Texas

(Makes ½ gallon)

Sorbet

2 pounds (8 cups) granulated sugar
1 quart water
3 cups pink grapefruit juice (about 4 grapefruit)
2 cups unsweetened pineapple juice
1 cup freshly squeezed lime juice plus grated zest of 3 limes (about 5 limes)
½ cup freshly squeezed lemon juice plus grated zest of 1 lemon (about 3 lemons)

¼ cup white tequila
6 egg whites, beaten lightly

Pomegranate sauce

Seeds from 5 fresh pomegranates, white pith and skin discarded
1 cup water
5 tablespoons granulated sugar
¼ cup *crème de cassis*
2 teaspoons arrowroot, dissolved in ¼ cup cold water

Bring the sugar and water to a boil and simmer for 5 minutes, or until it has a syrupy consistency. Add the juices and zests to the syrup and allow to stand 10 minutes. Add the tequila and place the liquid in an ice cream freezer.

Process according to manufacturer's instructions; 10 minutes into the freezing process, add the egg whites to the mixture and process until frozen and smooth. Transfer to a bowl and place in the freezer.

To make the sauce, place the pomegranate seeds in a blender or a food processor fitted with a steel

Strawberry Shortcake, Brennan's, Houston, Texas

blade and puree. Pour into a saucepan, along with the water and sugar. Bring to a boil and add the *crème de cassis* and arrowroot mixture. Simmer until thickened, remove from the heat, strain to remove the seeds, and chill well.

To serve, spoon the sauce around the *sorbet* and splash some tequila on top, if desired.

Note: The *sorbet* can be made a few days in advance, but it will become granular after that time. If you have some left, you can always allow it to melt, and then freeze it again. ■

Sweet potato pies are part of the Southern tradition in Southwest cookery, as are meringue-topped pies and pecan pies. This combination of all three is spectacular.

Maple Pecan and Sweet Potato Pie

The Mansion on Turtle Creek, Dallas, Texas

(Serves 8)

Pie shell

4 tablespoons unsalted butter
1½ cups unbleached all-purpose flour
1½ tablespoons sugar
1 egg yolk
2 tablespoons ice water

Pecan filling

3 eggs
½ cup brown sugar
1 tablespoon butter, melted
1 teaspoon vanilla extract
1½ tablespoons maple syrup
1 cup whole pecans

Sweet potato topping

¾ pound sweet potatoes, peeled and quartered (about 1½ cups)
Pinch of ground ginger
Pinch of ground cinnamon
Pinch of ground cloves
½ teaspoon salt
1 egg white
3 tablespoons sugar
Whipped cream for garnish

Texas Fruit Sorbet, Las Canarias, San Antonio, Texas

To make the pie shell, cut the butter into the flour with a pastry cutter or 2 knives until it has the consistency of fine meal. Sprinkle on the sugar and beat the egg yolk with the ice water. Sprinkle on and lightly blend together. This can also be done in a food processor fitted with a steel blade; be careful not to overprocess.

Form into a ball and wrap in waxed paper. Chill at least 20 minutes. Roll out on a floured surface and pat into a 10-inch pie plate. Prick with a fork and return to the refrigerator while making the filling.

Preheat the oven to 350°. Beat all the filling ingredients except the pecans together and blend well. Cover the pastry shell evenly with the pecans and pour in the filling. Bake 30 minutes, or until golden brown. Cool to room temperature before continuing.

While pie is baking and cooling, prepare the sweet potato topping. Cook the sweet potatoes in boiling water to cover until tender, about 15 minutes. Drain well.

In a mixing bowl, whip the potatoes with the spices until almost smooth; it should be slightly lumpy. Cool in the refrigerator 20 minutes.

In another bowl, beat the egg white until frothy at medium speed. Increase speed to high and slowly add the sugar. Beat until the meringue is stiff. Fold the meringue into the sweet potato mixture and spread on top of the pie.

Bake at 350° for 25 to 30 minutes. Serve at room temperature, garnished with whipped cream.

Note: Let the pie sit at room temperature at least 1½ hours but not more than 6 hours before serving. ■

Rice pudding is a favorite comfort food, and this version is creamier and more flavorful than most by adding custard to the cooked rice.

Rice Pudding

The American Grill, Phoenix, Arizona

(Serves 8)

Rice

1 cup long-grain white rice
½ cup water
2½ cups milk
¼ cup sugar
1 tablespoon unsalted butter
1 teaspoon vanilla extract
⅓ cup raisins
4 tablespoons apricot preserves

Pastry cream

6 tablespoons milk
¼ cup sugar
1½ teaspoons unsalted butter
1 tablespoon plus 1½ teaspoons cornstarch
1 egg yolk
¼ teaspoon vanilla extract

To finish the dish

¼ cup heavy cream
1 tablespoon powdered sugar

Blanch the rice in boiling water for 5 minutes and drain. In a large saucepan, combine the rice with the water, milk, sugar, butter, and vanilla. Bring the mixture to a boil over medium heat, then reduce the heat to low, cover the pot, and allow the rice to simmer for 30 to 40 minutes, or until the rice is tender and thickened. Stir the mixture occasionally to prevent it from sticking.

Pour the rice into a bowl to cool, then chill in the refrigerator until cold, stirring occasionally as it chills. Plump the raisins in boiling water for 30 minutes, drain, and add to the rice, along with the apricot preserves.

While the rice is cooking, prepare the pastry cream. Combine the milk, one-half of the sugar, and the butter in a small saucepan or in the top of a double boiler over simmering water, and stir constantly until it thickens;

do not allow the custard to come to a boil or the eggs will curdle. Combine the remaining sugar, cornstarch, and egg yolk and whisk. Add a small amount of the hot milk gradually, whisking constantly, and then pour the egg yolk mixture back into the saucepan and cook, stirring constantly, until it comes to a boil. Remove from the heat and beat until smooth. Stir in the vanilla and chill.

To finish the dish, whip the cream with the sugar until stiff. Fold the cream and ½ cup of the pastry cream into the chilled rice.

Serve in glasses or bowls, garnished with a dollop of whipped cream.

Note: The rice pudding can be prepared up to 3 days in advance and kept refrigerated, covered with plastic wrap. ■

Flan is a traditional Southwestern dessert, one of the many dishes of Spanish derivation now part of the repertoire. Pureed yams impart a vibrant color to the usually pale dish, as well as boosting the flavor and texture.

Red Yam Flan

Border Grill, Los Angeles, California

(Serves 6 to 8)

2 or 3 red or yellow yams (about 1¼ pounds total weight), to yield 1½ cups of puree
1½ cups sugar
¾ cup water
8 eggs
2 egg yolks
One 14-ounce can Eagle Brand Sweetened Condensed Milk
1 cup heavy cream
1 cup half and half
1½ teaspoons vanilla extract
½ teaspoon each ground cinnamon, allspice, and nutmeg

Preheat the oven to 325°. Scrub the yams and bake for 1 to 1½ hours, depending on size, until they are soft. Remove them from the oven, peel

Red Yam Flan, Border Grill, Los Angeles, California

yams, cut into chunks, and puree in a blender or a food processor fitted with a steel blade. You should have 1½ cups. Set aside to cool.

While the yams are baking, prepare the caramel. In a small heavy-bottomed saucepan, bring the sugar and ¼ cup of the water to a boil over high heat, washing down any crystals clinging to the sides of the pan with a pastry brush dipped in cold water. Watch the syrup carefully, not stirring, and when it turns a golden brown and is bubbling furiously, pour it into the center of an aluminum or glass 9-inch flan pan or soufflé dish, swirling the syrup around the bottom and partially up the sides of the pan. Pour any remaining syrup that does not adhere back into the pot, add the remaining ½ cup of water, and bring the syrup back to a boil to serve with the flan. Set aside.

Beat the eggs and egg yolks in a bowl until light and fluffy. Add the remaining ingredients, along with the cooled yam puree, and beat well.

Pour the mixture into the prepared pan, place it in a roasting pan, and pour boiling water into the roasting pan so it comes halfway up the sides of the flan. Bake for 1 hour, or until firm throughout. Do not overbake.

Remove from the water bath, cool to room temperature, and then chill. To unmold, run a knife around the edge of the flan, place a serving plate over the flan, and invert, rapping it on the counter to loosen the flan. Pour off any juice and serve with the caramel sauce.

Note: The flan can be made up to 4 days in advance and kept chilled in the refrigerator, tightly covered with plastic wrap. ∎

TOM EMERICK
Wine Connoisseur, Houston, Texas

In a city where grills and cafes abound, Tom Emerick, chef at the Wine Connoisseur, a small restaurant in the owner's house, believes there is a place for his love of classic cuisines. The thirty-seven-year-old Hartford native has been cooking in the Houston area for the past decade, and his personal interpretations of elegant dishes has been influential on other chefs in the area.

Emerick developed his philosophy through his classical training. After being discharged from the Army, he decided to visit friends in Europe and ended up attending the Cordon Bleu in London, then working in the kitchens at the Savoy and Carlton hotels. He next worked on a cruise ship in the Caribbean.

"While the hotels were classic Escoffier, they were still crushing the shells for lobster bisque with a mortar and pestle. The cooks on the ship were an international lot, and I really learned a lot about the foods of the world," he says.

After returning to land, he worked at the Hyatt Regency O'Hare in Chicago before entering the Culinary Institute of America, graduating in 1976.

It was then that he moved to Houston, where he first worked in the classic French kitchen at Foulard's before becoming chef in 1979 at Che, one of the most innovative restaurants that Houston had encountered. After it closed, he became chef at the exclusive Bayou Club.

"Although I had a daily printed menu, the members would call up and tell me about dishes they had eaten in Paris or New York, and I would try to duplicate the food for them. It was like doing twenty private dinners a night," he recalls.

In 1984 he moved to Austin, where his cooking at Gianni's garnered the first four-star review in the city's history, and then it was back to Houston, to become chef at 120 Portland and then the River Cafe.

"While I use some Southwestern ingredients in my food, I didn't fit the mold of the grill chef," he says.

This is a welcome variation on the classic floating island. The baked meringues have an appealing texture and appearance, and the custard sauce is velvety and rich.

Salzburg Nockerel with Vanilla Sauce

Wine Connoisseur, Houston, Texas

(Serves 4)

Custard

2 cups heavy cream
4 egg yolks
4 tablespoons sugar
1 teaspoon almond extract

Soufflés

4 egg whites, at room temperature
3 tablespoons sugar
½ teaspoon vanilla extract
½ teaspoon grated lemon zest
3 egg yolks, beaten
1 tablespoon flour or cornstarch
1 tablespoon unsalted butter
2 tablespoons milk or light cream

To make the custard, heat the heavy cream to the boiling point in a heavy saucepan over medium heat. Beat the yolks with the sugar and almond extract until thick and lemon colored. Whisking constantly, beat in about half of the heavy cream, then pour

the mixture back into the saucepan. Cook over low heat or in the top of a double boiler until the custard thickens and coats the back of a spoon. Do not allow it to boil or the egg yolks will curdle.

Preheat the oven to 450°.

To make the soufflés, beat the egg whites until soft peaks form. Add the sugar gradually and beat until stiff peaks form. Add the vanilla and grated lemon zest to the egg yolks, then fold the yolks into the whites. Sift the flour or cornstarch over the mixture and fold quickly to incorporate.

Heat the butter and milk or light cream in a baking dish, divide the meringue mixture into 4 ovals, and bake in the center of the preheated oven for 5 to 7 minutes, or until lightly browned.

To serve, rewarm the custard over very low heat if necessary, place a bed of the custard sauce on each of 4 plates, and place 1 of the meringues on top.

Note: The custard can be made up to 6 hours in advance and kept at room temperature; reheat over low heat. Do not make the meringues in advance. ∎

Salzburg Nockerel with Vanilla Sauce, Wine Connoisseur, Houston, Texas

If you are facile with your pasta machine, rolling out white chocolate to create this unusual trompe l'oeil dessert will be easy. The ravioli are like little individual candy bars, with the hazelnut sauce adding a perfect background flavor.

White Chocolate Ravioli

The Rattlesnake Club, Denver, Colorado

(Serves 8)

Chocolate mousse filling

8 ounces extra-bittersweet chocolate or other high-quality dark chocolate, coarsely chopped
4 tablespoons unsalted butter
2 eggs, separated and at room temperature
Pinch of salt
Pinch of cream of tartar
¼ cup sugar
¾ cup heavy cream, chilled
1 teaspoon vanilla extract

Hazelnut sauce

¾ cup hazelnuts
1¾ cups half and half, scalded
5 egg yolks at room temperature
¼ cup sugar
¼ teaspoon vanilla extract
Pinch of salt
2 tablespoons Frangelico (hazelnut liqueur)

Ravioli

Seven 3-ounce bars of imported white chocolate, preferably Tobler

Garnish

½ cup chopped toasted hazelnuts
8 mint sprigs

To make the mousse, melt the chocolate and butter in the top of a double boiler over barely simmering water. Stir until smooth, then transfer to a medium bowl. Whisk in the egg yolks quickly, one at a time. In a separate bowl, beat the egg whites with the salt and cream of tartar at medium speed until frothy. Raise the speed to high and gradually add 2 tablespoons of the sugar, beating until the whites are stiff but not dry. Beat the cream with the remaining sugar and the vanilla until lightly thickened. Fold the egg whites and then the whipped cream into the chocolate and chill, covered with plastic wrap, overnight.

To make the sauce, toast the hazelnuts on a baking sheet in a 350° oven for 10 minutes, or until browned. Place the nuts in the center of a tea towel, cover them with the towel, and let them steam for 2 minutes. Rub them with the towels to remove the skins. Place the nuts and hot half and half in a blender or a food processor fitted with a steel blade and blend until the nuts are coarsely chopped. Cool completely, or refrigerate overnight.

Combine the yolks, sugar, vanilla, and salt in a heavy saucepan or in the top of a double boiler and whisk in the nut cream. Stir over low heat until the mixture heats and slightly thickens; foam will come to the top and it will barely coat the back of a spoon. Stir constantly while heating and do not allow it to come to a boil or the yolks will curdle. Remove from the heat and strain into a bowl. Stir in the Frangelico and refrigerate until needed.

To make the ravioli, chill a ravioli mold in the freezer. Preheat the oven to its lowest setting for 5 minutes and then turn it off. Break the chocolate bars in half lengthwise and place them on a baking sheet in the turned-off oven for about 5 minutes, or until the chocolate is soft enough to be pliable and give to the pressure of a finger.

Roll 1 piece of chocolate out on a sheet of parchment paper to flatten it enough to fit through a pasta machine set on the widest setting. Run the chocolate through the pasta machine rollers, decreasing the setting each time until the chocolate sheet is 1/16 inch thick.

Quickly press the chocolate into the chilled ravioli mold and fill each ravioli with 1 to 1½ tablespoons of the mousse. Roll a second sheet of chocolate in the same manner and press it on the top of the ravioli, sealing it with a rolling pin.

Invert the mold, pressing gently to release the ravioli, and cut them into separate pieces with a ravioli cutter or knife. Place on a chilled baking sheet in the refrigerator and repeat with more sheets of chocolate, softening them in a warm oven as necessary.

To serve, let the ravioli stand at room temperature for 30 minutes. Spoon ¼ cup sauce on each plate, and place 4 ravioli on top. Sprinkle with nuts and garnish with mint.

Note: While no one will deny that this dessert is a lot of work, none of it need be last minute. The filling and sauce can be made 2 days in advance, and the completed ravioli can be refrigerated for 2 days, tightly wrapped, before serving. ■

JIMMY SCHMIDT
The Rattlesnake Club, Denver, Colorado

The dishes prepared by Jimmy Schmidt at The Rattlesnake Club in Denver are as vibrant and exciting as the artworks by Jasper Johns and David Hockney on the walls. Although soft-spoken and even more boyish in appearance than his thirty-two years, chef Schmidt is considered by his colleagues to be one of the most influential forces on American food today. He has been heralded by restaurant critics, and The Rattlesnake Club catapulted into prominence virtually months after it opened in 1986.

Schmidt's partner in the venture is Los Angeles restaurateur Michael McCarty, whose Michael's in Santa Monica is credited with establishing a beachhead for new American cuisine.

Chef Schmidt was raised on a farm in Champaign, Illinois, where he says he used to listen for the corn growing in the stillness of the night. He studied electrical engineering at the University of Illinois, and ventured into cooking purely by accident.

During a summer break in France in 1974, he studied both cooking and wine in Avignon, and it was there that he met Madeleine Kamman, who has been a force in his career. Rather than returning to engineering, he graduated from Kamman's Modern Gourmet cooking school in Boston, then worked in her restaurant, Chez la Mere Madeleine, before assuming the position as chef, and then limited partner, at the Detroit institution.

"There are no native dishes in Colorado, and what I'm doing is a regional style of cooking. I've learned that *tomatillos* really have an affinity for *poblanos*, and I've learned how to effectively use cilantro and wild mushrooms to achieve nuances in sauces," he says.

He is fond of blue corn tortillas, which he brings in from New Mexico, for the color and texture they impart. He uses flour as the basis for his Blini with Smoked Salmon, a dish given life with a confetti of chopped chilies sprinkled over a carefully composed rosette of fish topping the *blini*.

DONNA NORDIN
Cafe Terra Cotta, Tucson, Arizona

Donna Nordin's decision to open Cafe Terra Cotta, a light and airy restaurant in suburban Tucson, was the next step in a culinary progression that began more than twenty years ago when she decided to pursue her interest in French cooking.

"I was bitten by the food bug the first time I went to France during college, and I got tired of being confined to an office. I knew that if I went to Cordon Bleu it would make my life more interesting, and cooking would stop being my hobby," she says.

Her professional training continued with a professional pastry course from Gaston Le Nôtre a few years later, but just being in France had a marked effect on her. "I was in awe; France was a different world to me and the whole realm of ingredients and food being so much a part of their lives influenced me," she says.

By 1980 her roster of students numbered in the thousands; however, she decided to close her school, Cordon Rouge, to fulfill her wanderlust by giving cooking lessons around the country. The same year, she gained national exposure when a now-celebrated article on "Fabulous and Easy Chocolate Desserts" appeared in *Bon Appetit* magazine.

It was on one of these teaching trips, in 1983, that she first visited Tucson and became intrigued with the area and the idea of "contemporary Southwest cuisine," as she calls the style of cooking she now follows.

"The city was about five years behind the times, and needed to be brought up to the level of the rest of the country's cooking." The first step was a catering company; then she opened the restaurant in 1986.

She maintains that her style of cooking is simple, although based on classic French cuisine, and that it's the inclusion of Southwest ingredients that makes the difference. Her *coulis* of tomatoes underlying delicate shrimp stuffed with a mixture of goat cheese and cream cheese is an example: "The sauce is a concept from Cordon Bleu, but the cilantro and chilies are from me."

The pie is simultaneously rich and light, with the pecans in the crunchy crust and a hint of coffee in the filling providing nuances of flavor and texture.

Chocolate Cream Pie with Meringue Crust

Bistro Garden, Houston, Texas

(Serves 6)

Crust

3 egg whites
Pinch of salt
Pinch of cream of tartar
½ cup sugar
½ cup chopped pecans
½ teaspoon vanilla extract

Filling

9 ounces bittersweet or semisweet chocolate
⅓ cup espresso
4 eggs, separated and at room temperature
2 cups heavy cream
¼ cup powdered sugar
Chocolate shavings for garnish

Preheat the oven to 300° and lightly grease a 9-inch pie plate.

In a mixer, beat the egg whites with the salt and cream of tartar at medium speed until frothy. Increase the speed to high and slowly add the sugar, beating until stiff peaks form and the meringue looks glossy. Fold in the pecans and vanilla and spread the mixture into the pie plate, building up a rim of meringue. Bake for 30 minutes, then cool at room temperature.

To make the filling, melt the chocolate and remove from the heat. Add the espresso, stirring until smooth, and when the mixture has cooled, beat in the egg yolks, one at a time. Whip 1 cup of the cream until stiff and fold into the chocolate mixture. Beat the egg whites until stiff and fold into the chocolate mixture.

Pour into the baked pie shell and chill until set. Before serving, whip the remaining 1 cup of cream with the powdered sugar and spread on the pie. Sprinkle with chocolate shavings.

Note: If the pie is served the day it is baked the crust will remain crisp. It will become a chewy meringue by the next day. ∎

While there are a number of parts to this elegant dessert, none of them is complicated to make, and the dessert, with its contrasting colors and flavors, is well worth the effort.

Mocha Framboise

Cafe Terra Cotta, Tucson, Arizona

(Serves 16)

Cake

14 eggs, separated, at room temperature

1¾ cups sugar

5 ounces bittersweet chocolate, melted (semisweet or other high-quality dark chocolate can be substituted)

1½ cups walnuts, ground in a blender or food processor

1 teaspoon instant coffee dissolved in 1 teaspoon boiling water

Chocolate cream

6 ounces bittersweet chocolate, grated

1½ cups heavy cream

Coffee buttercream

1 cup sugar

½ cup water

2 eggs

1½ cups (3 sticks) unsalted butter, softened

2 tablespoons instant coffee dissolved in 2 teaspoons boiling water

For assembly

¼ cup Framboise or other raspberry liqueur

½ cup strained raspberry jam

⅓ cup finely chopped walnuts

32 chocolate "coffee beans"

Preheat the oven to 375°. Prepare two 10-by-15-inch jelly roll pans by greasing and flouring them, then lining the bottoms with parchment paper.

To make the cake, beat the egg yolks until light and fluffy. Slowly add 1½ cups of the sugar and continue to beat until the mixture is thick and forms a ribbon when it falls from the

Mocha Framboise, Cafe Terra Cotta, Tucson, Arizona

beaters. Divide the yolk mixture into two bowls; add the melted chocolate to one bowl and the ground walnuts and instant coffee to the second. Beat each well and set aside.

Beat the egg whites at medium speed until foamy, then raise the speed to high. Beat until stiff peaks form and then slowly add the remaining ¼ cup sugar. Fold half of the meringue into each of the yolk mixtures and immediately pour the batter into the 2 pans.

Bake for 20 to 30 minutes, or until lightly browned. Remove from the oven, cover the pans with tea towels, and let cool. Unmold and cut each lengthwise into two 5-by-15-inch pieces. Set aside.

To make the chocolate cream, bring the cream to a boil, remove from heat, then stir in the chocolate. Place in the freezer until cool, then whip to a creamy consistency.

To make the coffee buttercream, cook the sugar and water in a heavy saucepan until it reaches the soft ball stage, 240° on a candy thermometer. Beat the eggs, then slowly add the sugar syrup while beating, and

continue to beat until the mixture cools. This can be done with a mixer or in a food processor. Beat in the soft butter, bit by bit, then flavor with coffee extract. Chill until firm enough to handle, but do not allow it to become hard.

To assemble the cake, start with 1 layer of chocolate cake and brush with the liqueur. Spread with all of the jam and a layer of coffee buttercream. Top with a layer of walnut cake and spread with half of the chocolate cream. Top with the second walnut layer and the remaining chocolate cream. Finish with the chocolate layer and end with the remaining coffee buttercream on the top and sides of the cake.

Mark the cake into 16 pieces and pipe a rosette on each side of each piece. Sprinkle the sides with chopped walnuts and place chocolate coffee beans on each rosette.

Serve at room temperature.

Note: The cake can be prepared up to 2 days in advance and should be stored in the refrigerator. Allow it to sit at room temperature for 2 hours before serving. ∎

The combination of this dense chocolate cake with the creamy banana sauce is old-fashioned yet sophisticated; it's like a new twist on the banana split.

Chocolate Cake with Roasted-Banana Sauce

Cafe Annie, Houston, Texas

(Serves 8)

Cake

¾ cup (1½ sticks) unsalted butter, at
    room temperature
1⅓ cups sugar
3 egg yolks
1⅓ cups milk
⅓ cup heavy cream
1 teaspoon vanilla extract
6 ounces semisweet chocolate,
    chopped
1½ cups cake flour
1 teaspoon baking powder
½ teaspoon salt
2 eggs

Banana sauce

4 ripe bananas
2 tablespoons dark rum
¼ to ½ cup sugar
1 cup heavy cream
1 teaspoon vanilla extract

Garnish (optional)

Banana slices
Mint sprigs
Pecan halves

Preheat the oven to 350°. Prepare a deep-sided 10-inch-round cake pan (a springform pan can be used) by buttering the sides and bottom, lining the bottom with parchment paper, buttering the parchment paper, and lightly dusting with flour.

Place the butter and 1 cup of the sugar in a mixer bowl and beat until the butter loses its yellow color, about 15 minutes at low speed.

Make a custard by combining the egg yolks, ⅓ cup of the milk, the cream, and vanilla in the top of a double boiler. Whisk together and then stir with a wooden spoon over simmering water until the custard thickens and coats the back of a spoon; do not allow it to boil or the egg yolks will curdle. Remove from heat and stir in the chocolate. Allow to cool.

Add the whole eggs, one at a time, to the butter mixture, then add the chocolate custard. Sift the dry ingredients together and add to the mixture alternately with the remaining 1 cup of milk. When the batter is smooth, pour into the prepared pan. Place the pan in a larger baking pan, add hot water to halfway up the sides of the cake pan, and bake in the center of the preheated oven for 60 to 70 minutes.

Cool on a rack for 10 minutes, remove the cake from the pan, and place on a wire rack.

To make the sauce, place the bananas in a 350° oven for 20 minutes. Peel the bananas and place the pulp in a mixing bowl. Mash with a spoon, then add the rum, sugar, cream, and vanilla.

To serve, spoon the sauce over the warm cake and garnish with slices of fresh banana, a sprig of mint, and a pecan half, if desired.

Note: The cake is best if baked just prior to serving; however, a cooled cake can be heated slightly in a 100° oven before serving. ∎

Ibarra chocolate is a hard Mexican cooking chocolate already flavored with cinnamon. This recipe, a new twist on the classic flourless chocolate cake, replicates the taste. The cake is delicious and easy to make, and the glaze makes it look very professional when it's brought to the table.

Ibarra Chocolate Cake

Coyote Cafe, Santa Fe, New Mexico

(Serves 10 to 12)

Cake

2 cups unblanched almonds
3 oranges
3 ounces bittersweet chocolate, grated
1½ teaspoons ground cinnamon
6 eggs, separated and at room
    temperature
½ cup sugar
3 tablespoons freshly squeezed orange
    juice
3 tablespoons Grand Marnier

Chocolate Cake with Roasted-Banana Sauce, Cafe Annie, Houston, Texas

Glaze

5 ounces bittersweet chocolate
½ ounce unsweetened chocolate
1 tablespoon light corn syrup
¾ cup (1½ sticks) unsalted butter

Preheat the oven to 350°. Butter the bottom and sides of a 9-inch springform pan, line with parchment paper, and butter and flour the parchment paper.

Roast the almonds on a baking sheet for 5 to 7 minutes, or until slightly browned. Place them in a blender or a food processor fitted with a steel blade and grind finely. While the almonds are roasting, remove the orange zest from the oranges with a zester or vegetable peeler and chop finely.

In a bowl, combine the almonds, orange zest, grated chocolate, and cinnamon. Set aside.

Beat the egg yolks until light and lemon colored, incorporating as much air as possible, and when thick add the sugar in two parts. In another bowl, beat the egg whites until stiff. Beat the dry ingredients, orange juice, and one-third of the egg whites into the egg yolks, then rapidly fold in the remaining egg whites.

Pour the batter into the prepared pan and bake in the middle of the preheated oven for 35 to 40 minutes, or until the cake pulls away from the sides of the pan. Loosen the sides of the pan and cool 10 minutes. Invert the cake onto a rack to cool and remove the paper. When cool, paint with Grand Marnier.

To make the glaze, break the chocolate into small pieces and combine all the ingredients in the top of a double boiler. Heat the pan, and turn off the heat as the water comes to a boil. Beat with a whisk until smooth.

Place the cake on a rack over a pan or waxed paper and pour the glaze in the center. Tilt the cake to distribute the glaze evenly, and allow the cake to sit for 45 minutes. Repeat with the remaining glaze and let glaze set for 45 minutes before serving.

Note: The cake can be made up to a day in advance and should be kept at room temperature. ■

ROBERT DEL GRANDE
Cafe Annie, Houston, Texas

While some chefs have transferred talents from other art forms to cooking, Robert Del Grande, through his doctorate in biochemistry, entered the restaurant kitchen with an understanding of the scientific principles employed there. The success of Cafe Annie, where he is chef and his wife, Mimi, runs the front of the house, is the result of Del Grande's culinary talent combined with his scientific background. When asked about the influences on his cooking, he replies: "A dinner at Michael's in Santa Monica in 1980 when the entire California era was beginning, and the writings of Einstein and Bertrand Russell."

The thirty-three-year old California native began cooking while in graduate school at the University of California at Riverside. "I had not cooked before, but the principles I was learning applied to the kitchen, and I really enjoyed manipulating a recipe to make it taste better," he says.

In the summer of 1981, he went to Houston to visit his future wife. "I had been going to school for ten years without a break, and I fully intended to start postdoctoral work in the fall. Cafe Annie was a French bistro, and Mimi's sister and brother-in-law were the general partners, so they gave me a job and I'm still here," he says.

After a year he was the chef, and changed the food to new American cuisine, with an emphasis on the Southwest. "There was a European style of science as there is of cooking, and I read all the French books for the technique, and then went off and did dishes in an American way. Using local ingredients was a natural step, since it didn't take a cooking course to know that what was grown twenty miles from here was going to be fresher than what I had to have flown in."

His philosophy of cooking is that "each dish on the plate should be the manifestation of one single thought. It all fits exactly like a puzzle, and a tight, singular thought squeezes errors out. The main item, the technique, the vegetable, and the sauce equal the whole, so the more complicated you make the sauce the simpler you make the vegetable."

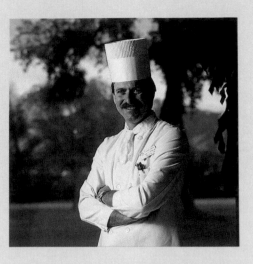

ALAN ZEMAN

Tucson Country Club, Tucson, Arizona

Alan Zeman, the executive chef at the exclusive Tucson Country Club, has achieved recognition for his cooking even though neither the public nor reviewers can sample his Sonoran Seafood Stew or his Pumpkin-Chocolate Cheesecake since the dining room is open to club members only.

The primary exponent for new Southwest cooking in his state, Chef Zeman's dishes have been featured on the pages of *Bon Appetit*. He participated with fellow chefs at the American Institute of Wine and Food dinner in Los Angeles in 1986, he was a speaker at the Symposium on American Cuisine held in Boston in 1984, and he now has a spice business, in hope of popularizing his Sonoran spice blend.

Zeman, a Chicago native, moved to Arizona to study political science, and returned briefly to Chicago when he first tried his hand at cooking. He entered the Culinary Institute of America in Hyde Park seven years after his initial acceptance, during which time he worked for a number of hotels and clubs in the Tucson area. In 1980, he was voted "Chef of the Year" by his colleagues in the Chef's Association of Southern Arizona, and graduated from the Institute first in his class with high honors.

"I knew I should get the academic training, but I love working in the kitchen. Cooking is one of the few businesses in which you get to handle something from start to finish, and you have almost an instant sense of satisfaction at seeing that flow of goods become a dish," he says.

After graduation, he immediately returned to his adoptive city, where he has changed the nature of the food served at the club. "When I first arrived we were serving beef to about 90 percent of the members, and now we're serving more than half of them fish," he says.

Although fish must be imported to the landlocked state, he has developed local resources for many of the other foods he likes to cook, such as pheasant and quail, apples, and pistachio nuts.

Pumpkin and spices are wonderful counterpoints to the richness of cream cheese in this cheesecake, and the chocolate swirl, as easy to create as in a marble cake, contrasts with the pastel filling and adds to the overall flavor.

Pumpkin-Chocolate Cheesecake

Tucson Country Club, Tucson, Arizona

(Serves 12)

Crust

¾ cup graham cracker crumbs
3 tablespoons light brown sugar
5 tablespoons unsalted butter, melted
1½ teaspoons vanilla extract

Swirl

3 ounces bittersweet chocolate, chopped
¼ to ⅓ cup heavy cream

Filling

Two 8-ounce packages natural cream cheese, at room temperature
⅔ cup sugar
½ cup canned pumpkin (not pumpkin pie filling)
¼ teaspoon ground cinnamon
¼ teaspoon ground ginger
⅛ teaspoon ground cloves
¼ cup heavy cream
5 eggs

Garnish

Marzipan Pumpkins, following (optional)

Preheat the oven to 275°. Combine the ingredients for the crust and press into the bottom of a buttered 9-inch-square cake pan with 2-inch sides.

Prepare the swirl by melting the chocolate with the cream in the top of a double boiler, or in a bowl over simmering water. Stir until smooth and then set aside, keeping it warm.

To make the filling, cream the cheese and sugar at medium speed with an electric mixer, scraping the bowl frequently and beating until smooth. Add the pumpkin, spices, and cream, and then add the eggs, one at a time, beating well between each addition.

Pour the filling over the crust. Drizzle a spiral pattern with the chocolate on top and draw it through the batter with a knife. Do not stir.

Place the cheesecake pan in a larger baking pan and pour ½ inch of boiling water into the baking pan. Bake in the center of the preheated oven for 1 hour, or until the center is firm and not soupy.

Cool at room temperature, then chill at least 2 hours. To serve, dip the bottom of the pan in very hot water for 1 minute. Invert onto a sheet of cardboard or a plate and then back onto a serving platter. Garnish each serving with a marzipan pumpkin, if desired. ▪

Using the same method, you can easily create a number of edible adornments— lemons, oranges, limes—for special desserts.

Marzipan Pumpkins

Tucson Country Club, Tucson, Arizona

(Makes 12)

4 tablespoons corn syrup
1 cup sifted powdered sugar
7 ounces almond paste
Red and yellow food coloring
½ teaspoon water
12 whole cloves

Work the corn syrup, powdered sugar, and almond paste together to form a smooth dough, kneading it with your hands. Mix a few drops of red and yellow food coloring together with the water and add to the dough, kneading to evenly color it.

Form into 12 balls, then indent the top of each to form a pumpkin shape. Use the cloves to make pumpkin stems. ▪

RICK O'CONNELL
Rosalie's and RAF, San Francisco, California

While in France apprenticeships may last a decade, Rick O'Connell accelerated the pace while working with the great chefs of France teaching at the Mondavi Winery in the Napa Valley.

"It was at those sessions assisting in the kitchen where I made the quantum leap to strive for perfection rather than good cooking. It was the most serious thing I'd ever seen, and the tension about a sauce breaking was like being in an operating room," says the former nurse, who started cooking while living in Japan prior to moving to San Francisco in the late 1960s.

She recalls Michel Guerard counting the peas to go on a garnish, and then saying the plate would have been better with one more pearl onion.

She planned the menu for Rosalie's a year before it opened in 1984. The restaurant, owned by Bill Belloli and Bill Miller, is one of the most stunning environments in the city; the space is dominated by mirrored columns, to which steel palm fronds have been attached to create fantasy trees.

The menu is a reflection of chef O'Connell's past: it combines regional American foods from New England, Texas (where she lived for a few years), and California. The Fried Crab Balls with Jícama Panache is an example of a combination of the Southwest and East, while her lobster and prawn tamales are drawn more directly from living in Texas.

Her desserts follow the pattern. They are elegant but simple in form, combining many flavors and textures. Chocolate and hazelnuts are combined in a roulade with a rich chocolate sauce, for example.

At RAF, which opened in late 1986, the food is Italian. The room, with plaster bas reliefs, looks like a Mediterranean grotto, and the antipasti and *risotti* vary daily.

"As Rosalie's is the me of today, RAF is my background, and what unites the two is that I'm cooking what I like to cook," she says.

Pinwheels of chocolate filled with light cheese and crunchy hazelnuts and a smooth chocolate sauce are an unbeatable match. This elegant dessert is very easy to make, and serves a large number of people.

Chocolate Roulade with Bittersweet Sauce and Hazelnut Filling

Rosalie's Restaurant, San Francisco, California

(Serves 10 to 12)

Cake

¾ cup sifted unbleached all-purpose flour
¼ cup unsweetened cocoa
1 teaspoon baking powder
¼ teaspoon salt
4 eggs
1 cup sugar
¼ cup water
1 teaspoon vanilla extract

Filling

1 cup hazelnuts
1 cup ricotta cheese
¾ cup (1½ sticks) unsalted butter, softened
¾ cup sifted powdered sugar
⅓ cup half and half
2 teaspoons vanilla extract

Chocolate sauce

1 pound bittersweet chocolate
6 tablespoons unsalted butter
1¼ cups heavy cream
½ cup milk
Pinch of salt
1 cup sifted cocoa
¾ cup light corn syrup

Garnish

Powdered sugar
Fresh raspberries

Preheat the oven to 350°.

Sift the flour, cocoa, baking powder, and salt together and set aside. In a mixer bowl, beat the eggs and sugar together until the mixture is very thick and lemon colored and forms a ribbon when dropped from the beater, about 10 minutes. Add the water and vanilla to the egg mixture, then add the sifted dry ingredients in two stages.

Line a 10-by-15-inch sheet cake pan with parchment and spread the batter evenly over the paper. Tap on the counter to remove any air bubbles and bake the cake for 12 to 15 minutes. Remove from the pan and trim to an even rectangle.

To make the filling, toast the hazelnuts for 10 minutes in a 350° oven. Remove the nuts from the oven, place the nuts in a tea towel, and fold the towel over them so they are covered. Let them steam for 5 minutes, then rub the skins off while they are still inside the towel. Chop and set aside.

Cream the ricotta, butter, and sugar together with a mixer, beating until light and fluffy. Add the half and half and vanilla, then fold in the nuts.

Spread the filling over the cake and roll the cake tightly, using the lining paper as a guide. Refrigerate for a minimum of 1 hour with the seam side down on a platter.

To make the sauce, chop the chocolate coarsely. Heat the butter, cream, and milk in a saucepan and stir in the chocolate, salt, cocoa, and corn syrup. Heat, whisking, until the mixture is combined and glossy. Set aside to cool and store in refrigerator.

To serve, cut the roll into thin slices with a serrated knife and place 2 slices on each plate. Spoon the sauce around the slices and dust the top with powdered sugar and a few raspberries.

Note: The cake can be made up to 2 days before serving, and the sauce keeps well in the refrigerator for 2 weeks. ■

From the time I saw my first meringue mushroom on a bûche de Noël, *I have always been delighted by trompe l'oeil food. This "baked potato" of ice cream, with all the appropriate* faux *trimmings, will delight your guests as well.*
P.S. And it's far simpler than carving a rabbit from a radish.

Y.O. Surprise

Sam Houston's, Kerrville, Texas

(Serves 4 to 6)

1 quart vanilla ice cream
1 cup sifted cocoa
1 cup heavy cream
½ teaspoon vanilla extract
3 tablespoons sugar
1 cup chocolate syrup
¼ cup chopped walnuts

Allow the ice cream to soften until it is pliable, then form it into irregular ovals resembling potatoes, making indentations with your fingers to look like eyes. Roll the "potatoes" in cocoa and place on a baking sheet in the freezer to firm up for at least 1 hour.

Whip the cream with the vanilla and sugar until it is the consistency of sour cream. Place in a strainer over a bowl in the refrigerator if not used immediately.

To serve, pool a few tablespoons of the chocolate syrup on each plate and place an ice cream potato on top of it. Cut the ice cream down the top and gently pull both sides away from the middle, as if opening a potato. Place the whipped cream in the center and sprinkle with the nuts. ■

Chocolate Roulade with Bittersweet Sauce and Hazelnut Filling, Rosalie's Restaurant, San Francisco, California

Menus for Entertaining

When I'm giving a party I envy the chefs I have observed while writing cookbooks over the past few years. They have a large number of hands ready to aid them in bringing dishes hot to the table, or to help them artfully arrange a plate. I think of them barking out orders to the line of cooks under their command when I am in my kitchen—as I hardly view two cats underfoot as adequate assistance.

I don't like last-minute preparation while my guests are enjoying themselves in the living room, and I'm assuming everyone using this book agrees with me. The first rule I followed in planning these menus was that the majority of the work can be done in advance, sometimes days in advance. This does not mean that the meal will cook itself, but at least three of the four dishes will be completed, and could be plated, before the doorbell rings. The last-minute work is no more than a few minutes of "hands-on time"—what I define as finishing a dish, not starting it.

When I plan a party menu, I start by looking at each recipe to see which dishes or steps of dishes can be done in advance. I then create a work order that might start with "Wednesday night— soak beans overnight" and extend to the last-minute grilling of the fish for the Friday-night dinner party.

On the day of the party itself, my trick to keep everything on course is a sheet of paper taped to the refrigerator door. It lists the menu, which steps need be taken with each dish, how long each will take, and what I plan to serve it in or on. It includes what might seem trivial, such as "open wine to breathe," but it means that nothing is left to memory at a time when I might be flustered. The bread I awakened at dawn to bake does not get forgotten in the rush of steaming vegetables, and the relish to complement the grilled fish does not end up being served as a separate course after the salad.

At the bottom of the sheet is my "battle plan": how long each dish will take to finish cooking and when to start each one so those to be served together finish at the same time.

If advance work is the first rule for a party, then the second rule is that every meal should contain a variety of colors, textures, and flavors. Food, more than any other art form, involves all of our senses. We eat with our eyes before our noses begin to detect aromas, and only then do our mouths enter the sensory process. I find it important to keep all these senses in mind, as well as textural sensations ranging from crunchy hard foods to soft foods that virtually melt away on the tongue.

I also believe that not every dish need be a star. I would prefer to see energy go into a spectacular appetizer and a dessert to be served with a simple entree, or keep the starter as unadorned as oysters on the half shell and spend the time and energy on a main course that will be memorable. That's why not every dish listed in each menu has a corresponding page number in the book. The thing that makes this book so special is that every recipe is a showstopper. The menus intersperse them liberally with simpler dishes that can be found in basic cookbooks.

And, regardless of the event, always start with the dishwasher empty, the sink and counters clean, and time enough to put your feet up for at least ten minutes before the guests arrive.

Peach Mousse with Raspberry Coulis, Austin's Courtyard, Austin, Texas

A Cocktail Party for 20 to 40

I prefer to have a mixture of hors d'oeuvres at a cocktail party, and enough of them that people don't really need to think about dinner after leaving. The only difference in my mind between a cocktail party and a cocktail buffet is that no forks are needed; all of the offerings—both those passed by servers and those on platters placed on tables—are finger foods. I usually put out stacks of small plates to encourage people to eat heartily.

As the guest list grows for a party, I tend to add more dishes rather than making huge quantities of a few things. This is a matter of personal choice. If you feel more comfortable with limited options, all the dishes listed below can be done in multiple batches.

Have enough fried tortilla chips (see page 16) to go with the various dishes, and remember that vegetables as well as chips can be served with the Guacamole.

Chimayó Cocktail, Rancho de Chimayó, Chimayó, New Mexico

Brie and Papaya Quesadillas, page 62
Crab Quesadillas, page 70
Chile con Queso, page 24
Assorted Hors d'Oeuvre, page 72
Spicy Beef Tartare, page 74
Guacamole, page 138
Exotic-Game Pâté, page 76
Chimayó Cocktails, page 143
Margaritas, page 143

A Southwest Thanksgiving for 8 to 10

Few meals are as bound with personal traditions as Thanksgiving dinner, and when people collaborate on a meal it often turns into a starch festival. One person must have candied yams, while another does not consider it a feast without mashed potatoes. This menu solves that problem, since all of the dishes relate to the traditional celebration, but in new ways.

Oysters with Cilantro Pesto, page 65, or Wild Rice Pancakes Garnished in Two Ways, page 77
Sweet Potato Bisque with Avocado, Pear, and Lime, page 83
Roast Wild Turkey with Blue Cornmeal–Chorizo Stuffing, page 92
Buttered Swiss Chard with Tomato, page 98
Ancho Chili Preserves, page 142
Maple-Pecan Sweet Potato Pie, page 161
Pumpkin-Chocolate Cheesecake, page 170

A Traditional Southwest Brunch for 8 to 10

I love attending relaxed brunches, but I shy away from giving them due to the early hour at which the last-minute work must be executed. This menu for a seated brunch is based on as much advance preparation as possible.

Sopa Azteca, page 26
Huevos Rancheros with Green Chili Sauce, page 29
Guacamole, page 138
Chimichangas, page 36
Sopaipillas, with honey, page 40
Biscochitos, page 49

Guacamole, Border Grill, Los Angeles, California

Two Formal Dinners for 6 to 8

Even though entertaining is becoming far more casual, with fewer courses and even one-course meals more common than long evenings at table, there are still occasions that call for a multi-course seated dinner. These menus follow the classic fashion of a fish and meat course, but I suggest that each be small servings. While the elegance of the menus is certainly in keeping with your best china and linens, use colorful flowers to reflect the Southwest origin of the food.

Catfish Mousse with Crayfish Sauce, page 68
Salmon Painted Desert, page 104
Herb Sorbet, page 137
Roasted Free-Range Veal Rack with Fresh Herbs and Natural Juices, page 121
Oven-roasted potatoes
Poppy Seed Cake, page 157

Wild Mushroom Gratin, page 62
Turbot and Tuna with Crustades of Black Olives and Smoked Tomato–Butter Sauce, page 106
Leg of Lamb Marinated in Mexican Spices with a Smoked Chili Sauce, page 122
Mexican Sweet Cinnamon Rice, page 141
Tossed salad
Chestnut Royal, page 159

A Buffet Dinner for 20

A buffet table that's a cornucopia of colorful foods can be a dramatic and delicious way to entertain a large group of friends. In the case of a buffet, when everything but the desserts is on the table at once, combining colors becomes all the more important. I plan buffet menus so that none of the foods requires a knife, since I don't think people were meant to be octopuses. I also try to choose foods that do not have to be eaten immediately from the oven, since people tend to finish conversations and not rush to the table when called.

Cornmeal Pizza with Wild Mushrooms, page 58
Avocado and Shrimp Terrine, page 66
Crepes Carmen, page 112

Pork Tenderloin with Date and Fig Chutney, page 126
Corn Pasta Ravioli with Cinnamon-flavored Chorizo and a Sauce of Texas Goat Cheese and Ancho Chili, page 128
Three-Tomato Salsa, page 139
Pahska Mousse Lilli with Fruit, page 154
Chocolate Roulade with Bittersweet Sauce and Hazelnut Filling, page 173

A Vegetarian Dinner for 6 to 8

It doesn't happen as often as it did in the seventies, when it seemed everyone was eating nothing but brown rice, but occasionally we are still faced with creating an interesting vegetarian meal for guests with dietary prohibitions. I find that even the confirmed carnivores among my friends agree that it is better for everyone at the table to eat the same dishes rather than to segregate out those persons who follow dietary guidelines.

Goat Cheese Rellenos, page 58
Guacamole, page 138
Sweet Potato Tortellini in Almond-Cream Sauce with Sautéed Onions and Cilantro, page 80
Baked Peaches with Macadamia Nuts and Apricot Coulis, page 155

A Dinner of Updated Foods Based on Southwest Tradition for 6 to 8

I've found it's better to demonstrate what you mean by new Southwest cooking rather than just talking about it. All the dishes in this menu have their ancestry in the traditional foods of the Southwest; however, interpretations by innovative chefs have placed them on a new level of sophistication.

For this dinner, the centerpiece was white mums, white statice, and large dried New Mexican red chilies. I used bamboo skewers to attach the pods to the base of florist's oasis.

Pumpkin-Chocolate Cheesecake, Tucson Country Club, Tucson, Arizona

Fresh-Berry Mousse in Pizzelle-Cookie Bowls, Wolfdale's, Lake Tahoe, California

A Traditional Buffet for 20

This could also be called "Back to the Roots"—a menu planned to evoke the strains of mariachi bands and the vision of thorny cacti. These dishes are native to the Southwest, favorite foods in both homes and restaurants. Rather than wine, I suggest serving a Mexican beer and Margaritas.

A Casual Sunday Supper for 10

I am a great fan of Sunday entertaining. Dinners can begin and end early, and the meal and dress are usually more casual than for Saturday nights. Another benefit is that dishes can be long simmered since there are fewer demands to take you away from the house.

A Children's Birthday Party for 6 to 8

Children's food should be fun, and a birthday party is a festive opportunity to introduce children to new tastes while giving them some of their favorite foods.

A Dinner of Down-Home Favorites for 8

There is a decided Southern influence in the Southwest, which melds with the Mexican to create dishes unique to the region. The dishes on this menu reflect that influence, and can form the basis for a casual supper.

This is a meal for your checked or gingham napkins, and perhaps straw place mats in lieu of a tablecloth.

A New Southwest Brunch

A theme of new Southwest cooking is assertive flavors that make foods sparkle with excitement. Several dishes are especially good for brunch, and make interesting departures from bacon and eggs or corned beef hash.

While there is some last-minute preparation involved with the meal, many steps—from roasting the chilies to the preparation of the corn fritter batter—can be done in advance.

A Casual Seafood Supper for 10 to 12

It's the chicken and egg dilemma: are more varieties of fresh fish and seafood available because of popular demand, or are people becoming more enthusiastic about aquatic creatures because they are more plentiful in the marketplace? Regardless, the versatility of fish and seafood make them a marvelous basis for menu planning. This menu features diverse methods of presentation.

There are a number of dishes listed below; make just one recipe of each and then the group can have a sampling of all the options.

A Romantic Dinner for 2

There are times when just two people make a party, such as Valentine's Day or a special birthday. The following menu tempts the tastebuds with subtle yet tantalizing flavors, but is not heavy, since food may not be all that's on the diners' minds.

A Dinner for 6 to 8 for Accomplished Cooks

Some recipes require more culinary prowess and more time in the kitchen than others. While I believe that every recipe in this book can be accomplished successfully in the home kitchen, this menu concentrates on those that are fairly complex.

A Spring and Summer Dinner Outdoors

In the Southwest, outdoor dining is an option a great percentage of the year, but those of us in less temperate climates also relish the opportunity to cook and eat al fresco. This menu utilizes a charcoal grill and features dishes appropriate to warmer times of the year.

Black Bean Chili with Sirloin and Asiago, Cafe Terra Cotta, Tucson, Arizona

DECORATING IDEAS FOR A SOUTHWESTERN PARTY

The set for a party is as important as it is for a play. What visually greets guests whets their appetites and helps create a mood for the evening. Even if the dinner is formally served and seated, decorative touches will signal that the food to follow is inspired by the Southwest.

You don't have to go as far as buying *piñatas* and straw donkeys to set the scene for a Southwestern meal, any more than you need a dragon with flashing red lightbulbs for eyes if you want to create a Chinese ambience. But the assertive spirit of the flavors of the food will be conveyed by bright colors and materials native to the region. A Southwestern theme is not the time for the starched damask linen and a centerpiece of baby's breath, unless the linen is dyed turquoise and the baby's breath is arranged with dried chili pods and heads of garlic.

I have an array of brightly colored napkins, and I use a mixture of red, turquoise, yellow, orange, hot pink, emerald green, and purple (you can also buy a few smaller packages of paper napkins rather than just one color). For a buffet, I roll the utensils in the napkins and tie them with raffia twine. Instead of arranging them on a tray or the tablecloth, I place them in a basket or a low terra-cotta flower pot, or cover a tray with dried corn husks, so the variety of colors is showing. For a seated dinner, I'll use the same napkins on the table, festooning them out of the wineglasses.

Since we have all been supporting the economies of Third World nations by collecting baskets for the past few years, it's time to take them off the walls and use them on the table. Transform them into serving pieces by lining them with platters or mixing bowls. If there is a gap between the rim of the bowl and the sides of the basket, fill it in with napkins. For serving breads or rolls, place different-colored napkins at an angle so the brightly colored corners will fall over the top. Flat-bottomed baskets need only be lined with aluminum foil–covered cardboard to become utilitarian serving trays.

Terra-cotta is another material reminiscent of the desert. Small flowerpots can be used as cigarette cups or cocktail napkin holders, while the deep saucers intended as underliners for large urns can be made into wine coolers (place plastic underneath them on a wooden table, since they do "sweat" when filled with ice). Small plant saucers become votive candle holders, and a medium-sized flowerpot can be used as a salad or serving bowl if lined with another bowl.

For centerpieces, a panoply of brightly colored Shasta daisies, miniature carnations, poinsettias, zinnias, marigolds, and any other bold bloom works well, and so does a grouping of small cacti bought at a supermarket. I've always liked mixing flowers and vegetables to combine colors and shapes, and your arrangement can be as simple as a pyramid of green and red peppers or as elaborate as a mix of artichokes, chilies (both fresh and dried bell peppers and chilies), dried strawflowers, and fresh flowers.

If you're hosting a buffet, a table with different elevations resembling a Cubist still life is easy to achieve and quite dramatic. Drape cake pedestals and overturned boxes with napkins, or use overturned baskets to create different heights on the table. Just make sure that all props are sturdy enough to support a serving bowl, and that the front levels are low enough that people can reach over them to serve from the back of the table.

Southwestern food is spirited, so don't be afraid to be adventurous. If you don't own any Mexican or Spanish pottery, anything that is brightly colored or with a bold floral pattern will work nicely. ∎

Pairing Wine with New Southwest Cooking

BY DAVID VAUGHAN

Conventional wisdom mandates that beer accompany all Southwest cuisine; only a heretic or an easterner would suggest wine. Even as an avid wine lover, I agree that a Dos Equis or a Tecate deserves a prominent place at the traditional Southwestern table; however, I urge you not to overlook the pleasures to be gained through the proper pairing of wine with the dishes from the new Southwest cooking. There are many native foods, such as *chimichangas*, barbecue, and chile con carne, for which beer is the natural companion. On the other hand, the numerous more subtle and more complex dishes in this book, such as Avocado and Shrimp Terrine, Two-Salmon Pasta, and Rabbit with Apple Cider and Mustard Seeds, marry beautifully with an appropriate wine.

The immense variety in the spicing level of new Southwest cooking makes it difficult to offer general wine advice. One must start with the central guideline for pairing all wine and food: to balance the intensity of flavor of the wine with the intensity of flavor of the food. Serve intensely flavored wine with intensely flavored food and mildly flavored wine with mildly spiced dishes. Neither the food nor the wine should overpower the other.

Thus, with a spicy dish, such as those prepared with *serrano* or *jalapeño* chilies, consider a spicy zinfandel from California, or a hearty red from the Rhône Valley in France, such as Côte Rotie or Hermitage. With more mildly flavored dishes, such as Prawns Stuffed with Goat Cheese on Tomato Coulis or Blue Corn Blini with Smoked Salmon, consider a mildly flavored white wine such as a macon from the Burgundy region of France.

The fresh taste of cilantro is used extensively in dishes in this volume. It is enhanced and balanced by the grassy flavors of some of the California sauvignon blancs and fumé blancs; however, the overall taste of the dish is what should be judged. If cilantro predominates, as in Cream of Cilantro Soup with Mussels, that is what should be matched. If, on the other hand, the cilantro flavor is blended with chilies, then a more intense wine is required.

As a rule, red wines are more intensely flavored than white wines; however, there are exceptions. For instance, a big spicy Gewürztraminer from Alsace or one of the "monster" chardonnays from California would in all likelihood be more fully flavored than a light red from the Loire Valley in France.

Richer white wines, even those that verge on the edge of sweetness, go well with spicy food. The richness or trace of sweetness enables the flavor of wine to come through the spiciness of the dish. Many of the so-called "blush" wines now being promoted fit into this category. Also, many of the bigger, richer California chardonnays and white zinfandels can match up to a relatively spicy dish.

Many Southwestern dishes are casual and, therefore, call for a simpler wine. Although 1929 Château Latour would be a wonderful companion for Enchilada of Filet Mignon with Chanterelles and Sorrel Sauce, there are probably better uses for your 1929 Latour. Most of this cuisine is fun, casual fare and calls for fun, casual wines. It is a cuisine to be enjoyed, not pondered, and I recommend that the accompanying wines be similarly straightforward. ∎

W hen we started shopping for ourselves, no one had to tell us to select yellow bananas instead of green, or that apples should be firm and free from soft spots, or that tomatoes are eaten when they are bright red. These basics of our culinary knowledge come from the observations of childhood, watching what our parents selected from the market, and from familiarity with the flavors of what we eat.

In the same vein, it is not necessary for us to be told that a hamburger does not contain ham, or that a hot dog is not a breed of canine.

Unless we grew up in traditional Southwestern families, however, we have no such subliminal reference points for the selection of ingredients such as *tomatillos* or plantains, or what constitutes an enchilada or a *chimichanga*. In compiling this glossary, I had the following purposes in mind:

• to define specific ingredients as to their flavor characteristics, and explain how to select them and what to substitute if a substitution is possible.

• to define various terms and names of specific Southwestern dishes, both to aid in the selection of dishes and to explain the traditional bases from which the chefs are improvising.

• to add to your bank of culinary trivia so you can dazzle your dinner guests by explaining the history of a dish or the derivation of a name.

• to make every reader fluent in "restaurant Spanish."

Assorted Herbs

Fresh Lemons

achiote (ă-chē-ō′-tā):
Dark, brick-red seeds from the annatto tree that are often made into a paste; these are especially popular in the Yucatán for adding color and an earthy flavor to food. They must be soaked in water overnight before grinding, or you can bring them to a simmer, let them soak for an hour, and then grind them.

acitrón (ă-sē-trŏn′):
Cactus leaves that have been candied by simmering in a sugar syrup.

aguacate (ă-gwă-kă′-tā):
The Mexican word for *avocado;* in English also called alligator pear. The name comes from the Aztec word *ahuacacuahatle,* meaning "testicle tree" (avocados grow in pairs), and may explain claims that the avocado is an aphrodisiac. Though roughly the shape of a pear and technically a fruit, the light green flesh of the avocado is eaten as a vegetable, dip, garnish, or butter substitute. Its skin may be smooth and green or dark and rough; a ripe avocado should be

soft when touched, but not mushy unless it is to be mashed. Do not allow the flesh of any avocado to be exposed to air or it will turn brown. Sprinkle cut surfaces with lemon juice, and for dips such as *guacamole,* press plastic wrap directly into the surface of the food.

albóndigas (ăll-bōn′-dē-găs):
Spanish for *meatballs,* which are traditionally served in a chicken soup.

añejo cheese (ăn-yā′-hō):
A firm Mexican cheese that is strong-flavored, salty, and white. Feta cheese is an acceptable substitute, although it can be more crumbly.

anise:
Two types of unrelated spices that impart a licorice flavor to food: European or green anise is in the form of small seeds from a bush related to parsley; and star, badian, or Chinese anise takes the form of small brown star-shaped pods. In Southwestern cooking the European type is used, although the Chinese can be substituted.

antelope:
Black Buck antelope is harvested in Texas; the meat is finely textured and sweeter than venison.

armadillo:
A game animal, covered with protective plates, that is indigenous to the Southwest and has a flavor comparable to duck.

arroz (ăr-rōts′):
The Spanish word for *rice,* which is one of the staples, along with beans, in the Latin American diet. Long-grain rice is preferred for Southwestern cooking.

arroz con pollo
(ăr-rōts′ kōn pŏ′-yō):
Spanish for *rice with chicken,* this variation on Spanish *paella* consists of poultry, rice, and vegetables cooked together in a tomato sauce.

asadero cheese (ă-să-dā′-rō):
Also called Chihuahua, Mennonite, or Oaxaca cheese, *asadero* is a white Mexican cheese that is milder than *añejo* and is frequently sold braided. Longhorn cheddar, Monterey jack, or Swiss may be substituted.

atole (ă-tō′-lā):
Corn gruel.

azafran (ă-tsă-frăn′):
See *saffron.*

backstrap:
A tenderloin steak, which should be so tender that it does not require a long marinating period.

BEANS
The species of bean used in Latin American dishes varies regionally more than the methods of preparation. Here are the basic bean types and their characteristics:

black:
Also called *frijoles negros,* or turtle beans, these small black kidney-shaped beans are from the Yucatán and central Mexico and have a smoky mushroom flavor stronger than pinto beans. They are used for black bean soup, and have a black-purplish cast when cooked.

bollito (bōy-ē′-tō):
A boiling bean native to the Southwest.

garbanzo (găr-băn′-zō):
Also called chick-peas and originally

from Spain, these tan or golden beans, roughly spherical in shape, have a mild, slightly sweet flavor, are widely available dried or canned, and are also available fresh in some markets. It's preferable to use the dried ones, soaked and cooked, rather than the canned ones, which have a mushy texture.

pinto (pēn′-tō):
Frijoles, small brown kidney-shaped beans with pale spots. These are the beans used in traditional Mexican cookery, and they have migrated across the border to Texas as well.

red:
Named "Mexican strawberries" by Southwestern cowboys, red beans are similar to and interchangeable with pinto beans.

bison:
Called "hunchbacked cows" by Coronado when he encountered them in Texas, bison are the largest mammals in North America. An important source of meat since prehistoric times, they were almost exterminated in the 1890s. They are now raised in the western United States. The meat is richer, more tender, and less gamey than that of wild bison. The taste is similar to beef, but slightly sweet.

biscochitos (bǐs-kō-chē′-tōs):
A crispy anise flavored cookie that is native to New Mexico. They are cut into star or other decorative shapes and are traditionally served at Christmas.

black-eyed peas:
Introduced into the Southwest by African slaves, each of these little, slightly kidney-shaped beans is marked with one black spot, or "eye." Black-eyed peas are sold dried or canned, and are now available fresh.

blue corn:
A variety of corn with blue-gray kernels, indigenous to the Southwest and originally grown by the Pueblo Indians. Dried and ground blue corn is similar in taste to but more flavorful than regular cornmeal.

boar:
Wild pig, served both roasted and smoked.

bolillos (bō-lē′-yōs):
Spanish for hard rolls that have a texture similar to French bread.

buñuelo (boon-wā′-lō):
Crispy fried pastries that are sprinkled with cinnamon and sugar.

cabrito (kǎ-brē′-tō):
A kid goat, usually roasted whole, and considered a delicacy both in Mexico and the Southwest.

cactus:
The pads of the *nopal* cactus, or prickly pear cactus, are usually served raw or cooked as a vegetable and taste similar to green beans, but are more tart. Green or red in color, the small, unblemished pads are preferred.

cajeta (kǎ-hā′-tǎ):
A heavy, sweet paste with a caramel flavor made by the slow simmering of milk and sugar. Used for dessert, or for a sauce to top desserts such as bread pudding.

calabacita (kǎ-lǎ-bǎ-sē′-tǎ):
Spanish for *squash*.

caldo (kǎl′-dō):
Spanish for *clear broth*. A soup described as a *caldo* is a liquid in which foods are simmered, versus a *sopa*, which is a thick puree.

capers:
The small pickled flower of a shrub thought to have originated in the Orient or the Sahara Desert. Mexican capers are large, large Italian capers are widely available and can be substituted.

capirotada (kǎp-ēr-ō-tǎ′-dǎ):
Spanish for *bread pudding*.

carne (kǎr′-nā):
Spanish for *meat*.

carne adovada (kǎr′-nā ǎ-dō-vǎ′-dǎ):
Meat—usually pork—cured in red chili sauce. A traditional New Mexican dish.

carne asada (kǎr′-nā ǎ-sǎ′-dǎ):
A dish of grilled marinated meat.

Chilies

Fresh Chilies

carne seca (kăr′-nă sā′-kă):
New Mexican jerky, this dried meat served as one of the staples of the Southwestern diet before refrigeration, and was one of the "trail foods" utilized on the range.

cecina (sā-sē′-nă):
Salted, cured, or smoked dried meat strips, similar to *carne seca*.

chalupas (chă-loo′-păs):
Tortillas fried into the shapes of canoes and filled with meat and vegetables.

chauquehue (chŏw-kā′-hāy):
Mush made from blue cornmeal, native to the New Mexican Indians.

chayote (chī-yō′-tā):
A mild-tasting (reminiscent of cucumber), pale-green squash with a wrinkled skin and a large, edible disclike seed. Also called *merliton*, or vegetable pear. Available autumn through spring; buy firm, unblemished squash with medium green skin. If small, they do not require peeling.

cherimoya (chăir-ē-mŏy′-ă):
A fruit with the consistency of banana, and a taste reminiscent of a cross between banana and pineapple. It was known to the ancient Aztec and Peruvian Indians. It has a hard brown shell, and the flesh is dotted with black seeds that must be removed before eating.

chicharrones (chē-chăr-rōn′-ās):
Spanish for *pork cracklings*, a popular snack.

chicos (chē′-kōs):
A term applied to dried whole kernels of corn still in the hull. *Chicos* are softened by soaking before cooking.

chile con queso
(chē′-lā kŏn kā′-sō):
Melted cheese flavored with green chilies, used as a dip for fried tortilla chips.

CHILIES
Indigenous to South America and cultivated by the Incas and Aztecs, chilies were used as a seasoning and spread north through Mexico City to the Pueblo Indians in New Mexico. In lore, chilies are credited with everything from increasing sexual potency to aiding digestion. We do know they are high in both vitamins A and C,

and cause a secretion in the stomach that may aid in digestion.

Chilies may be named for their use, appearance, flavor, creator, or potency. Chili potency is commercially rated from 1 (for the weakest) to 120 (for the strongest), with *jalapeños* rated at 15. When shopping, look for firm, unblemished, and fairly straight chilies with smooth skins. Dried chilies should be free from mold and unbroken.

Anaheim (ă′-nă-hīm):
Also called California, California greens, *chiles verdes* or, when canned, mild green chilies, Anaheim chilies are dark green, about 7 inches long, 1½ inches wide, and mild to hot in flavor. When the chilies ripen completely in the fall, they turn red and are sweeter and milder. Their large size makes Anaheim chilies ideal for stuffing.

ancho (ăn′-chō):
Dried *poblano* chilies, *anchos* come from California (where they're sometimes incorrectly called *pasilla* chilies) and Mexico and range from dark red to almost black. They're about 4½ inches long and 3 inches wide and are moderately hot, with a smoky undertaste. They are wrinkled and should still be pliable if fresh. *Pasilla* chilies, though difficult to find, may be substituted.

California chili pods:
Dried Anaheim chilies. Substitute pure ground chili powder.

California red:
Also called red chilies or Colorado chilies, these are ripened green Anaheim chilies that have turned red. Relatively smooth and shiny, California red chilies are often strung to make decorative *ristras*. Spiciness ranges from mild to hot.

caribe (kă-rē′-bā):
See *guero*.

cascabél (kăs-kă-bĕl′):
Meaning *jingle* or *sleigh bells*, *cascabéls* are roughly shaped 1½-inch spheres that are brownish brick-red in color and have seeds rattling inside. They are moderately hot and only available dried in the United States.

cayenne (kā-yĕn′):
Also called *finger* or *ginnie peppers*, cayenne chilies are long (3 to 8 inches) and slender. The bright green chilies turn red when ripe and are very hot. Cayennes are usually dried and ground; the powder may be used interchangeably with pure red New Mexico chili powder.

chiles del arból
(chē′-lās dăl ăr-bōl′):
Literally "chilies of the tree," these bright-red chilies are very small and very hot.

chimayó (chē-măy-ō′):
A richer-tasting version of the Anaheim chili from Chimayó, New Mexico.

chipotle (che-pot′-la):
Jalapeño chilies that have been dried, smoked, and often pickled, *chipotles* are usually a dark shade of brown and have a very hot smoky taste. If packed in tomato sauce, *chipotles* may be called *mara* and are a dark, brick red.

Colorado:
Red chili. See *California red*.

guahillo (gwă-hē′-yō):
Also called *mirasol*. A yellow to burnt orange–colored dried chili from Mexico and Peru, *guahillos* are about 2½ inches long, ¾ inch wide, and fairly hot, though subtly sweet. *Cascabél* chilies can be substituted.

guero (gwā′ rō):
Also called Hungarian yellow wax chili. A hot yellow or yellow-green chili similar in shape to the *jalapeño*. It turns red when ripe.

Hatch:
See *New Mexico green*.

hot cherry:
Also called Hungarian cherry pepper, bird cherry, or Creole cherry pepper. Up to 2 inches wide, this spherical chili can get very hot. Though it can be used when dark green, it is best when completely ripe and red. Cayenne, *sándia*, or Mexican improved chilies may be substituted.

Hungarian yellow wax:
See *guero*.

Prickly Pears

jalapeño (hă-lă-pān'-yō):
A fairly small, dark green hot chili approximately 2 inches long and 1 inch wide. One of the most widely available fresh chilies. *Serrano* is a common substitution, although the heat from *jalapeños* is immediate while the *serrano* provides more of an afterburn. *Jalapeños* can vary in the level of hotness, and those with striations on the skin are older and usually hotter. It's better to start with less than the required amount, and add to suit personal taste.

japones (hă-pō'-nās):
Japanese hot chilies that are actually *serrano* chilies and quite hot.

manzano (măn-tsă'-nō):
A yellow-green chili, milder than the *jalapeño*.

Mexico improved:
A very hot chili, used when green for salsa, and when ripe, dried, and ground, for chili powder.

mulato (moo-lă'-tō):
A deep-green chili that turns a burnt red when ripe. This chili is often confused with the *ancho* until it's dried, when its color and taste are reminiscent of chocolate. *Mulato* chilies are quite hot and often used in *mole*.

New Mexico green:
Similar to the Anaheim chili, but shorter and more potent.

New Mexico red:
Also called *chiles de ristra*, since the long and shiny peppers are used to make *ristras*. New Mexico chili powder is pure ground New Mexico red chilies.

Numex Big Jim:
A large (7 to 12 inches long), mild green chili that was developed by a botanist and a New Mexican farmer named Jim. Anaheim chilies may be substituted.

pasilla (pă-sē'-yă):
Named for *pasa*, which means "raisin" in Spanish, the chili is also called *chilaca* when fresh, brown, and

ripe, and *negro* when dried and black. *Pasillas* are mild to hot in temperature, are used in *mole*, and may be substituted with *ancho* or *mulatto* chilies.

pequín (pā-qwēn'):
Small dried red chilies that have the shape of an elongated sphere and are extremely potent. The Indians used *pequín* to help preserve dried meat. Also called *chilepequeno*, bird pepper, *petine*, and *chiltecpin*, *pequíns* grow wild in Mexico and the Caribbean, and along the U.S. border, but little is harvested and they are quite expensive. Cayenne may be substituted.

poblano (pō-blă'-nō):
Large tapered chilies about 4 inches long, 2½ inches wide, and shiny dark green in color. *Poblanos* are mild to hot. When used in sauces, they may be interchanged with Anaheim green chilies, though the flavor will be different. If you're desperate, green bell peppers can be substituted for stuffed *poblanos,* but increase the spice level of the filling.

sándia (săn'-dē-ă):
Also called "hot green chili," this is a fairly hot pepper that grows up to 7 inches long and 2 inches wide. *Sándia* is used fresh when bright green and dried when red. Anaheim may be substituted.

Santa Fe grande:
A cultivated variety of the *guero* chili. Best when yellow, but it can be used when it ripens and reddens. Hungarian yellow wax chili can be substituted.

serrano (săr-ră'-nō):
A tapered, thin, bright-green chili that is similar to but smaller than a *jalapeño* and often pickled or canned in oil. Good for cooking or as a garnish, it varies in hotness as much as a *jalapeño*. *Jalapeño* chilies may be substituted.

tepín (tā-pēn'):
A small round version of the *pequín*, resembling a red peppercorn. *Pequíns* may be substituted.

tequila sunrise:
A new species of chili that takes its name from the drink. They are very hot, have the shape of a large *jalapeño*, and are orangy pink in tone.

Jalapeños or *serranos* may be substituted.

Thai:
Very powerful chilies that are about 1 inch long, slender, and dark green or deep red. Cayennes or *pequíns* may be substituted.

chimichanga (chĕm-ē-chăn′-gä):
A specialty from Arizona. A large flour tortilla is filled with meat, deep-fried, and topped with *guacamole, cheese,* or *salsa.*

chorizo (chō-rē′-tsō):
A spiced Mexican pork sausage found either raw or smoked. A hotly spiced pork sausage reinforced with chili powder, vinegar, and cilantro may be substituted, although some fresh chorizo also includes cinnamon and other spices.

cilantro (sē-lăn′-trō):
Also called *fresh coriander* or *Chinese parsley,* and used as extensively in Asian cooking as it is in Southwestern. Cilantro resembles flat-leaf parsley, but is much more flavorful and aromatic. Its flavor is pungently sweet, and its scent has been compared to that of orange or lemon peel; a combination of caraway and cumin; honey; and lastly, bedbugs. Cilantro was first introduced to the Mexican Indians by the Spanish; its use then spread to the Southwest. Look for crisp, green, and unwilted leaves. Though much less interesting, parsley may be substituted.

cinnamon:
The inner bark from shoots of a tree called *Cinnamomum zeylanicum.* Cinnamon was originally imported from Spain and Mexico, where it continues to be more heavily used than in the Southwest; however, the Mexican variety of cinnamon (originally from Sri Lanka) is a lighter brown, softer in texture, and has a milder taste than the American variety.

cloves:
Originally from the Spice Islands and now grown in Madagascar and Zanzibar, supposedly all clove trees are descended from one tree saved when Frenchman Pierre Poivre's collection was destroyed by members of Louis XV's court for political reasons. Cloves are a labor-intensive and expensive spice, as clove buds must be hand picked from the trees just before they are ready to bloom. Ground cloves will impart a brown shade along with their flavor.

coconut:
Coconuts were introduced to Latin America centuries ago, probably when they washed up on shore from the Pacific Islands and took root. Early on the North Chilean Indians used coconut palm sap as a sweetener. Today coconuts are grown, primarily around the equator, to produce the coconut milk and dried white coconut meat used in Southwestern cooking.

cojack:
An American cheese that blends Colby cheddar and Monterey jack.

comal (kō-mäl′):
A flat griddle used for dishes such as *fajitas.* A low-sided skillet can be used instead.

cómino (kō′-mē-nō):
Spanish for *cumin.*

coriander:
The seed of cilantro, or Chinese parsley. See *cilantro.*

corn husks:
Dried husks are used for encasing tamale dough before steaming them. Before using, husks are usually soaked in hot water for a minimum of a few hours, preferably overnight, and the inner corn silk is removed.

cream of coconut:
The thick sweetened "milk" extracted from coconut flesh and used in desserts and drinks such as piña colada. Coco Lopez is the most widely available brand.

cumin (kŭ′-mĭn):
Cómino in Spanish. Seeds from pods of the indigenous and plentiful Southwestern cumin plant. Used whole and ground, they are mixed with ground chilies to make commercial chili powder, and are also used in curry powder. If a recipe calls for ground red chilies and cumin, do not add additional cumin if substituting chili powder.

empanadas (ăm-pă-nä′-däs):
Baked or fried pastry dough turnovers stuffed with sweet or savory fillings. A street food eaten all through Latin America.

empanaditas (ăm-pă-nă-dē′-täs):
Small empanadas that are a traditional New Mexican Christmas food when filled with a Southwestern version of mincemeat.

enchilada (ăn-chē-lă′-dä):
Soft corn tortillas rolled around a filling or stacked like a torte, often topped with green or red chili sauce and baked.

ensalada (ăn-să-lă′-dä):
Spanish for *salad.*

epazote (ĕ-pă-tsō′-tā):
Also called Mexican tea, wormseed, or goosefoot, and occasionally mistaken for lamb's lettuce, *epazote* grows wild in the United States and Mexico. With a flavor similar to winter savory, older leaves are used as a seasoning in Mexico and the Southwest and are believed to decrease the discomfort caused by beans; younger leaves are eaten as a vegetable.

escabeche (ăs-kă-bā′-chā):
Spanish for *pickled;* a technique usually applied to various fish dishes.

farmer's cheese:
An uncreamed cottage cheese; also called baker's or pot cheese. Dry-curd cottage cheese may be substituted.

feijoa (fē-jō′-ă):
A fruit native to Mexico with a thick green skin, which should always be peeled, and pale yellow flesh. It has a subtle flavor, which is as succulent as pineapple, with a hint of freshness akin to mint. The flesh gives to gentle pressure when ripe, and can be used in fruit sauces. Substitute pineapple with a touch of lime juice.

flan (flän):
The traditional Mexican and Southwestern custard dessert similar to the French *crème caramel* or *crème brûlée.*

flautas (flăoo-täs):
The Spanish word for *flutes* has been given to a dish of slender deep-fried enchiladas.

frijoles (frē-hō′-lēs):
The word means *beans,* and usually refers to stewed pinto beans.

frijoles refritos
(frē-hō'-lēs rā-frē'-tōs):
Refried beans. A paste of stewed
pinto beans fried in fat with onions,
garlic, and frequently chilies.

fruit paste:
A firm but gelatinous sweet paste of a
fruit such as guava, mango, and papaya, eaten for dessert.

fry bread:
Also called Indian fry bread. Flat
discs of dough that are deep-fried and
served with honey, such as the New
Mexican *sopaipilla*.

garlic:
Mexican garlic has a dark pink-blue
hue to the husk and is sharper than
California white garlic. Garlic is usually mashed or roasted for Southwestern cooking.

gazpacho (găts-pă'-chō):
A spicy vegetable soup made from a
puree of raw vegetables seasoned with
pepper and vinegar and served
chilled.

ginger:
A rhizome originally grown in the
Asian tropics and now imported to
the United States from Jamaica.
Southwestern recipes usually call for
ground dried ginger as opposed to
fresh.

grits:
Ground white hominy, eaten as a
cereal that is similar in texture to
pudding.

guacamole (whă-kă-mō'-lā):
An avocado-based dish, usually
mixed with onion, tomato, cilantro,
hot pepper, and lime, used both as a
dip with tortilla chips and as an accompaniment to tortilla specialties.

guava:
A fruit cultivated in Peru and Brazil
for over five hundred years, the guava
is very sweet but has a strong odor
and a profusion of abrasive seeds. It
is acid when unripe and ripens at
room temperature, at which time it
has a sweet aroma.

hearts of palm:
The tender inner portion of a palm
tree, eaten as a vegetable, or as a garnish for salads. Only available canned
in the United States, although it is eaten fresh in Latin America.

hominy:
Large dried kernels of corn, or *chicos,* that have been treated with
slaked lime to dissolve and remove
the hulls.

huevos (huā'-vōs):
Spanish for *eggs*.

jackrabbit:
A hare native to North America and
originally called "jackass rabbit" because of its long ears. Five-pound
jackrabbits are about one year old
and are best for roasting. Jackrabbit
meat is dark, rich, and more gamey
than rabbit.

jalapeño cheese:
Asadero cheese blended and molded
with *jalapeño* chilies. The most frequent substitution is *jalapeño* jack
cheese made with Monterey jack;
however, a *jalapeño* Havarti is becoming more common.

jícama (hē'-kă-mă):
A large root vegetable with the flavor
of a very mild and slightly sweet radish. *Jícama* is crisp and white with a
thick brown skin. Choose *jícamas*
that are small, firm, and not visibly
damaged. Peel both the brown skin
and woody layer underneath, and use
raw or slightly cooked as a vegetable.
Fresh water chestnuts have a similar
flavor.

lard:
Almost flavorless rendered pork fat
resembling vegetable shortening and
used for frying and as an ingredient
in baked goods.

lardons:
Strips of fat, bacon, or salt pork.

laurel:
The tree on which bay leaves are
grown. Used as a seasoning in many
dishes, the leaves should always be removed before serving.

limones (lē-mō'-nās):
Spanish for *limes*.

longhorn cheese:
A mild cheddar cheese produced in
the United States. Any mild cheddar
can be substituted.

maiz (mă-ēs'):
The Spanish word for *corn*, or Indian
corn. While corn is indigenous to the
Southwest, its domestication is credited with the creation of settled civili-

zations such as the Incas, Aztecs, and
Mayas. When choosing fresh corn,
look for small, pest-free ears with
uniform small kernels.

mango:
Mangoes have been cultivated since
the beginning of history, but were
only introduced to the United States
through Brazil in the early eighteenth
century. A ripe mango has a smooth
yellow to red skin and smells sweet,
with the pale to bright orange-yellow
flesh tender to the touch and having a
very pleasant but complex taste, simultaneously sweet and tart. A fi-
brous but gracefully shaped fruit, the
mango looks something like a
smooth, elongated curved disk or
partial kidney bean that is 5 to 6
inches long and 3 to 4 inches wide.
The skin should be peeled and the
flesh cut away from the stone in
strips. Papaya can be substituted in
many recipes.

marjoram:
Often confused with and substituted
for oregano. Sometimes called "wild
oregano," marjoram is an herb in the
mint family and is related to thyme.
Though similar to oregano, marjoram is sometimes called sweet marjoram because it tastes sweeter and
milder. Marjoram grows up to 2 feet
high, with closely bunched purple and
white flowers that resemble knots. It
is used to season pork or game.

masa (mă'-să):
A cornmeal dough used to make tortillas and tamales.

masa harina (mă'-să hă-rē'-nă):
Finely ground cornmeal that is usually commercially prepared and used
to make the dough for tamales and
corn tortillas.

menudo (mă-nŭ'-dō):
A tripe soup traditionally served for
breakfast in Mexico and the Southwest, where it is believed to relieve
hangovers.

Mexican chocolate:
Coarsely textured sweetened squares
or large discs of chocolate made with
cinnamon and ground almonds and
melted in milk to make Mexican hot
chocolate. Ibarra is the most common
brand in the United States. Adding a
dash of cinnamon to bittersweet
chocolate is the best substitution.

Mexican mint marigold:
Also known as sweet mace, the flavor of the leaves is similar to tarragon with a subtle anise flavor. Both the petals and leaves can be used in sauces and relishes and as a garnish.

Mexican strawberry: See *red beans*.

mole (mō′-lā):
A rich and spicy chili sauce, sometimes seasoned with chocolate, used in Mexico as a topping for chicken or turkey.

molletes (mō-yā′-tās):
Yeast rolls flavored with anise.

nachos (nă′ chōs):
Corn tortilla chips, usually triangles or circles, that are fried crispy and covered with toppings, such as refried beans and hot peppers, along with melted cheese. Unlike most tortilla specialties, this one originated in El Paso, Texas, rather than Mexico.

natilla (nă tē′ yă):
A dessert similar to floating island, with stiffly beaten egg whites layered on top of an egg custard.

nixtamál (nēx-tă-măl′):
The Indian name for a cornmeal paste made with *masa harina*, spices, leavening, lard, and water and used to make tamales.

nopales (nō-păl′-ās):
Pads of the *nopal*, or prickly pear, cactus, similar in taste and unfortunately in sliminess to okra. Eaten raw or cooked as a vegetable and, when green, traditionally scrambled with eggs. The *nopales* found in most supermarkets have had the thorns removed; if not, remove them with tweezers. Sliced green beans can be substituted.

nopalitos (nō-păl-ē′-tōs):
Pieces or strips of cactus pads, often pickled.

okra:
Introduced from Africa by Afro-American slaves, okra resembles a large green chili with longitudinal ribs outside and an abundance of round, slimy, but edible seeds inside. Use small unblemished okra for soups and stews, and to thicken gumbos.

oregano:
Also called wild, bastard, or dwarf marjoram, oregano is used to season many foods, especially sauces and soups. Though similar to marjoram, oregano plants grow wild in the Southwest and are shorter, heartier, huskier, and more potent than marjoram. The best substitute for oregano is marjoram or, if preferred, sage.

panela (pă-nā′-lă):
A mild white Mexican cheese made with rennet. Monterey jack is a good substitute.

papaya:
An attractive fruit with shiny round black seeds surrounded by bright orange or pink flesh. It is tender to the touch, shaped like a gourd or a large, elongated pear, and has a mottled yellow-green skin. Papayas are available year round. They have a sweet, musky flavor with a slight citrus tang and are used primarily for dessert. They must be ripe when used or they will be bitter and acid. The skin of the papaya contains a natural enzyme that tenderizes meat, and is frequently included in marinades for that reason.

pecans:
Native to the United States, pecans probably originated in Texas and were introduced to Mexico by the Texans. Pre-Columbian Indians used ground pecans as a thickener and flavoring, and pressed whole pecans for oil.

pepitas (pā-pē′-tăs):
See *pumpkin seeds*.

pheasant:
One of the most preferred and leanest of game birds, pheasant should be eaten when it is a year old or younger. To test for age, press the space above the breastbone; if the pheasant is young enough, the bone will give. While the hen pheasant is more flavorful than the cock, it is legally protected and difficult to find.

picadillo (pē-kă-dē′-yō):
A thick stew of ground meat, spices such as cinnamon, and dried fruits, used most frequently as a stuffing for tamales.

picante (pē-kăn′-tā):
Spanish for *sharp, hot, spicy*. A word for those not fond of spicy food to watch for, since a *salsa picante* always is.

pico de gallo (pē′-kō dā gī′-yō):
Although the Spanish literally means *chicken beak*, this is a relish made from cooked or raw vegetables and served with traditional Southwestern tortilla specialties.

piloncillo (pē-lōn-sē′-yō):
Unrefined cane sugar molded into brown cones and used as a popular general sweetener in Mexico. It is now available in Latino stores, but dark-brown sugar can be substituted.

piñones (pen-yo′-nas):
Spanish for *pine nuts*. White seeds that resemble corn kernels and come from cones of a Southwestern pine tree, the piñon tree. Any pine nuts can be substituted.

plantains:
Similar to a banana in both shape and texture, plantains are a member of the same family. The green skin will develop black spots as it ripens, and the slightly pink flesh must be cooked to be edible. Most commonly sliced thin and fried.

pollo (pōy′-yō):
Spanish for *chicken*.

posole (pō-sō′-lā):
Another name for hominy; *posole* is also the name for a traditional stew of New Mexico, made with pork and red chilies.

praline:
A candy eaten in the South and Southwest; made from brown sugar and pecans.

prickly pear:
The egg-shaped fruit of the *nopal* cactus, ranging in color from yellow to deep red. The sweet fruit is filled with edible seeds, and the skin is usually covered with small spines.

pumpkin seeds:
Also called *pepitas*; the husked inner seed of the pumpkin. The seeds are roasted and used as a snack or garnish and, when ground, as a thickener and flavoring agent.

quail:
The American quail or bobwhite quail is a Galliformes, a different family than the European quail. There is some possibility that the bird in this hemisphere is named for its resemblance to the European species and is not a quail at all; however, the

Fresh Raspberries

name has stuck. Quail have pale meat, usually weigh about 4 ounces, and are subtly flavored.

quelitas (kā-lē′-tăs):
Also called *lamb's lettuce*, *quelitas* are fresh greens that grow in the elevated deserts of the Southwest. They are used for salad and cooked like spinach.

quesadillas (kā-să-dē′-yăs):
Flour tortillas folded around fillings, usually including cheese, then crisped in a pan or the oven.

queso (kā′-sō):
Spanish for *cheese*.

queso fresco (kā′-sō frās′-kō):
Also called *ranchero seco*, this is a white Mexican cheese made with rennet. It is similar to farmer's cheese but is slightly saltier. White cheddar or a mixture of farmer's and feta cheese may be substituted.

quince:
A fruit introduced to Latin America by the Spanish and/or the Portuguese, the quince looks like a large pear, but is hard and very sour. Before it is eaten, quince is usually cooked with sugar, after which it becomes a faint pink.

rajas (ră′-hăs):
The word means *strips* in Spanish, and usually refers to a garnish of strips of roasted or sautéed green chilies and onion.

ristra (rēs′-tră):
A string of red chilies, usually Californian or New Mexican, strung together. *Ristras* are used as decoration on the inside and outside of houses; the peppers, once dried, can be broken off and used in cooking.

saffron:
Saffron (*azafrán* in Spanish) is the most expensive food item in the world. It is made up of the dried stigmas of the *Crocus sativus*, which are laboriously hand picked from each flower. One acre of crocus plants produces about forty-four pounds of saffron. Unique and slightly medicinal in taste, saffron is used both as a flavoring and to impart its characteristic yellow color to food. It takes only a few threads to achieve the desired flavor and color.

sage:
The predominant spice in American turkey stuffing and a relative of mint. Leaves of the woody sage plant are used for seasoning meat, pork, poultry, and game birds. Native to the Mediterranean, sage was introduced to the United States hundreds of years ago, and now often grows wild.

salsa (săl′-să):
Spanish for *sauce*. Usually refers to a fresh tomato and onion sauce used for dipping tortilla chips.

sopa (sō′-pă):
The Spanish word for *soup*. It usually refers to thick soups, while *caldo* is for broths.

sopaipillas (sō-pă-pē′-yăs):
Puffy fried breads native to New Mexico, made with a dough similar to flour tortillas. The round rolled shapes are cut into quarters and fried in hot oil. They can be served with honey or topped with *natilla* as a dessert.

taco (tă′-cō):
A corn tortilla fried crisp in a V-shape, stuffed with seasoned meat, cheese, and beans, and topped with garnishes such as *guacamole*, onion, shredded lettuce, and tomato.

tamale (tă-mă′-lā):
Cornmeal dough stuffed with either sweet or savory fillings and wrapped in corn husks, then steamed.

tamarind:
A fruit that resembles a long brown bean pod, it contains large, pulp-filled seeds used as a flavoring for drinks or sweets.

tequila (tā-kē′-lă):
A clear or golden liquor, it is a distillation of the agave plant. It is usually marketed in the United States at 80 proof, and is the basis for Margaritas.

tomatillos (tō-mă-tē′-yōs):
Related to red tomatoes, *tomatillos* are small and dark green (even when ripe), with a protective brown paper-like husk. Also called *frescadillas* or green tomatoes, *tomatillos* belong to the nightshade family and were originally eaten by the Aztecs. Fresh *tomatillos* should be green and firm, with dry husks. The best substitution is small green tomatoes.

tortilla (tōr-tē′-yă):
Round flat breads made from either wheat flour or cornmeal and lard. The tortilla is the staple of all Latin American cookery.

tostados (tō-stă′-dōs):
Deep-fried corn tortilla chips. Small triangles are used for dipping with *salsas*, or the whole tortilla is fried flat, then topped with a variety of ingredients.

tripe:
Technically the lining of the first two stomach chambers of a ruminant, such as a sheep, but also the linings of various stomachs of other animals, such as pigs. Tripe is used to make *menudo*, a savory stew introduced to the Southwest from Mexico.

venison:
Technically game of any kind, but it more commonly refers to deer meat. Though originally from Eurasia, deer have populated both North and South America for millions of years. The U.S. deer population was almost exterminated as early as the 1600s, and commercial hunting has not been permitted for some time. Most of the venison served today is still imported from Europe, Australia, or New Zealand; however, Axis and Sika deer are now being harvested in Texas.

yam:
A sweet root vegetable similar in appearance to the sweet potato, but with pointed ends and a subdued yellow-orange color. Though *Dioscorea sativa* is the most popular commercial type, a darker variety called yampee, or cush-cush (*D. trifida*) grows in the Southern United States and Mexico and produces clusters of smaller, tastier yams. Yams are often candied. They should be firm, unwithered, and unblemished when purchased.

yerba buena (yār′-bă bwā′-nă):
A wild mint, the name means *good herb* in Spanish. Cilantro, although substantially different in taste, works well as a substitute.

yucca (yŭ′-kă):
A plant native to Latin America and the Southwest. The petals, fruit, and root can all be eaten, and the root is also used as a thickener for soups and stews.

ALAN ZEMAN'S SONORAN SPICES
P.O. Box 31283
Tucson, AZ 85712

A spice blend developed by the chef, featuring peppers with orange.

ALBUQUERQUE TRADERS
P.O. Box 10170
Albuquerque, NM

Chili powders and dried pods.

THE BLUE CORN CONNECTION
8812 Fourth St. N.W.
Albuquerque, NM 87114
(505) 897-2412

Blue cornmeal, popcorn, chips, and muffin mix.

CASA LUCAS MARKET
2934 24th St.
San Francisco, CA 94110
(415) 826-4334

Dried chilies, Mexican ingredients, fresh *epazote*.

CASA MONEO
210 W. 14th St.
New York, NY 10014
(212) 929-1644

A large selection of chilies and canned goods.

CASADOS FARMS
P.O. Box 852
San Juan Pueblo, NM 87566
(505) 852-2433

Ingredients and decorative items.

DURHAM—NIGHT BIRD GAME AND POULTRY COMPANY
650 San Mateo Ave.
San Bruno, CA 94066
(415) 543-1099

Many kinds of furred and feathered game.

FLOR DEL RIO DECORATIONS
P.O. Box 6
Velarde, NM 87582
(505) 852-4457

Red chili *ristras* and wreaths, sprays with corn cobs.

H. ROTH & SONS
1577 First Ave.
New York, NY 10028
(212) 734-1110

Mexican canned chilies and dried chilies.

H. ROTH & SONS
1577 First Ave.
New York, NY 10028
(212) 734-1110

Mexican canned chilies and dried chilies.

JANE BUREL'S PECOS VALLEY SPICE CO.
142 Lincoln Ave.
Santa Fe, NM 87051
(505) 988-2940

JOSIE'S BEST TORTILLA FACTORY
1130 Agua Fria
Santa Fe, NM 87501
(505) 983-6520

Cornmeal, chips, *salsas*, dried chilies, and chili powder.

KITCHEN BAZAAR
4455 Connecticut Ave. N.W.
Washington, D.C. 20008
(202) 363-4600

Utensils for the cooking and serving of Southwest foods, from taco racks to *salsa* bowls.

KREUZ MARKET
208 S. Commerce St.
Lockhart, TX 78644
(512) 398-2361

They will ship their famous sausages.

LAZY SUSAN, INC.
P.O. Box 10438
San Antonio, TX 78210
(512) 534-1330

An extensive catalog of everything from *fajita* grills to red plastic chilies to push over your Christmas lights.

LE MARCHÉ SEED COMPANY
P.O. Box 566
Dixon, CA 95620

Seeds for everything from blue corn to chilies.

MADAME CHOCOLATE
1940-C Lehigh Ave.
Glenview, IL 60025
(312) 729-3330

The chocolate lady, Elaine Sherman, sells every brand of high-quality imported chocolates, including Mexican chocolate.

THE MEXICAN CONNECTION
142 Lincoln Ave.
Santa Fe, NM 87501
(505) 988-2940

Southwest food writer Jane Butel's store features everything from her spice blends and other ingredients to tableware and furniture.

THE MOZZARELLA CO.
2944 Elm St.
Dallas, TX 75226
(214) 741-4072

In addition to mozzarella, cheesemaker Paula Lambert makes rolls with various fillings such as *ancho* chilies, and also sells Texas goat cheese and *scamorza*, a smoked mozzarella.

TEXAS WILD GAME COOPERATIVE
P.O. Box 530
Ingram, TX 78025

Axis venison for stews, chili, and roasts; smoked venison and pork sausage; smoked wild boar; Axis deer hides.

WEBER-STEPHEN CONSUMER SERVICE
They will answer questions on grilling and smoking, and where to find Weber products, including chunks of wood. Call 1-800-323-7598 or, in Illinois, (312) 934-5800, Monday through Friday from 9 a.m. to 4:30 p.m. (Central Time).

SOUTHWEST TASTES

Book Production

Publisher	HP Books
Proprietors	Great Chefs Television Productions
Editorial and Production Services	Jack Jennings, David Crossman Mimi Luebbermann, Carolyn Miller
Book Design·	Amanda Bryan, Thomas Ingalls
Writer	Ellen Brown
Photography	Eric Futran
Public Relations	Linda Nix

GREAT CHEFS OF THE WEST

Television Production

Television Producers and Writers	John Beyer Terri Landry
Presenter	Mary Lou Conroy
Narrator	Andres Calandria
Camera	David Landry
Audio	Ray Peterson
Post Production by	Teleproductions, Inc., New Orleans, Louisiana
Director	John Beyer
Executive Producer	John Shoup
Music	Charlie Byrd Trio Silver Sage Bill Monroe
Official Airline	Continental Airlines
Official Hotel	Sheraton Hotels
Distributed in association with	KLRU-TV Capital of Texas Public Telecommunications Council

Where there's smoke, there's flavor.

Bring out the best in your outdoor cooking with Weber® FireSpice® Natural Cooking Woods.

Nothing brings out the mouth-watering flavor of outdoor cooking like real hardwood. And Weber FireSpice Natural Cooking Woods give you four ways to get that great taste: Mesquite, Hickory, Alder or Oak.

Each adds a taste-tempting, smokey flavor to your fare—without adding calories, cholesterol or sodium.

You'll find FireSpice Natural Cooking Woods in your choice of chunks, chips or bits. Simply add them to your briquettes (or lava rocks), or use them by themselves when you barbeque.

So go ahead. Make the most of your outdoor cooking with FireSpice Natural Cooking Woods from Weber.

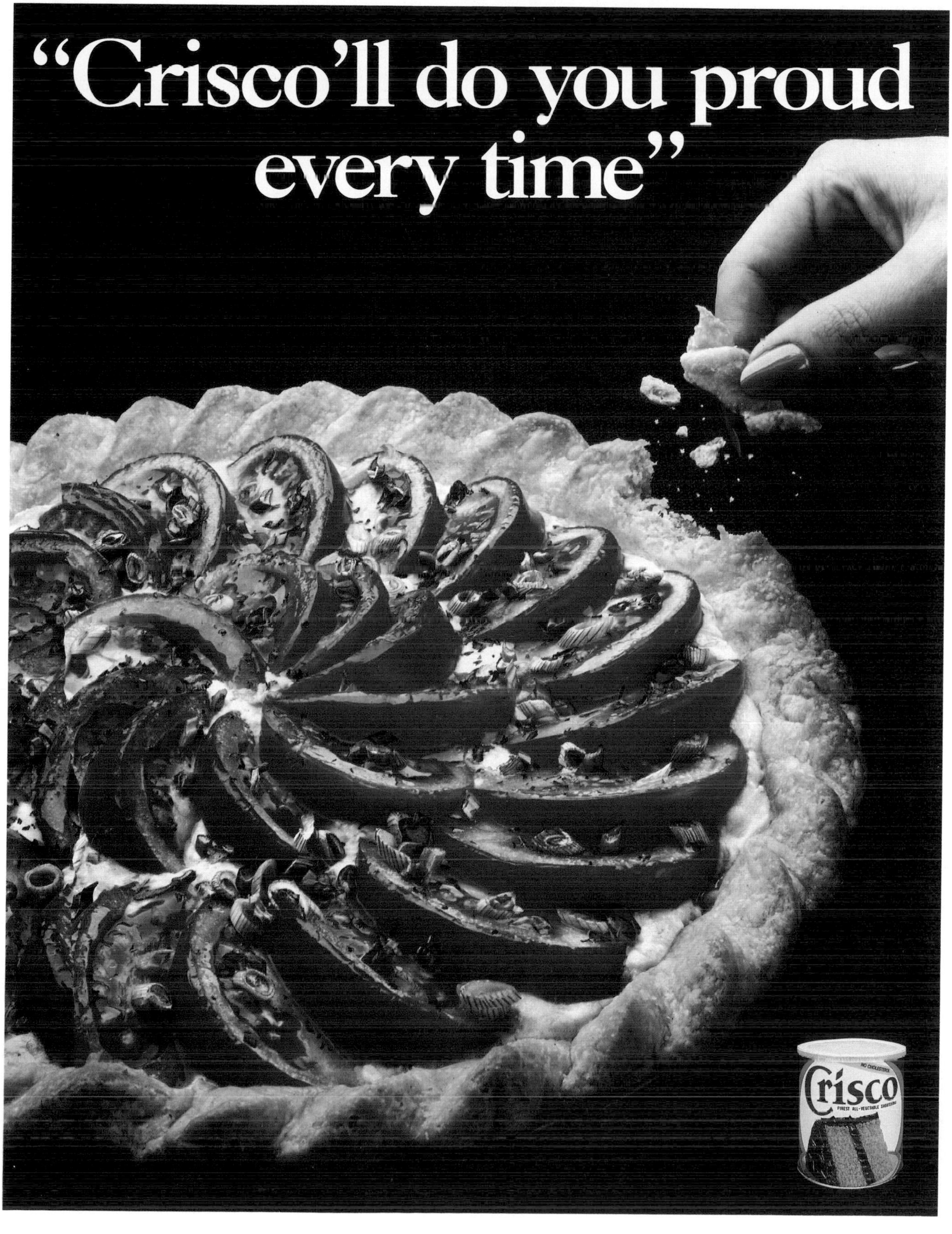
"Crisco'll do you proud
every time"
Crisco

NOTES

NOTES